# PACIFIC STAR

*Endpapers*

**Russell Clark** (1905-66) was appointed an Official War Artist during the latter stages of the Second World War. In February 1944 he joined 3NZ Division in the Pacific as a temporary second lieutenant. He remained in the Pacific until November 1944, spending most of his time in the Solomon Islands. The four examples of his work shown here are:

(upper left) *Bringing out wounded at Mono Island.*
(Archives New Zealand, AAAC 898 NCWA 50)

(lower left) *Action, Falamai Village.*
(Archives New Zealand, AAAC 898 NCWA 56)

(upper right) *Fox holes, evening, Mono Island.*
(Archives New Zealand, AAAC 898 NCWA 127)

(lower right) *'A' Company going out, leaving Malsi, Mono Island.*
(Archives New Zealand, AAAC 898 NCWA 63)

# PACIFIC STAR

## 3NZ Division in the South Pacific in World War II

REG NEWELL

EXISLE PUBLISHING

First published 2015

Exisle Publishing Limited,
P.O. Box 60-490, Titirangi, Auckland 0642, New Zealand.
'Moonrising', Narone Creek Road, Wollombi, NSW 2325, Australia.
www.exislepublishing.com



A catalogue record for this book is available from the National Library of New Zealand.

ISBN 978-1-927187-83-8

10 9 8 7 6 5 4 3 2 1

Text design and production by IslandBridge
Cover design by Nick Turzynski, redinc
Maps by Fran Whild
Printed in China

# Contents


Acknowledgements 6
Note on nomenclature 8
Preface 9

1 The Great Pacific War: A brief overview 13
2 Defence Dilemmas and Strategic Nightmares 17
3 New Zealand's Achilles Heel: The vulnerable northern approaches 21
4 Into the Pacific: Fijian genesis 25
5 Japan Enters the War 34
6 Confusion and Obfuscation: Forming a division 43
7 Growing Pains 51
8 New Caledonia: The land of the Niaouli trees 58
9 To the Solomons: Into the forward area 71
10 Fighting on Vella Lavella: Initiation to battle 76
11 The Treasury Islands: Operation *Goodtime* – A diversionary operation 93
12 The Green Islands: Operation *Squarepeg* 109
13 Death of a Division 123
14 'Mud, Mosquitos and Monotony': The hard slog 133
15 Columbia's Apprentice: Fighting with the Americans 157
16 Aftermath 182
17 The Achievements of 3NZ Division 196

Notes 200
Appendix: The organisation of 3NZ Division at its height, early 1943, New Caledonia 212
Glossary 213
Bibliography 220
Index 226

# Acknowledgements

In producing this book I have incurred personal debts to many people. I would particularly like to thank the veterans of 3NZ Division and their families who have shared their experiences, some none too pleasant. I also acknowledge the help of Archives NZ and Alexander Turnbull Library, my typist Kirsty Nolan, and Ian Watt of Exisle Publishing for his support and guidance. Above all, I would like to thank my wife Heather Newell and my son Michael for their encouragement.

*To all those who fought for freedom*
*in the South Pacific.*

# Note on nomenclature

In the First World War New Zealand sent overseas the New Zealand Expeditionary Force (amounting to a full infantry division), which fought at Gallipoli and later in France. A Mounted Rifles Brigade also fought at Gallipoli and later in Sinai and Palestine. When war broke out again in 1939, the Second New Zealand Expeditionary Force (2NZEF) consisted of the Second New Zealand Division (2NZ Division), which fought in the Middle East and Italy. When it was decided to send an expeditionary force into the Pacific, rather than call it '3NZEF', it was named 'Second New Zealand Expeditionary Force in the Pacific, 2NZEF (IP)'. The reason for naming it so was probably to save the army from repeating the same set of regulations that applied to the force in the Mediterranean. The Pacific force was composed of army personnel. New Zealand air and naval forces fought in the Pacific but under separate commands. The land component of 2NZEF (IP) was known as the 'Third New Zealand Division – 3NZ Division'. The term '3 Division' had been initially used by Major General Owen Mead on 14 May 1942 in Fiji. However, the division was never formally gazetted or designated as such. When Major General Harold Barrowclough was appointed as the commander of 3NZ Division he was simply referred to as 'General Officer Commanding 2NZEF in Pacific'. The official date for the creation of 3NZ Division can be considered to be 15 November 1942 when Barrowclough issued Administration Order No. 1, 2NZEF (IP). For the sake of simplicity I will refer in this work to '3NZ Division' to describe New Zealand's land force in the South Pacific.

The Pacific Star is a medal awarded to New Zealand soldiers, sailors and airmen who served in the combat zone of the South Pacific in World War II.

# Preface

In the grey early morning drizzle the American destroyers began the preparatory bombardment to soften up the Japanese defences. The well-practised gun crews sent shell after shell shrieking across the water to explode on the distant jungle-clad island. Meanwhile, the transport ships of the American invasion force began lowering the frail wooden landing craft from davits into the water. The soldiers in full kit and carrying weapons began forming up on the decks of the transport ships, as they had done so many times before. They then began their perilous descent down rope cargo nets slung over the side of the transport ships and into the swaying landing craft at their feet. The bombardment suddenly stopped and the landing craft began their journey through rifle, machine-gun and artillery fire to their designated invasion beaches. Operation *Goodtime* was under way.[1]

This scene was repeated many times during the Great Pacific War. However, *Goodtime* was different. The naval gunfire, the transport ships and the landing craft may have been American but the soldiers were New Zealanders. These soldiers were making the first opposed amphibious assault undertaken by New Zealanders since the ill-fated Gallipoli landing in 1915.

Strangely, however, the story of *Goodtime*, the close-quarter jungle fighting on Vella Lavella and the even larger invasion of the Green Islands, all undertaken by units of 3NZ Division, have been lost to public memory. It is the purpose of this work to remember the sacrifices and contributions made by the men and women of 3NZ Division to Allied victory in the South Pacific.

The story of 3NZ Division is memorable if only for the fact that the division is utterly unique. It remains the only New Zealand Army formation created as a result of an invasion threat to New Zealand and deployed to fight an enemy in the northern approaches to New Zealand. It was cobbled together from a sprinkling of regular army personnel, garrison units, reinforcements designated for 2NZ Division in the Middle East and untrained soldiers. It was intended to be trained in amphibious assault techniques and to be used as a combat unit in the tropics. What was really unusual, however, was that it was to operate under American command as part of an American strategy to blunt Japanese power in the South Pacific. The division has the distinction of being one of the most under-strength units New Zealand has ever deployed on overseas military operations. It was also hugely reliant upon its major ally for support and choice of combat operations. Yet it was successful in carrying out what was required of it.

## The Drive in the Pacific 1942–1945

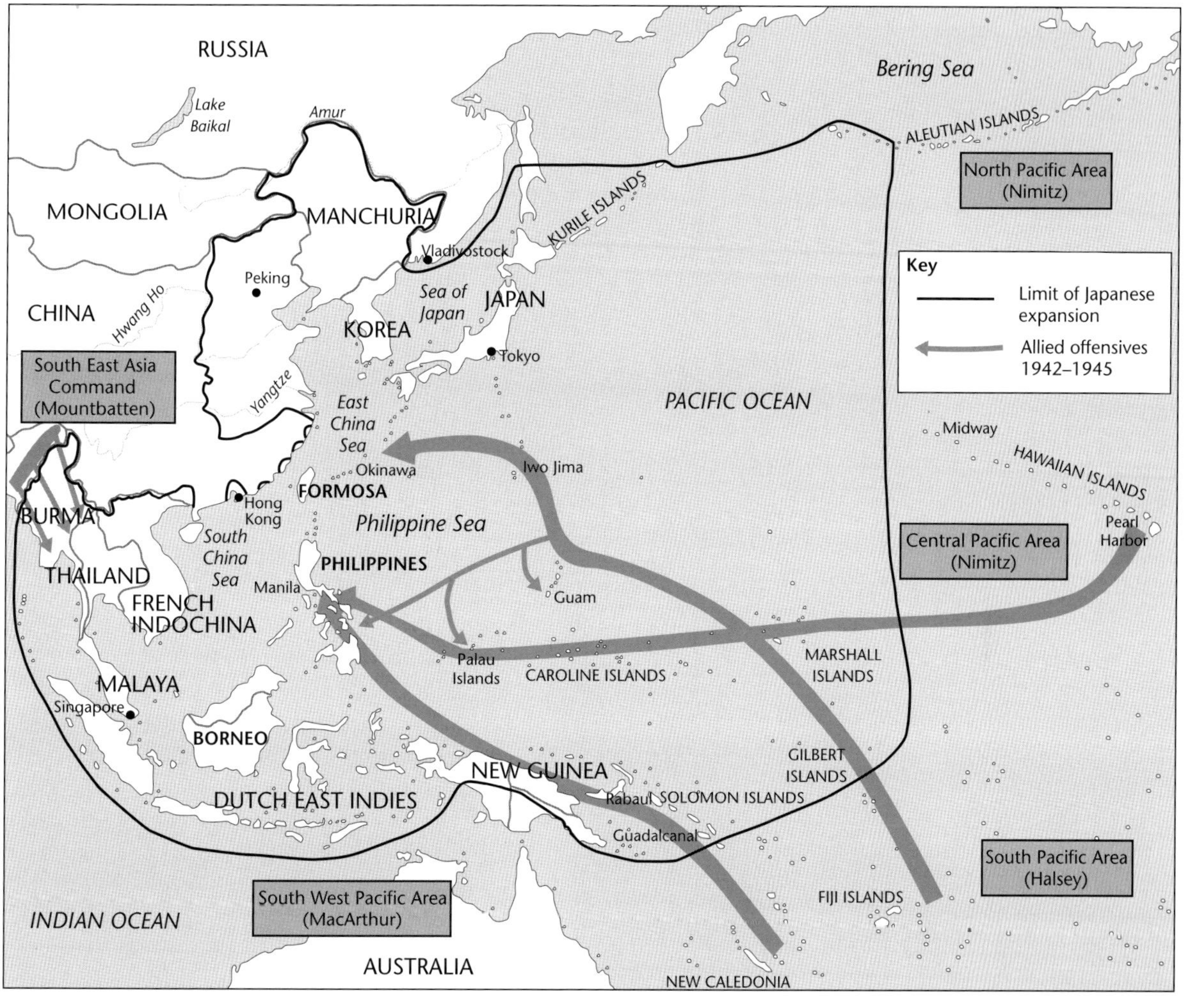

# 1 The Great Pacific War

## A brief overview

The origins of the Great Pacific War can be traced back to the rapid modernisation of Japan in the 19th century and the carving out of a Japanese empire on the mainland of Asia. Japanese leaders were only too aware of the country's burgeoning population and limited natural resources, and this gave impetus to their drive for empire.

In the 1930s the Japanese government was controlled by ultra-nationalistic military leaders intent on expansion into China. Manchuria was seized in 1931, and by 1937 a full-scale war had erupted with China. The Chinese held on grimly, even though large parts of China fell under Japanese control. As the Japanese became mired in the Chinese war, their economy became increasingly strained and dependent on American and Dutch oil. The answer seemed to lie in gaining control of the resource-rich area of south-east Asia, especially the oil-rich Dutch East Indies (modern Indonesia). Plans were made to strike south, seize these resources, create fortifications and make it prohibitively costly for the western powers to recover their lost territories. With the outbreak of the European war in September 1939, Britain and France became preoccupied with a life-and-death struggle against Germany and Italy, with a consequent military weakness in Asia. It seemed to the Japanese that there was a window of opportunity, particularly after the fall of France in 1940, to create their 'Greater South-East Asia Co-prosperity Sphere' and gain mastery over Asia. The major problem was the American Pacific fleet based at Pearl Harbor, the one force that could disrupt Japanese plans. The United States, led by President Franklin Delano Roosevelt, had remained neutral, and the prevailing American sentiment, while sympathetic to Britain, was that America should not get involved in the European war. Under the dynamic leadership of Admiral Isoroku Yamamoto, the Japanese military devised a plan to attack the American fleet through the use of carrier-based aircraft. In the aftermath of the Japanese seizure of French Indo-China and a threatened oil embargo by Roosevelt, it was evident that there could be no negotiated settlement. Yamamoto was given the green light to implement his attack.

The Great Pacific War began with an air raid of devastating proportions on Pearl Harbor on 7 December 1941, which sank or disabled the battleships of the American fleet. Fortunately, American aircraft carriers were absent and submarines and their facilities were undamaged. The Japanese would pay a fearful price for their failure to eliminate these elements.

The Japanese had not understood the psychological effect of their 'sneak attack' on Pearl Harbor. At one stroke it united the American people in their resolve to strike back at Japan and rendered the Japanese hopes of a negotiated settlement void.

As the Japanese struck south in a series of brilliant amphibious operations, they rolled over the weak, ill-equipped, badly led and disunited Allied defenders. The sinking of the British battleships HMS *Prince of Wales* and *Repulse* on 10 December 1941 was a portent of things to come. This was followed by a series of Allied disasters as the Japanese completed the conquest of Hong Kong, Malaya, Singapore, Burma and the Philippines. A multi-national Allied naval force was eviscerated at the Battle of Java Sea in 1942. The only force capable of checking the Japanese was the American carriers.

The Japanese pushed into New Britain and seized the strategically important harbour at Rabaul in January 1942. They also thrust into the Solomon Islands and Papua New Guinea, intent on cutting Australasian supply lines with the US and securing their conquests. A Japanese attempt to send an invasion fleet to seize Port Moresby on the south coast of Papua New Guinea was thwarted at the Battle of the Coral Sea on 7–8 May 1942. Although the Americans lost the aircraft carrier USS *Lexington*, they succeeded in turning back the Japanese invasion convoy – Japan's first strategic defeat.

The Japanese landed on the north coast of Papua New Guinea in 1942 and established themselves on the Kokoda track, opening up the possibility of an overland strike against Port Moresby. Initially the battle-hardened Japanese got the best of the fighting, but the Australians committed more resources and pushed the Japanese back.

Yamamoto hoped to destroy the American carriers by forcing them to defend the island of Midway. Unfortunately for him, brilliant code-breaking by the Americans revealed enough of Japanese plans for Admiral Chester Nimitz, the American commander in chief in the Pacific, to set up an ambush. In the space of five minutes, American carrier aircraft sank three of the main Japanese aircraft carriers and later in the day finished off a fourth. The demolition of the Japanese navy's main striking arm blunted their most deadly weapon. However, there were other Japanese carriers and their air power remained extremely potent. It would take two more years of brutal fighting to eviscerate Japanese naval and air power.

The two areas where attrition occurred were Papua New Guinea and the island of Guadalcanal in the Solomon Islands. An attempt by the Japanese to land at Milne Bay, Papua New Guinea, on 26 August 1942 was decisively defeated. Earlier, on 7 August 1942, American Marines of the 1st Marine Division landed on Guadalcanal. The battle for Guadalcanal would see-saw backwards and forwards as both Americans and Japanese committed more of their troops, planes and ships to the battle. By January 1943 the Japanese had accepted their defeat and withdrawn from 'the island of death'. Similarly, in Papua New Guinea, Australian and American forces throughout 1943 rolled up the Japanese beachheads at

US infantrymen on Vella Lavella, 13 September 1943.

*(US Army Signal Corps)*

Gona, Buna and Salamaua in a series of amphibious thrusts which isolated Japanese garrisons. Arguably, it was the grinding battles at Guadalcanal and the Solomon Islands, together with that in Papua New Guinea, which tilted the scales against the Japanese.

The American commander in the South-West Pacific, General Douglas MacArthur, was determined to return to the Philippines and liberate the islands. Having been trounced as the commander there in 1942, he was determined to restore his honour. In October 1944 he got his way and American forces landed at Leyte and began the costly process of eliminating the Japanese defenders. This in turn triggered mammoth naval battles which destroyed major elements of the Imperial Japanese Navy in the Marianas and at Leyte Gulf.

While MacArthur's forces 'island-hopped' up the coast of New Guinea in their drive to the Philippines, American forces under the command of Nimitz began a central Pacific drive, starting with the costly invasion of Tarawa in November 1943, and progressively invading the islands of Kwajalein, Guam, Saipan and Iwo Jima, culminating in the costly battle of Okinawa in April 1945. By early 1945 the supremacy of Allied air power was such that Japanese air and naval power had been written down, enabling American carrier planes to launch strikes against mainland Japan.

By mid-1945, US forces were poised to invade Japan. American submarines had decimated the Japanese merchant fleet and American carrier power had finished off the remnants of the Japanese battle fleet. The Japanese faced starvation. American bombers reduced Japanese cities to cinders. Arguably, the two atomic bomb raids on Hiroshima and Nagasaki provided the Japanese government with the ability to save face and surrender. The Russian declaration of war and smashing victories in Manchuria sealed Japanese demoralisation.

Japanese forces officially surrendered in Tokyo Bay on the deck of USS *Missouri* on 2 September 1945. World War II came to an end.

The war in the Pacific was essentially an American war and dominated by the twin elements of air power and sea power. US forces were joined by Filipino, British, Canadian, Fijian, Tongan, Papua New Guinean, Solomon Islands, Australian, Dutch, Chinese, Malay, Indian and New Zealand forces, which all played a role in the Allied victory.

# 2 Defence Dilemmas and Strategic Nightmares

The idea that a New Zealand wartime government would send the cream of its fighting men overseas, leaving New Zealand vulnerable to attack, now seems absurd, but that is precisely what occurred in the Second World War. New Zealand pursued two competing defence strategies. One, which recognised that New Zealand's destiny was inextricably tied to that of Britain, meant that the bulk of New Zealand's manpower was dispatched to the Mediterranean, which was, until 1944, Britain's principal theatre of combat. New Zealand's leaders were not blind to the country's vulnerability, however, and the second strategy involved garrisoning the islands to the north. These efforts at direct defence would ultimately manifest themselves in New Zealand's major contribution to the land war in the South Pacific, 3NZ Division.

New Zealand was obliged to take more responsibility for its own defence because there had been a seismic shift in British defence capabilities between 1918 and 1939. By the First World War the challenge of German sea power had forced the Royal Navy to concentrate its forces in the North Sea. This was counterbalanced in the Far East by the Anglo-Japanese Alliance of 1902, but dependence on Japan exposed cracks in British defence. Britain's strategic nightmare of simultaneous threats in Europe and the Far East developed in the 1930s. British defence weakness was exacerbated by the Washington Naval Conference of 1921–22, which reduced the size of the Royal Navy, limited the ability of the British to fortify their possessions in the Pacific and ended the Anglo-Japanese

Alliance. War weariness, economic problems and an aversion to military spending contributed to a decline in British military power, while the rise of fascism focused British attention on Europe and the Mediterranean, resulting in further weakness in the Far East and Pacific.

British Pacific strategy centred on the creation of a naval base in Singapore.[1] The British problem was that the Royal Navy lacked sufficient battleships to defend the global British Empire. The British plan, 'War Memorandum Eastern', contemplated Royal Navy battleships being sent from other areas to Singapore if war with Japan seemed imminent. The plan was that the British would then force the Japanese fleet to fight a decisive battle in the South China Sea where it was envisaged that the Japanese would be far from their home bases and therefore at a disadvantage.[2]

The Singapore strategy was sold to the New Zealand government on the basis that 'even an inferior British Fleet at Singapore would have the effect of preventing an invasion of Australia and New Zealand.'[3] Governments on both sides of the Tasman contributed troops, equipment and money to the base, which became the symbol of British power in the Far East.

There were weaknesses in the strategy. It would take an estimated 60–90 days before the fleet could relieve Singapore, and it was unclear how many ships (if any) could be sent and what they could accomplish. Canberra and Wellington accepted the Singapore strategy, but, extremely mindful of growing Japanese military power, they urged Britain to strengthen its position in the Far East, which was their 'Near North'. Faced with inadequate resources, the British responded with a mixture of indecision, wishful thinking, miscalculation and even duplicity. As Christopher Thorne comments, 'the assurances given to Australia and New Zealand at the Imperial Conference of 1937 (even if Germany and Italy were to join in a war against Britain, they were told, "no anxieties or risks in the Mediterranean ... can be allowed to interfere with the despatch of a fleet to the Far East"), and again in 1939 ("it is our full intention to despatch to the Far East a fleet of sufficient strength to make the position of any Japanese major expedition precarious") were, to put it mildly, less than frank.'[4]

Since British sovereignty had been established in 1840, New Zealand had been cocooned by the naval supremacy of the Royal Navy. It had dealt with the limited threat of naval raiders and the perceived threat from Czarist Russia in the 1880s by developing coastal defences. Some New Zealand politicians were aware of the strategic importance of the arc of islands to the north. Prime Minister Richard Seddon had lobbied Whitehall to assert sovereignty over Pacific territories and Wellington had been greatly concerned when Germany acquired Western Samoa in 1900.

In 1914 both Australia and New Zealand had taken the opportunity to seize German territories in the South Pacific. A British review of New Zealand's defence needs in 1919 had highlighted the strategic importance of Fiji to New Zealand.

New Zealanders viewed with disquiet the emergence of Japan as a great power after its defeat of Russia in 1905, even though Japan was formally allied to Britain and in 1914 would supply a naval escort for an Anzac troop convoy. There was considerable discomfort at the thought of Japan's immense, burgeoning population with little arable land in contrast to the relatively underpopulated, almost empty, spaces of Australia and New Zealand. The palpable threat of 'The Yellow Peril' was heightened in 1914 when the Japanese seized the Caroline and Mariana Islands and retained them under a League of Nations mandate in the post-war settlement. The termination of the Anglo-Japanese Alliance ratcheted up Australasian defence anxieties. In 1927 the New Zealand military conducted an anti-invasion exercise based on the concept of a Japanese invasion convoy staging through the Caroline and Mariana Islands and reaching New Zealand shores.[5] Japanese atrocities in the Second Sino-Japanese War, which was fought from 1937 to 1945, cemented the fear of Japan. Equally concerning was the marked proficiency the Japanese displayed in amphibious operations along the Chinese coast.[6]

Whitehall was not reluctant to share its defence responsibilities, especially the cost. As early as 1929 the Committee of Imperial Defence asked New Zealand to garrison Fanning Island and in 1930 Wellington agreed to do so when requested by Britain or when war seemed imminent. In 1936 the British Overseas Defence Committee recommended that New Zealand should take over the defence of Fiji, although this entailed some complexity as Fiji was a British Crown colony with a governor, a limited defence and police force, and was economically controlled by Britain. These factors would eventually be overcome by high-level negotiations.

In December 1938 a report from the New Zealand Chiefs of Staff (NZCOS), a committee made up of senior air, naval and army commanders, to the New Zealand government noted with alarm that the Japanese fleet of fast liners had increased, that Japan had developed amphibious capabilities and that Japanese vessels had been observed in Fijian and Tongan waters, clearly involved in intelligence gathering. If Japan established a base in Fiji or Tonga, the Japanese could cut strategic lines of communication and threaten Australasia. The NZCOS recommended that the Fiji Defence Force be increased to 1300, that Suva be defended by two 6-inch guns and that if war broke out with Japan, New Zealand should send an infantry brigade and aircraft to Fiji. They suggested that New Zealand should store part of its strategic reserves of fuel and munitions in Fiji and Tonga, and that Tonga should raise a battalion of troops for its own defence.[7] The New Zealand Defence Council accepted the report.

None of the Allied-held Pacific Islands could defend themselves, and New Zealand's military resources, especially trained manpower, were minuscule. Concerned about its defence, New Zealand hosted the Pacific Defence Conference in Wellington in April 1939, attended by government and military representatives from Britain, Australia and New Zealand. The British reiterated their belief that, properly reinforced, Singapore would repel a Japanese seaborne invasion. To seize Australasia, the Japanese would have to penetrate the barrier of New Guinea, the Solomon Islands, New Hebrides, Fiji and Tonga Islands, and the conference concluded that patrol aircraft could provide a warning of Japanese intentions. Accordingly, New Zealand was tasked with aerial patrols of Tonga, Fiji and the New Hebrides, while the Australians were responsible for New Guinea and the Solomons through to the New Hebrides. When the New Zealanders asked what would happen if Singapore fell to the Japanese, one British representative flippantly replied that the New Zealanders would have to seek shelter in the Waitomo Caves.[8]

The conference endorsed the 1938 NZCOS report and New Zealand was recommended to supply rifles, webbing and expert personnel for Fiji and Tonga. In addition, it recommended that the New Zealand Army should be expanded and a platoon dispatched to Fanning Island if war seemed likely. Fiji required at least a brigade group from New Zealand and one should be formed. New Zealand did not, however, have the industrial infrastructure to produce large quantities of arms and munitions. Desperate efforts by the British to rearm, coupled with shipping difficulties, would mean a significant delay in meeting orders in Britain. New Zealand was told to develop its own armaments industry, a pious hope in the short term.[9]

Financing defence was a problem for the country. In April 1939, Britain's Minister for Co-ordination of Defence, Ernle Chatfield, declined a New Zealand application for a defence loan on the basis that New Zealand defence was not a high priority. The British were also concerned about New Zealand's ability to pay its overseas debts.[10] Despite these concerns, Wellington accepted the conference recommendations and set about trying to implement them. A detachment of infantry left New Zealand on 30 August 1939 for Fanning Island.

# 3 New Zealand's Achilles Heel

## The vulnerable northern approaches

On 3 September 1939 New Zealand followed Britain in declaring war on Germany, and the vulnerability of its strategic situation was laid bare. For the next six years its prime military effort was in supporting British Commonwealth interests, first in the defence of Britain and then, from late 1940, in the Mediterranean. However, with relations between the West and Japan severely strained, the NZCOS would spend an anxious three years looking at the pathetic state of military defence to New Zealand's north.

The development of the bomber had made this area particularly critical.[1] In the 1930s the Japanese had bombed Chinese cities, notably Canton in 1938, with considerable and devastating effect, and in 1940 and 1941 they launched deliberate terror bombing of Chinese cities. Aircraft such as the Mitsubishi G4M *Betty*, a twin-engined medium bomber, had a potential range of 3000 miles. Japan also had carrier-borne air power, although its exact capabilities would not become evident until the attack on Pearl Harbor.

Because Auckland and much of the North Island were within the range of bombers possibly based in Fiji, a scant 1100 miles north, the NZCOS in 1938 believed it was 'essential that an enemy should be prevented from establishing himself in this area' and that 'landing grounds and other facilities for the operation of air reinforcements' be built, especially in Fiji, to provide bomber bases and allow for effective reconnaissance patrols.[2] For the New Zealand government air power had powerful advantages: it was seen as a cost-effective alternative to naval units, it fitted in with its preference for local defence and it was considered to be somehow more 'defensive' and less 'imperialist'.[3]

The NZCOS warned against the danger to New Zealand shipping, and the trade that depended on it if the Japanese took one of the islands to its north, especially Fiji. Fiji was also a critical point for wireless and cable (telegram) communications, since the British Trans-Pacific cable ran through Suva. Suva had importance as a naval fuelling base as well. Operating in the Pacific, where typhoons frequently occur, navies needed secure anchorages for replenishment and shelter. The US Navy would develop fleet oiling and replenishment capability as the Pacific war progressed, but pre-war thinking emphasised advanced bases. Suva, with its harbour facilities, became of considerable strategic significance, as did the ports at Tonga, Norfolk Island and Noumea.

If the forward defences in the islands fell or were bypassed, New Zealand would be exposed. Every trained soldier or piece of military equipment sent north potentially weakened homeland defence. Wellington had to choose how many resources to devote to forward defence in the islands, how many to retain in New Zealand and how many to send overseas in support of the Commonwealth's war effort.

When the European war broke out in September 1939, Fiji's defences were virtually non-existent. There were only a few ill-trained volunteers and no coastal artillery or anti-aircraft guns. Late in September 1939, the cruiser HMS *Leander* made a high-speed trip from New Zealand to Suva to deliver dummy guns that were eventually replaced by real 4.7-inch guns the following December. (Requests had been made to London for 6-inch guns but none were available.) The Suva Battery was formed in November 1939, with the assistance of New Zealand artillery officers, but a modern cruiser could easily outrange it. To protect against surprise land assaults, the Fijian Defence Force (FDF) was built up with specialist New Zealand Army personnel, but it was considered inadequate and badly trained, with NCOs unlikely to fulfil their role as leaders. Ten members of the New Zealand Army were seconded to the battery, and its performance improved, but Fiji's defences remained critically weak. A New Zealand Army officer and four NCOs were seconded to the FDF, arriving in Suva on 6 October 1939 to set up an officers' training course for 1 Battalion FDF. This was the start of a long association between the FDF and the New Zealand Army. By February 1940 the building of airfields on Fiji was under way and Wellington decided also to build airfields on Tonga.

Apart from the threat of sudden Japanese seizure, there was a second reason why Fiji needed a garrison. The sizeable Indian population felt considerable resentment at their lack of political rights and inability to own land. A strike by Indian sugar workers in 1920 had been seen as being anti-British, and New Zealand troops had played a role in breaking the strike. There was a fear that the Indian population was disloyal to the British Crown and constituted a potential 'fifth column' who would welcome a Japanese invasion. Internal security was obviously a major concern.[4]

If Fiji was so strategically vital to New Zealand, why had it been left so vulnerable? The answers lay in both will and resources. New Zealand had a tiny army, which was underequipped and undermanned with no reserves to spare for forward defence. It also lacked the capacity to train and equip soldiers en masse. In 1939 New Zealand did not have the facilities to train more than one intake of soldiers at a time, and those already trained would have to be sent overseas to make room for the next wave. The first Labour government, elected in 1935, contained men who had opposed conscription during the First World War and tended to view the military with suspicion. Labour had embraced the concept of collective defence within the League of Nations framework, but had not embarked on a strong programme of rearmament. It only reluctantly accepted that New Zealand's security rested with the wider defence of the Commonwealth. Even then there was a focus on local defence and intense debate about sending an expeditionary force to Europe. The government, believing that air power would solve the local defence problem of New Zealand's northern approaches, had developed air resources at the expense of ground forces.[5]

Initially, the NZCOS did not regard large reinforcements for Fiji as urgent. But after the fall of France in June 1940 and the increased likelihood of Japan entering the war on the side of the Axis powers, the NZCOS decided that it was necessary to send an infantry brigade to Fiji. They proposed that three New Zealand infantry battalions be stationed on Viti Levu with a battery of New Zealand field artillery, that the FDF should be mobilised, and that coast-watching stations be set up and makeshift mines laid. They also proposed that the commander of New Zealand forces in Fiji should direct all land forces in Fiji, Tonga and Fanning Island, with a combined operations headquarters in Suva for intelligence collection and analysis. The NZCOS furthermore recommended that the Tongan Defence Force be increased from 357 to 480, leavened with experienced New Zealand personnel, and trained.[6] Tonga, with its good anchorages and airfield, was critical to the defence of both Fiji and New Zealand, but also constituted another call on New Zealand's limited military resources. Western Samoa, likewise, was inadequately garrisoned.

The obvious answer to the need for troops was to use the Third Echelon reinforcements intended for 2NZ Division, and in February 1940 the NZCOS had presumed this would happen. However, New Zealand troops were desperately needed in the Middle East, something Wellington knew was vital for Britain, particularly for oil supplies. Eventually the Third Echelon was dispatched to the Middle East, but 3053 troops were formed into a brigade group for Fiji, initially known as B Force[7] and later as 8th Infantry Brigade Group.[8] It became the foundation of 3NZ Division.

The deployment to Fiji was so inadequate that it invited disaster. However, any garrison Wellington could have provided would still have been reliant on a friendly navy maintaining maritime dominance in the South Pacific. If naval or aerial supremacy were lost, even the strongest garrisons could be reduced to impotence, as the Japanese on Rabaul between 1943 and 1945 would discover. Unquestionably, New Zealand's commitment to defending its northern ramparts was inadequate and strategically risky, but there was simply no alternative.

# Into the Pacific

# 4

## Fijian genesis

On 20 July 1940 Colonel William Henry Cunningham was appointed from the New Zealand Army Reserve to command the brigade to be sent to Fiji, and was promoted to temporary brigadier on 28 October. Cunningham faced a series of challenges unique in New Zealand military history. He had to defend the more than 250 islands, islets and reefs that made up Fiji, with no realistic means to do so. His command lacked heavy weapons, anti-aircraft guns, machine guns and that most basic of military commodities, the trained combat infantryman. Fortifications and even a bare military infrastructure were lacking.

As if all this was not bad enough, Cunningham was confronted by a division of control between the civilian administration and the military authorities. Such matters as requisitioning land and supplies had to be handled with delicacy. He was required to deal with the British colonial administration headed by the governor, Sir Harry Luke. Cunningham would have to deploy his chronically limited resources as best he could and hope that he would have time to train his men and construct fortifications and defence infrastructure before the Japanese blow fell. He identified the Suva Peninsula as critical because of its airfield, port and wharf facilities, and considered that three battalions would be needed, preferably with one sufficiently mobile to be a strategic reserve. Without sufficient vehicles, however, this problem would not be resolved for some months.

Since the brigade's engineer unit was not yet fully trained, a company of engineers from the Third Echelon was sent to Fiji as an advance party.

Brigadier William Henry Cunningham.

*(Alexander Turnbull Library, Ref. DA-01148)*

The 18 Army Troops Company, made up of eight officers and 280 men, disembarked at Suva on 12 October 1940 and began the construction of facilities for the main body. Their priority was the creation of Samambula Camp, four miles from Suva. Another camp was established at Namaka, 17 miles from Lautoka. The troops built huts and roads, and installed electrical lighting and water piping. Work on headquarters with an underground 'battle chamber' was started at Borron's House, a residence on a hill overlooking Suva. However, this would not be ready until early 1942. On 28 October 1940, the first 942 men of B Force sailed from Wellington on SS *Rangatira*, escorted by HMS *Monowai*, into the teeth of a gale. As the little convoy surged along the coast of New Zealand, most of the men became profoundly seasick. This first group arrived in Suva on 1 November. A second group of 910 men arrived on 14 November, followed by a third on 22 November. By the end of November 1940, the formation now known as '8 Brigade' consisted of 3053 men in two mixed infantry battalions and a field battery of six 18-pounder guns. A third battalion of infantry was made up of reinforcements and metamorphosed from a Training Battalion to a Reserve Battalion and then to its ultimate form, 34 Battalion. Cunningham established a headquarters at Suva in the basement of Government Buildings pending completion of the command facilities at Borron's House, and his men began laying out barbed wire, digging weapons pits and emplacing guns. 29 Battalion was assigned to defend the east of Viti Levu and 30 Battalion the west. To ensure unity of command, the Governor of Fiji appointed Brigadier Cunningham Commandant of the Fiji Defence Force on 6 November.

So that the men were 'not kept in a tropical climate for too long a period',[1] for health reasons the troops were rotated. Originally reliefs were supposed to happen every four months but shortage of shipping and escorts lengthened that to six months.

The first relief occurred in January 1941 with 18 Army Troops Company embarking for New Zealand and being replaced by 20 Field Company. The new arrivals had been given three months' basic training but their engineering expertise had been limited by a lack of engineering equipment. They would find the same conditions in Fiji, where there was a severe shortage of basic tools and equipment.

These first arrivals were short of uniforms, weapons and equipment. Cunningham was concerned about the lack of uniformity in clothing and the fact that 'some of the men were dressed in rags', but the rapid expansion of the New Zealand military meant there were insufficient uniforms.[2] As a soldier of 30 Battalion in Fiji in 1940 commented:

> We were like a bunch of tramps in those days ... We were issued with shorts that had been stowed away in ordnance stores since the last war. The metal buttons had rusted through on to the cloth. The shirts, also of World War I vintage, started to rot across the back. Our felt hats refused to assume the prescribed shape and our knee length puttees were moth eaten. We scrubbed our worn out old-time web and cleaned both sides of our brass. No wonder they gave us smartening-up exercises.[3]

A soldier in 29 Battalion, who arrived in Fiji in April 1941, recalled that 'initially we were issued with what looked to me second hand shorts and shirts. I distinctly remember the metal buttons being rusted into the material'.[4]

Moreover, the uniforms were inappropriate. They included puttees that rapidly became soaked with perspiration and attracted thorny seeds, woollen battledress that was extremely uncomfortable in the heat and humidity, and rain capes that gave little protection against torrential downpours. As the American historian Eric Bergerud has commented, 'the South Pacific was no place for an officer who was a stickler for proper dress',[5] but in pursuit of good discipline Cunningham insisted on the soldiers' clothing being smart and shirts and tunics being buttoned up. Harry Bioletti remembered that 'in our knapsacks when on parade we had our oilskin capes, not to keep us dry but to give a square tidy look to our knapsacks'.[6] The lightweight felt hats rapidly became sodden with sweat as their wearers struggled to work in the heat and humidity. The ubiquitous leather military hobnail boot soon fell apart in the heat. Some soldiers wore out their clothing during their stint on Fiji and used the remnants as rags for cleaning weapons. Since they could not account for the items, the army docked their pay and insisted on the soldiers authorising the deduction before they were allowed to return to New Zealand.[7] Tropical conditions not only sapped the energy of the soldiers, it also affected their gear. Mould grew overnight, damp conditions rotted items and uniforms had to be replaced frequently. However, there were insufficient stocks of uniforms in New Zealand despite clothing factories working round the clock. The soldiers had to make do.

In the words of one officer: 'We were woefully short of equipment and had to improvise at every turn until gradually our stores came through and conditions improved.'[8] Grenades were in such short supply that local craftsmen were given the task of making dummy wooden grenades for use in grenade-throwing practice. This may have been the origin of the term 'coconut bombers'. Imitation Bren guns and mortars were carved out of wood and piping in order to provide training. One battalion had four Lewis guns but only one return spring without which the guns were not operable. The return spring was handed from company to company as the soldiers trained with the Lewis gun.

The inadequacy of their gear and equipment was not lost on the soldiers defending Fiji. Morale suffered and a secret intelligence report commented on the level of defeatism among officers. The NCOs felt the same. Basil Renshaw of 8 Brigade recalled his sergeant major remarking not long after they arrived in Fiji that 'the best thing we can do if the Japs come is to hand this bloody island over to them and apologise for the state it's in'.[9] The pessimism was justified: if a Japanese force of substantial size had struck Fiji in early 1941 it would undoubtedly have fallen.

The men had to create barracks and infrastructure. Armourers were forced to work with ammunition that was exposed to the elements because of lack of storage facilities. The two major New Zealand camps were located 152 miles apart linked by rough, unpaved, sometimes dangerous road.

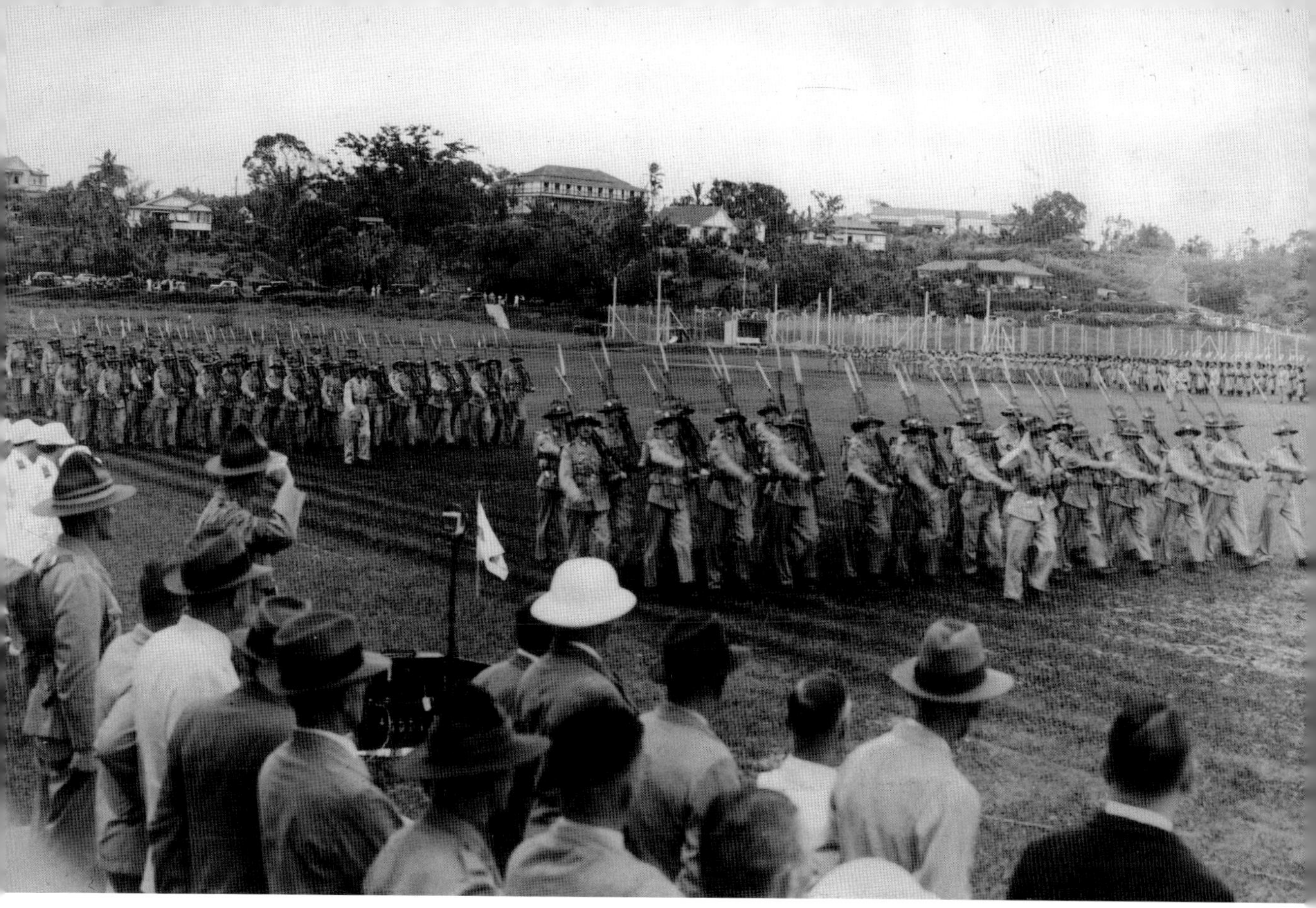

In creating a garrison out of virtually nothing Cunningham also faced a problem with his men. Most of his officers, drawn from the reserve, were over age – many were veterans of the First World War – and unfit for tropical warfare. (It has been suggested that Cunningham himself failed the medical examination for overseas service – he had shrapnel wounds from 1914–18 – but that Prime Minister Peter Fraser overrode this and approved his appointment.)[10] Cunningham had limited success with purging the unfit. For the 'other ranks', young fit men who had expected to serve in the Mediterranean, deployment to Fiji was a letdown. They were derisive of the 'Retreads' and 'Blood Pressures' who commanded them. For a force obliged to do garrison duty there was a sense of purposelessness and maintaining morale was difficult, with instances of drunkenness and a failure to enforce disciplinary standards such as saluting officers.[11] Even worse, the troops felt they were the object of scorn, and that they were simply 'playing at soldiers'. Although the war experience of the older officers was valuable, it sometimes proved restrictive for the troops under their command. Orthodox army methods prevailed and initiative was discouraged. Junior officers were kept in the dark about defence plans for Fiji.

Brigadier William Henry Cunningham, CBE, Commander of New Zealand troops on Fiji 1940–42, taking the salute during the ANZAC Day parade in Suva, 1941.

*(War History Collection, Alexander Turnbull Library, PAI-Q-294-057-518, photographer unknown)*

Training, even allowing for the lack of equipment, was unimaginative. The process of turning civilians into soldiers entailed elementary drill in the 'bull ring', which the men found particularly trying in the tropical heat and rain. January was one of the hottest times of year and the troops would have three or four showers a day and sometimes another at night because they could not sleep in the heat, especially if they were quartered in canvas tents. Water consumption was so high that the Suva reservoir began to get low and orders were issued to reduce the rate of usage. Showers were cut off for periods of time.[12]

Rations were also a problem. Supply ships brought food from New Zealand but there was insufficient cool storage in Fiji and food spoiled rapidly in the hot climate. In the tropics the New Zealanders ate less meat than they did at home, preferring instead to consume more fruit and vegetables. Apples were a popular item but had to be treated as a luxury. Attempts were made to obtain food from local sources, and on 6 January 1941 a purchasing arrangement was organised with the Fiji Agricultural Department. Potatoes were difficult to obtain. Kandavu Island, sixty miles south of Fiji, was the only place where potatoes could be grown successfully and the troops did not like taro, which was used as a substitute. Efforts were made to grow potatoes at Namaka Camp.

There was little to see or do for recreation. The troops rapidly discovered that local trinkets and souvenirs skyrocketed in price when they appeared. Fraternisation with the local people, particularly females, was discouraged unless officially sanctioned. The men had to obtain special permission to play any kind of sport with the Fijians. The experience of 30 Battalion at Momi Bay captures the problem:

> The soul-searing monotony of life was relieved only by mail days. Of entertainment there was none and only a varied assortment of rumours gave a fillip to the deadly sameness of garrison duties. The food was poor and if leave was available where could one go? There was nothing to do but get up in the morning, throw on a pair of mud bespattered shorts or underpants, a pair of boots (socks for 'cissies') and dig and sweat, and swat the mosquitoes that drove one to distraction.

Only the 'camaraderie among the boys which produced laughs and good natured banter … allowed them to become inured to tinned yellowtail for breakfast, to kumala [sweet potato], dala [taro] and tough stringy beans, to sweating by day and night, to long intervals between mail days, to bouts of dysentery and the pin pricks of communal life.'[13]

To add to these woes, Fiji experienced its worst hurricane in 21 years in February 1941. With winds raging in the vicinity of 130 miles an hour, trees were uprooted, corrugated iron flew through the air and rain fell in sheets. Military telephone lines were destroyed, debris blocked Suva's water supply intake, camp buildings at Samambula were wrecked and a stores hut caught fire, causing the loss of scarce battledress and 13,000 rounds of rifle ammunition. Miraculously no one died. Repair work began immediately. The hurricane did have had some benefits. For months afterwards quartermasters would blame any missing items on 'the blow'.[14]

For the first time the New Zealand Army was confronted by the challenge of tropical diseases and a climbing sick rate which threatened the fighting ability of the garrison. On 22 November 1940, 23 New Zealand Army Service sisters, led by Matron Gladys Thwaites, arrived in Suva to work in a temporary hospital set up in a girls' school hostel. They cared for some 25 patients initially, most of them suffering from heat and the effects of a change of climate. They also had to cope with the outbreak of a measles epidemic. Medical officers from 7 Field Ambulance were kept busy ensuring that the newly established camps were sanitary and dealing with 'hill diarrhoea', which broke out in early December 1940. The shortage of water for drinking, cooking and washing as troop numbers built up contributed to outbreaks of septic sores. Sea water used for washing was found to contain traces of coral and to be contaminated by insects. These were lessons learned only by experience. There were also epidemics of gastroenteritis, 'dhobi's itch' (a groin infection called *Tinea cruris*), ringworm and dysentery. In August 1941 the temporary hospital in Suva was replaced by a new 140-bed hospital (though it could take up to 200 patients) built some five miles away, on Tamavua Heights. A regular flow of men returning to New Zealand medically unfit would continue until a convalescent depot was established at Nukulau Island on 23 January 1942.[15]

Because Suva Harbour was strategically important, the British provided two 6-inch guns, which arrived on 1 December 1940. Between August and November 1940 German raiders were active in the South Pacific and an attack on Fiji was expected. On 6 December 1940 a Japanese cargo ship failed to stop when ordered and a warning round was fired. It was later thought that the ship had provoked the fire to plot the location of the battery.[16] Six days later searchlights were installed and the Suva Battery was manned around the clock.

In August 1941, a British adviser to the New Zealand government, Lieutenant-General Guy Williams, suggested that New Zealand take overall responsibility, expedite defence work, base a squadron of fighter bombers in Fiji, organise coastal batteries and increase the garrison.[17] In line with previous defence reports, Williams considered that New Zealand would be exposed only to commerce raiders or limited attack so long as Singapore held and the United States Pacific Fleet remained in existence. Williams also appraised New Zealand's strategic situation if Singapore fell, and noted the deficiencies of its troops in Fiji. Most had not completed their basic training, and regular rotation made the creation of an effective cohesive military force difficult. He recommended that the men should have at least three months' training before arriving in Fiji and that the tour of duty should be a minimum of 12 months. Williams considered 8 Brigade's proficiency in weapon handling and the artillery needed live firing exercises. In many respects Williams was simply reflecting the views of senior New Zealand army officers, but as a British general and outsider his views had weight. Wellington accepted his report,[18] which would profoundly affect the government's view of Fiji's defence needs.

Nevertheless, the New Zealand Army continued with a Second Relief on 14 August 1941. Apart from some senior officers, the brigade was again made up of fresh personnel with limited training. The new officers, mostly second lieutenants, had only recently graduated.[19] The return of ten captains to New Zealand left subalterns as company commanders and there were insufficient NCOs. The relief process meant that, at a critical time, the brigade was undertrained, underequipped, short on officers, lacking in cohesion and largely unused to the Pacific climate. On the other hand, an infantry brigade had been established, equipped and deployed to Fiji, despite shipping being in short supply and German raiders disrupting New Zealand's coastal shipping. In undertaking the relief, Cunningham was only too aware that the sick rate was increasing and many of the older officers were suffering in the tropical conditions.

By October 1941 war with Japan seemed increasingly likely and 8 Brigade's status changed to that of a frontline unit rather than merely being a garrison and a reservoir of trained personnel for 2NZ Division. When Cunningham returned to New Zealand, he made Fiji's defence needs clear to the newly appointed Chief of General Staff, Lieutenant-General Edward Puttick, who promised weapons and equipment, including grenades, armoured cars and mortars, together with more soldiers.

Anticipating that London would accept Williams' proposal that Wellington take control in Fiji, New Zealand Minister of Defence, Fred Jones, and former prime minister Gordon Coates, now a member of the War Cabinet, and the NZCOS flew to Suva on 14 November 1941. Four days later Jones, Coates, the Governor of Fiji, Sir Harry Luke, the Colonial Secretary for Fiji, C.W.T. Johnson and the Secretary to the Western Pacific High Commission, H. Vaskess, signed an agreement defining New

Zealand's defence responsibilities in Fiji, which extended to all British territories within the New Zealand Naval Station. Another outcome was an agreement on the importance of airfield construction. Under the influence of General Douglas MacArthur, the earlier American decision to write off the Philippines as indefensible had been revised now that the revolutionary B-17 *Flying Fortress* was considered capable of devastating any Japanese invasion convoys.[20] The Americans needed staging airfields capable of handling the huge bombers and Wellington agreed to lengthen the runways at Nadi airfield. Construction started immediately, using 1400 New Zealand Department of Public Works men.[21]

Lewis and Bren guns began to arrive from New Zealand and rifle ranges were fully used. Fortification construction proceeded apace as anti-tank defences, gun emplacements, roads and deep tunnels for storage of petrol and ammunition were completed. The Suva Peninsula came to resemble a gigantic rabbit warren as the soldiers tunnelled into the hard soapstone. Much of this backbreaking work was done with picks, shovels and hand barrows because few mechanical tools were available. The difficult and unpleasant task of stringing barbed wire along beaches and mangrove swamps became a regular chore. Barbed wire sixteen feet wide and 4½ feet deep was staked into the key coastal areas.

New Zealand also deployed coastwatchers to report on enemy movements. Personnel skilled in wireless telegraphy were scarce, so volunteer New Zealand Post and Telegraph workers were employed, though as civilians they were likely to be shot as spies if captured. The first coastwatching stations had been established on the Campbell and Auckland Islands in March 1941. On 19 July 1941, 22 soldiers and 15 wireless operators sailed from Suva to the Gilbert, Ellice and Ocean Groups. They were placed on small islands where there was nowhere to hide and no hope of rescue in the event of Japanese invasion. To lend them some legitimacy and provide company, 'soldier companions', volunteers selected from 8 Brigade, accompanied them. The men were unarmed in the belief that this would enhance their chances of survival if captured. Arguably, the coastwatchers sent to the South Pacific were a sacrificial force designed to act as a tripwire to warn of Japanese advances. Peter Fraser affirmed that they had to remain at their post until 'a Japanese places his hand on their shoulder'.[22] This would have fatal consequences for some of the men.

# 5 Japan Enters the War

When news of the attacks on Malaya and then Pearl Harbor was received in Fiji on the morning of 8 December 1941[1] all the New Zealand units were on a training exercise and occupying defensive positions. Morale soared: at last the troops had a meaningful role. New Zealand declared war on Japan that morning. Outside Fiji, Tonga and Western Samoa, New Zealand's defence deployment in the Pacific consisted of the coastwatchers stationed in the Gilbert and Ellice Islands, Phoenix Island, Tokelau, Line and Cook Islands, linked by wireless to a New Zealand naval liaison officer in Suva. Fanning Island had a 6-inch gun and 105 New Zealand garrison troops. Fiji was defended by a manifestly inadequate force consisting of 12, mainly obsolete, military aircraft, five small patrol boats, two and a half New Zealand infantry battalions, three FDF Territorial companies and an FDF Home Guard company.[2] On 8 December the New Zealand War Cabinet approved an increase in troop numbers from 3050 to 6050,[3] which placed a huge strain on New Zealand's limited supply of shipping, manpower and equipment.

Even after the devastating aerial bombing of Pearl Harbor, the NZCOS initially underestimated the severity of the Japanese threat and still considered naval raiders the main threat to Fiji. Since the Middle East was 'a vital theatre', they felt that the reinforcements for 2NZ Division should be dispatched unless the Japanese attacked Fiji in force.[4] Nevertheless, because of the strategic value of Nadi airfield, they recommended that the garrison be increased to two brigades, a squadron of bombers and a squadron of fighters, and that the United States should be asked to contribute.[5]

Within one week 14 Brigade was organised and embarked. Its equipment was obtained from training camps, the National Military Reserve and various Home Guard units, leaving the army at home short of weapons and equipment. The measure of how desperately troops were needed in Fiji is shown by the experience of 37 Battalion. Formed at Burnham Camp on 29 December 1941, the battalion would sail from Lyttelton to Wellington on 9 January 1942, travel by train to Auckland and embark on SS *Rangatira* the next day. It would disembark on the 14th at Lautoka, from where it would be transported to its camp at the Sambeto River. There it would build roads and assist with camp organisation for the next month.[6] Two weeks from formation to deployment was not enough time to develop any unit cohesion.

By 20 December the NZCOS were recommending that Fiji should have precedence for equipment and that New Zealand's only four anti-aircraft guns should be deployed there.[7] 'Whereas formerly the Islands were the first line of defence for New Zealand, their retention by us is now vital, for the prosecution of war against Japan. So long as we hold the Islands, large scale operations against New Zealand are unlikely. It is therefore necessary to take all possible steps to defend those islands adequately.' They concluded that the Japanese would realise the increased importance of Fiji and were therefore likely to attack in greater numbers than estimated by Williams.[8]

The hammer blows of Japanese victories profoundly shocked the Allies. The invasion of Malaya started on 8 December, Guam was captured on the 10th, the same day that Japanese aircraft sank the British ships HMS *Prince of Wales* and HMS *Repulse* off Kuantan in the South China Sea and Japanese troops invaded the Philippines. Wake Island was taken on 23 December, and Hong Kong finally fell on Christmas Day. MacArthur abandoned Manila and retreated to Bataan, and Singapore appeared to be in danger. These events caused consternation in Wellington. In a cable to Winston Churchill on 24 December, Fraser indicated that although the extensions to Nadi airfield were proceeding apace, he was concerned that it could be a liability if not properly defended. New Zealand could provide a brigade, but there were difficulties in equipping it. Significantly, Fraser asked Churchill to impress on American President Franklin Roosevelt the strategic importance of Fiji and the chronic need for weapons. New Zealand had lost faith in the Singapore strategy.[9]

On 26 December 1941 Fraser raised with General Bernard Freyberg, who was commanding 2NZ Division, the prospect that all or part of the

8th Reinforcements intended for the Middle East should be diverted to Pacific defence.[10] The prime minister noted that there was 'no intention of ignoring our responsibility for maintaining the Middle East Forces at proper strength' but 'neither we nor you can disregard the possibility that events in this part of the world may greatly increase our difficulties in this respect.' On 27 December the sailing of the 8th Reinforcements to the Middle East was postponed indefinitely and a week later the 9th Reinforcements were allocated to the defence of New Zealand and Fiji. Freyberg replied that his recent 5000 reinforcements could maintain his division until August 1942.

During December 1941, 771 soldiers arrived in Fiji, bringing 34 Battalion up to full strength. Fortification work continued at a frenetic pace. Little leave was allowed. Necessity required invention. Given the paucity of AA guns, six antique 18-pounder field guns were emplaced and put to a novel use as anti-aircraft weapons. As Third Division history *The Gunners* records, 'they had their trails dug deep in miry pits. With a false setting on their "TP 80" fuses and a false angle of sight they were prepared to provide a barrage from 4,000 ft down to 500 ft over Kings Wharf and other important objectives.' Even though their range was limited to a height of 4000 feet, shrapnel shells were fired across Suva by way of experiment, in the hope that they could be used to deter low-flying aircraft.[11] Ammunition arrived in significant quantities and 35 Field Battery was put to work digging tunnels to create storage. Motor mechanics, medics, searchlight crews and communications specialists were in short supply. In early January 1942 four troopships arrived from New Zealand bringing 35 Battalion, artillery units and Divisional Headquarters staff. 36 Battalion and 37 Battalion soon followed in mid-January 1942. The garrison had risen to 7600 soldiers. The troops resented the 1000-plus civilians who were employed constructing airfields because of their better pay and conditions. As the garrison grew, Cunningham relinquished his command of 8 Brigade and was promoted to Major-General and overall command of New Zealand troops. On 6 January 1942, Brigadier L.G. Goss took command of 8 Brigade and Brigadier Leslie Potter assumed command of the newly formed 14 Brigade.

February 1942 was a bad month for the Allies. The Japanese advanced in the Philippines, completed the capture of Malaya and Singapore, invaded the Dutch East Indies, landed in New Britain, launched air raids on Darwin and completed the destruction of Allied ships in the Battle of the Java Sea. Japan seemed to be unstoppable and there was an almost palpable sense of panic in Wellington as plans were made for the destruction of key facilities and even the evacuation of the government from the capital in the event of Japanese invasion. Fear gripped the New Zealand population. It was uncertain where the Japanese would strike next, but it seemed likely that they would exploit their newly acquired bases in the Gilbert and Ellice Islands, and coastwatchers confirmed a build-up of enemy shipping. New Zealand Army HQ anticipated an attack on Fiji on 8–11 February 1942 and the troops were told that air and naval attacks, even an invasion, were possible. Fortunately the intelligence was incorrect.

The Deputy Chief of Staff, Brigadier K.L. Stewart, visited Fiji on 8 February 1942 and took command of New Zealand troops temporarily when Major-General Cunningham was hospitalised with dysentery. Cunningham was so sick he was returned to New Zealand and was then replaced by Brigadier Owen H. Mead, who arrived on 25 February. Colonel Robert A. Row took over 8 Brigade and Brigadier L.G. Goss was sent for liaison duties in Australia. The title of the New Zealand Force was changed to 'Pacific Section 2NZEF'.[12]

On 12 March 1942, 1032 reinforcements arrived in Suva. However, Mead was told he should expect no more than small parties and should incorporate Fijians in New Zealand units. After discussions with the Fijian governor, it was decided that 3 Battalion of the FDF would be formed at Lautoka and, once trained, would come under the operational command of 14 Infantry Brigade. Although New Zealand officers and NCOs were to be seconded to the FDF, it would consist of as many native Fijians as possible.[13]

The crisis in the Pacific called for one overall theatre commander. However, rivalries between the American Army and Navy led to the Pacific being divided into various command areas. To the consternation of the Australasians, the US Joint Chiefs of Staff decreed that the South West Pacific Area encompassing Australia would be commanded by General Douglas MacArthur and dominated by the US Army. The South Pacific Area including New Zealand would be commanded by a US Navy officer responsible to Admiral Chester Nimitz and would be dominated by the US Navy. These command areas were imposed on Australia and New Zealand. The issue remained, however, whether American resources could be deployed in time and in sufficient quantities to head off the rampaging Japanese.

On 20 March the United States took responsibility for defending Western Samoa. New Zealand troops there were to be used as military police to deal with the local population, one of the first instances where New Zealand soldiers were placed under American operational command.[14] By this time the Tonga Defence Force, controlled from Fiji, comprised 110 New Zealanders and 650 Tongans, two 4-inch guns and two 18-pounders.

In the light of the possible invasion of Fiji, the New Zealand Army, the Fijian civil administration and the Fijian chiefs discussed the possibility of guerrilla warfare. Brigadier Leslie Potter suggested raising guerrilla units to harass the Japanese, gather intelligence and provide enclaves where Allied troops could reform. They would have access to caches of food, weapons and explosives. Recruits were obtained from Fijian villages and in April 1942, under the command of New Zealand officers and NCOs, they began guerrilla training. In May three commando units were formed from New Zealand and FDF personnel. One of these, Northern Independent Commando, was mounted on horseback and operated in the western area of Viti Levu. Some later Fijian units were described as 'guerrillas'. Led predominantly by New Zealanders, they were employed by the Americans on Guadalcanal, New Georgia and Bougainville, and proved extremely adept as scouts.[15]

Mead believed that any Japanese invasion would consist of at least one division supported by tanks and aircraft. He was also concerned that the Japanese would strike against not only Viti Levu but also other Fijian islands, stretching Allied resources. Because the naval strength in Fiji was

Private P. Wacquawai of 1st Commando Fiji Guerrillas waiting in ambush.

*(Archives NZ WAII, 7, 3 Official Photograph Album, photographer unknown)*

insufficient, the first line of defence consisted of aircraft: a squadron of twenty-four P-39 *Aircobra* fighter planes, nine *Hudson* light bombers, five *Vincent* bombers, three *Singapore* flying boats and three *De Havilland* light planes. All these aircraft were obsolete and would have been decimated if exposed to the full force of Japanese air power. Even the most modern American fighter available, the P-39 *Aircobra,* was completely outmatched by the Japanese *Zero*, whose pilots viewed the P-39 as 'easy meat'.[16] Mead understood that he could rely on his air assets only for reconnaissance and transportation. He believed that extra brigade groups were required, and that tanks were desirable, together with a motorised infantry battalion and a 25-pounder artillery battery.[17] Although efforts had been made to provide weaponry and equipment, some specialised units of artillery, engineers and signals remained so poorly equipped that their capabilities in combat were questionable.

Brigadier Robert A. Row assumed command of 8 Brigade Group on 4 March 1942 and decided to test his unit by holding an exercise that only senior officers would be aware was just a training exercise. Accordingly, on 8 March all units in Suva were told that an enemy convoy was approaching Fiji and later they were informed that half of the convoy was heading towards Lautoka and the other half was heading for Suva. Because the troops believed that this was the real thing, they occupied their posts and set up fields of fire by uprooting trees and shrubs and damaging private property. On 9 March the troops were told that the enemy had landed and established a beach head at Nausori. They were then required to force march to Nausori. After the units had gone ten to fifteen miles they were told that it was simply an exercise. There was some degree of anger on the part of the troops that they had been hoaxed. The exercise did, however, reveal weaknesses such as that there were insufficient vehicles, that the signals system had been inadequate, emergency rations had not been issued to the troops and there had been inadequate attention to anti-aircraft defences.

On 20 April 1942, the NZCOS told the War Cabinet that Fiji urgently required further forces – at least two brigade groups and a battalion on Viti Levu and one brigade group and a battalion on Vanua Levu. Coastal artillery and anti-aircraft guns were essential, as were fighter aircraft. These additional forces could come only from the United States or New Zealand. American troops were not immediately available so Wellington had little option but to send more men to Fiji.

The Chiefs of Staff recommended that the serious situation be drawn to the urgent attention of Vice-Admiral Robert Ghormley, USN, who had recently been appointed Commander of the South Pacific Area, and American reinforcements requested. If the United States refused, the NZCOS considered the situation serious enough for the New Zealand Army Reserve Brigade Group to be sent to Viti Levu. Their recommendation was approved on 22 April and Fraser cabled Walter Nash, the New Zealand representative in Washington, asking him to point out to Admiral Ernest J. King, the Chief of Naval Operations, that the NZCOS considered six divisions necessary for the defence of New Zealand, but only the equivalent of three divisions were available. The New Zealand Cabinet approved the dispatch of 2000 additional troops to Fiji to man weapons and equipment supplied by the United States.[18] The Americans told Nash that the security of the Pacific area had to be looked at as a whole and that they expected New Zealand to supply 12,000 troops to Fiji by the end of 1942.[19]

Fraser instructed Nash to make it clear in Washington that New Zealand had already sent to Fiji 'greater forces than we could reasonably be expected to spare, amounting to approximately a quarter of our effective strength at that time' and 'all the anti-aircraft guns, both light and heavy, that we possessed'. Providing 12,000 men 'would cripple the defences of this Dominion' and 'denude New Zealand of equipment'. Even if 2NZ Division were brought home to supply troops for Fiji, it would take too long. 'Suggest either United States or Canadian reinforcements.'[20]

The strategic situation worsened when the island of Corregidor fell to the Japanese on 5–6 May, ending formal American resistance in the Philippines. By this time the Japanese had taken Burma and were advancing into New Guinea and the Solomon Islands. A planned Japanese amphibious operation to take Port Moresby triggered a naval battle in the Coral Sea on 7–8 May. The Japanese won a tactical victory by sinking USS *Lexington* in exchange for a light Japanese carrier, but the Japanese troop convoy was prevented from carrying out its mission. Imperial Japanese Army forces, however, remained intact and potent.

The Battle of the Coral Sea focused American military attention on the South Pacific. On 9 May Admiral King told Nash that both he and Admiral Chester Nimitz, the Commander in Chief of the United States Pacific Fleet, believed that it was urgent that Fiji and Tonga should be strengthened and that this was best accomplished by the United States taking over. When Nash suggested that six divisions were needed for the defence of New Zealand, King pointed out that the supply of American troops was limited and there were many demands on them. Troopships had already been sent to Fiji to disembark American troops and repatriate the New Zealand garrison. Nash suggested that New Zealand troops be trained for amphibious warfare, provided that they could be equipped and that these soldiers could take part in later American offensives. The following day Nash learned that American troops for Fiji had been delayed, that one division had been intended for Fiji and that this would be strengthened by support personnel and anti-aircraft guns. In the meantime it was proposed that New Zealand guns and personnel should remain, but the United States would eventually take over operational command of the FDF. Fraser obtained Whitehall's approval, then indicated New Zealand's acceptance.

Mead was instructed to prepare camps for the American troops and told that a shuttle service would be run by troop transport USS *President Coolidge*, returning troops to New Zealand. It was, however, vital that the garrison strength be maintained during the transfer period. New Zealand anti-aircraft and coastal units would remain in Fiji until approximately August or September. Matters were complicated by further delays in the dispatch of troops from the United States. The Americans requested that New Zealand send further troops to Fiji, and these arrived during May. On 12 May Fiji and the other islands in the South Pacific were placed under the command of Vice-Admiral Ghormley, who inspected the Fijian defences before continuing to Auckland. In the meantime Mead took command of all forces on Fiji, the first occasion when a New Zealander had military control over American troops.

In early June 1942, at the Battle of Midway, the main Japanese carrier force of four fleet carriers was sunk, removing that threat. Although substantial Japanese surface and submarine units continued to operate, the Japanese Navy had been dealt a severe blow. Planned Japanese operations for August 1942 to seize Samoa, Fiji and New Caledonia were cancelled on 11 July.

Although the New Zealand government had agreed to the Americans' proposal that they have defence responsibility of Fiji for the duration of the war and six months thereafter, Fraser was surprised that New Zealand troops were not to be retained. He 'felt that these troops would be of greater value in Fiji than in New Zealand',[21] but the Americans did not agree. Although they intended to have 23,000 ground and air personnel in Fiji by September, Fraser believed this number was still inadequate and he renewed the offer of troops. King was adamant that the New Zealand troops be repatriated, apparently because of an American preference for homogeneity of forces and unity of command. The Americans also seem to have been concerned that if New Zealand troops remained, 'the New Zealand War Cabinet would subsequently feel an aching void in New Zealand and demand a further US Division for New Zealand'.[22]

Once the decision had been taken, arrangements were made to send the New Zealanders home and the Americans took over New Zealand facilities. Jack Cantwell was a signaller with headquarters. He and his comrades were encamped at the bottom of a hill and the telephone and radio centre was sited at the top of the hill. He recalled climbing the hill one morning, as usual, with his comrades to begin their daily work. On this day, however, they found their way barred by an American sentry who told them that they could not enter. Undeterred, the Kiwis gained access to the facility by a tunnel. One of them then approached the American from behind and tapped him on the shoulder.[23]

For some of the troops the journey home was not a comfortable one. USS *President Coolidge* was so crammed with troops – three infantry battalions together with artillery units – that the men received only two meals a day during the three-day voyage to Auckland.[24] By the end of July the two brigades had returned to New Zealand. There would be no return for Mead. On 25 July 1942 he flew from Suva intent on a final inspection of troops on Tonga. His *Hudson* was never found.

# Confusion and Obfuscation

# 6

## Forming a division

Even before its soldiers returned from Fiji, questions arose about what New Zealand's contribution would be to the land war in the South Pacific: home defence, combat troops, garrison units, labour units or a combination of these? Answers would inevitably involve the United States.

It would also involve a convoluted and torturous process with both Wellington and Washington talking past each other and misunderstandings, obfuscation and hidden agendas (sometimes changing) abounding. But for the driving force of Japanese pressure in the South Pacific, it is doubtful that New Zealand land forces would have returned to fight in the South Pacific alongside their American ally.

Fraser had initially focused on protecting New Zealand by garrisoning Fiji, but after those troops were repatriated he began to think of using the garrison troops as a cadre for a division for combat operations. Fraser's desire for New Zealand troops to take part in offensive operations in the South Pacific stemmed from a mixture of motives: the fear that Allied preoccupation with the European war would allow the Japanese to launch fresh attacks in the Pacific, the need to secure New Zealand's defence, ensure a 'British' presence in the Pacific War and establish a claim for a New Zealand voice in the post-war settlement in the Pacific, and to deflect Australian criticism of New Zealand's failure to withdraw 2NZ Division from the Middle East to fight in the Pacific.

Peter Fraser, Prime Minister of New Zealand, c.1940.

*(Alexander Turnbull Library, PA Coll 5547-033, photographer S. P. Andrew)*

Yet Fraser continued to qualify his enthusiastic offers to participate in land operations with the Americans. He sought to have the RNZAF placed under American command and told Nash that Wellington wished to provide 20 squadrons of modern aircraft by 1943. However, the Americans would have to provide the aircraft – and it would entail a huge allocation of personnel. In a draft cable to Nash dated 12 July 1942 but never sent, Fraser indicated that although 'New Zealand would be willing to detach certain army formations and place them under American control for amphibious operations' – this had been much discussed – this 'would not permanently release them from their defence functions in New Zealand until the time came for them to move out of New Zealand.' The bitter experience of New Zealand losses in the Greek and Crete campaigns had made Fraser wary of high-risk operations.

This wariness increased when Ghormley told the New Zealand Chief of General Staff, Lieutenant-General Edward Puttick, about the impending invasion of Guadalcanal (Operation *Watchtower*) but specified that he not tell the War Cabinet until 7 August. When an affronted Fraser eventually learned of *Watchtower* from MacArthur and John Curtin, the Australian prime minister, he remonstrated with Ghormley that he did not want another Crete in the Pacific and demanded to be advised of plans for any proposed use of New Zealand troops.

General Edward Puttick.

*(Alexander Turnbull Library, PA Coll 5547-05)*

Puttick also had an influence on the constitution and role of what would become 3NZ Division. His responsibility for the defence of the New Zealand homeland coloured his attitude, often making his advice cautious and tinged with reservations. He had begun his career as a draughtsman for the Public Works Department and was familiar with the ways of the civil service. A First World War veteran, Puttick became a member of New Zealand's Permanent Force and held various staff positions. He had commanded 4th New Zealand Infantry Brigade in the disastrous Greek campaign, and after Crete Fraser had offered him the position of Senior Land Force Commander in New Zealand. Based in Wellington, Puttick was attuned to politics and Fraser's desire for New Zealand participation in South Pacific offensive operations.

Puttick attempted unsuccessfully to ascertain American requirements for New Zealand units when Ghormley arrived in New Zealand. The War Cabinet then authorised Puttick to discuss with the Americans amphibious training for New Zealand troops. Puttick wrote that 'on the assumption that it is the wish of War Cabinet that NZ troops should take part in offensive operations, that a reinforced division (Force D) be the basis for planning, that the cadre of forces returned from Fiji be its foundation and that a divisional commander be appointed immediately.' The choice of the reinforced division would enable Wellington to keep its options open for garrison or combat operations.

Puttick sought advice, not from the Americans, but from the British, on the possible organisation of New Zealand troops in amphibious and garrison operations. His assumption that New Zealand troops would be involved in offensive operations was 'confirmed by cables from Washington suggesting that the 3rd NZ Division on return from Fiji should train with the 1st United States Marine Division for amphibious operations.' He thought that brigade groups with reduced equipment would be suitable.[1]

In late July Puttick visited Ghormley and again discussed the role of New Zealand troops. Ghormley indicated they would be used as follow-on troops to secure captured areas, freeing up American amphibious assault troops. He suggested that New Zealand prepare four different force configurations 'so as to be able to meet any contingency at short notice' and 'be ready to embark after 25 August'. This date probably fitted Ghormley's conception of when American positions on Guadalcanal would be secured and the island could be handed to garrison forces. All the configurations featured anti-aircraft and heavy artillery and were best suited to defensive operations. Ghormley also indicated that he did not require New Zealand troops to be amphibiously trained because he had sufficient and special equipment was scarce. In his opinion, New Zealand should supply garrison troops.[2]

On 31 July Puttick told Defence Minister Fred Jones of his support for Ghormley's request, while acknowledging that there was 'considerable work and no time to spare'. The proposed division would need to obtain men from throughout New Zealand but most would have to come from the Reserve Brigade Group and Home Defence forces. He pointed out that New Zealand home forces were stronger due to the creation of the Army Tank Brigade, better equipment and training, together with an improved strategic situation. He acknowledged the danger of sending forces offshore but urged the War Cabinet to assist Ghormley 'to the maximum possible extent'. In the meantime he was 'proceeding with the reorganisation of the 3rd Division'.[3]

Within a few days Puttick was reporting on 'the major difficulties' involved. These included the necessity of rcplacing unsuitable and medically unfit personnel, the needs of 2NZ Division, the under-strength nature of most units, the need to inoculate troops, administrative problems associated with leave, equipment and uniform, requirements of operational security and the fact that the units returning from Fiji would not be available until 30 August, five days after Ghormley's deadline. Puttick also touched on the deficiencies in training. Yet he believed that 'the scope and nature of operations' justified the risk of employing 'incompletely trained troops'. Puttick warned that it was dangerous to assume that the New Zealanders would be used only in limited roles. Sending 3NZ Division overseas would mean the disappearance of the Army Brigade Group and a weakening of the defences around Auckland, but this could be accommodated by redeploying units.

There were, Puttick emphasised, no certainties. American forces had built up in the South Pacific and seemed intent on offensive operations. He thought Japan would probably confine operations to where it had air superiority, but might attempt 'vigorous offensive operations' in New Guinea or New Caledonia. However, he considered a major Allied naval defeat, and the fall of New Caledonia and Fiji, were prerequisites for an invasion of New Zealand. He believed New Zealand should participate 'to the fullest extent in offensive operations against the Japanese' while strengthening Home Defence forces. Provided forces were brought up to strength, and that proposed American operations were reasonable and enhanced New Zealand security, sending a reinforced division to Fiji made sense.[4] The War Cabinet agreed: a division would be 'established and trained in New Zealand for offensive purposes – the basis of the Division to be the Fijian Force and the 7th Brigade Group'. On 11 August it approved the appointment of Major General Harold Eric Barrowclough as commander.

A battle-hardened veteran of the Western Front in the First World War and North Africa in the Second World War, Barrowclough was a combat soldier, but one with considerable administrative skills. He had been recalled from Egypt on 22 February 1942, with the expectation that he would command the Pacific Division, but discovered that the command of the forces in Fiji had been given to Mead because the suddenness of Cunningham's departure and the worsening of the situation had necessitated an immediate appointment. He was extremely angry and initially considered demanding to be returned to North Africa. He rejected command of the South Island Home Defence Division in favour of his home area of Northland, the most likely focus of Japanese invasion, and characteristically threw his energies into forming units, training and welding them into an effective fighting force.

Barrowclough was then asked to assess New Zealand's defence against possible invasion, more specifically North Auckland and the Bay of Islands. He gloomily concluded 'with our present grouping of forces I am certain that we cannot hold any of these positions for more than a few hours'. However, following Mead's death, Puttick arranged for Barrowclough to take command of 3NZ Division. Barrowclough's instructions referred to 'offensive operations',[5] which would have fitted his inclinations.

On 10 August 1942 Brigadier Stewart, the New Zealand Deputy Chief of Staff, was told by Ghormley that the New Zealand force would relieve the 1st US Marine Division on Guadalcanal. Stewart made enquiries and in his report he favoured a first echelon made up of an infantry brigade, anti-aircraft units, artillery and supporting forces. He stressed the unhealthy nature of Guadalcanal (malaria, blackwater fever, dysentry, jungle sores), water supply problems, lack of roading, need for cover from rain and weather and problems with local intelligence. Stewart had strong reservations about logistics and the need for the Americans to commit to this. He concluded that 'a reinforced div[ision] is the minimum force which can do the job. Anything smaller is asking for trouble.' He also concluded that 'casualties from disease alone will be heavy and will necessitate a constant flow of reinforcements'. He warned that New Zealand could expect shipping losses from air and submarine attacks.[6]

Major-General Harold Eric Barrowclough, Commander of 3NZ Division.

*(Alexander Turnbull Library, War History Collection H-346/7/43, photographer unknown)*

Ghormley had in mind that the New Zealanders would supply garrison troops. Although Ghormley did not want New Zealand combat troops, Wellington told him on 10 August that a reinforced division would be made available to him 'as requested' from 25 August.[7] Realistically, the offer could not be fulfilled and Stewart would have known that. He would also have known that he was on safe ground. Importantly, the despatch of the force was subject to New Zealand Government approval after Fraser had consulted personally with Ghormley. This provided an opportunity for non-performance while seeming to co-operate.

Ghormley declined the offer.[8] His reasons appear to have been his aversion to dealing with foreign troops, shipping and support problems, reservations about the combat-worthiness of New Zealand troops, unwillingness to deal with Wellington and his focus on Guadalcanal. The American foothold there was tenuous. Although the landings on 7 August 1942 were successful, the disastrous naval Battle of Savo Island two days later triggered the withdrawal of transports and the USN covering force. Thereafter the battle see-sawed. These uncertainties were conveyed to Fraser in November 1942: 'operations in the South Pacific have entered a critical phase. The serious naval losses which the Americans have sustained ... render their ability to command the seas problematical ... Should Guadalcanal fall, as well it may, and should Espiritu Santo also be taken, ... the Americans will be thrown back on New Caledonia and Fiji'.[9] The New Zealand force was to be held in abeyance. Ghormley later complained that the New Zealanders were always asking questions and he felt that Wellington was 'so afraid that they will run into a second Crete that they are very backward in coming forward'. He concluded that 'they do not want to put their troops into a hot spot [and] in some ways you cannot blame them'.[10]

Meanwhile Fraser's confidence in Ghormley had been fundamentally undermined, changing his attitude towards a forward deployment of the division. Fraser had called into Noumea on 12–13 August 1942 on his way to Washington. He wished to clarify Ghormley's requirements for fighting the Japanese in the Solomons. Ghormley had just received the news of the loss of four Allied cruisers at the Battle of Savo Island, one of the greatest defeats in US naval history.[11] He crumbled before Fraser's eyes. The prime minister lost confidence in him, cancelled his trip to Washington, returned to New Zealand and began to think again of home defence. This is what Stewart was referring to when he wrote to the American Lt. Col. Mead that 'there have been certain developments regarding the use of New Zealand troops for offensive operations' and that it was 'most unlikely that the New Zealand Government will agree to the despatch of any New Zealand troops for operations outside New Zealand until it is fully informed of the nature of the operations.'[12]

Stewart attached a questionnaire for the Americans to complete. It asked about the tasks to be allotted to New Zealand forces, the size and composition of the force, its naval and air support, who its commander would be, what arrangements were proposed to protect the troop convoy, what the logistical arrangements would consist of, an appreciation of enemy strength and capabilities and shipping and loading details. The government, Stewart said, could take several days coming to a decision and suggested that the Americans make the request for troops 'at the earliest moment after you know that our assistance will be required'. In the meantime steps were being taken to form a minimum force, Kiwi A. A larger force, Kiwi C, was also being formed. Ghormley had wanted a maximum force, Kiwi D, but this was being held in abeyance, although it could be formed if needed. Stewart hoped he had made 'the position perfectly clear': 'we must avoid misunderstandings'. Mead replied that 'the time and place of possible New Zealand participation is still indefinite'.[13]

Puttick also began to have doubts about the desirability of sending troops overseas and told Jones so on 3 September. He indicated that 'Kiwi A', the smallest force, 'will not be sufficiently well trained to undertake an active role in the forward theatre of operations until it has had a period of at least six weeks training from date', although that could perhaps be reduced if needed. And War Cabinet approval would be needed.[14] A clear message had been sent to the Americans: even the smallest New Zealand force was not up to standard, and there were likely to be problems getting Wellington's consent to overseas deployment. This effectively killed the prospect of New Zealand involvement in combat operations on Guadalcanal.

When Ghormley had turned down New Zealand's offer of a full division, Wellington decided to proceed with creating Kiwi A, which was essentially no more than the follow-on garrison force sought by Ghormley but with a stronger artillery component. Although Kiwi A was to have top priority, the formation of Kiwi C also went ahead. This option included both 8 and 14 Brigades with supporting troops. Kiwi D was shelved.

Although Kiwi C was in many ways a flexible option combining the possibilities of both offensive and garrison roles, there were problems. Organisation was hampered by delays in establishing the Base Headquarters Staff. There was also fuzziness with the relationship between Kiwi A and Kiwi C. The impression had grown that Kiwi A was the priority and anything to do with Kiwi C could be resolved after Kiwi A had been deployed overseas. When this led to unnecessary duplication and delays in training and equipping, Barrowclough sought a ruling that units would be brought up to Kiwi C levels. He asked for priority because 'I may be called upon to go into action immediately on landing at my destination, and the problem confronting me is very different from and much more difficult than that which confronted General Freyberg when he took the 2NZEF out of this country to an admirable training ground in Egypt'.[15]

Raising the troops proved difficult. Kiwi A seemed to be more viable since it was smaller and more easily equipped, but this conflicted with Puttick's direction to 'Proceed with Force C including full scale transport'.[16] This could not have been achieved because the organisation and the transport were simply not available.

The US Headquarters made it clear that the division would not be expected to carry out assault landings. It would most likely be needed for garrisoning small islands and possibly land operations on larger islands. Since units would be operating in the tropics, medical and other support would be needed. As heavy counter-attacks from air, sea and land-captured areas were likely, beachheads and ports would need to be strongly defended. This required anti-aircraft and coastal defence units. There was little chance that the division would be sent into the combat zone while the danger of invasion to New Zealand remained high.

As Fraser told Nash in September 1942, Ghormley had 'made it clear that the time to ask for [a New Zealand force] has not yet arrived and our impression is that when requested the force will not be as large as a Division. In the meantime, we are preparing a Division ... which at present will be retained intact for the defence of New Zealand but could be made available either in whole or in part for transfer to the islands if in our opinion circumstances warrant it.'[17]

Oblivious to the controversies regarding their role, the units of 3NZ Division began to coalesce. The units repatriated from Fiji formed the cadre and specialist supporting units were created around them. This was against a backdrop of continuing uncertainties about Japanese capabilities and, despite the American victory at Midway, the possibility that New Zealand might still face a Japanese invasion.

# Growing Pains

# 7

Homecoming was bittersweet for the troops returning from Fiji. They had travelled from the oppressive heat of the tropics to the frosts and bone-chilling rain of a severe New Zealand winter. Most of the soldiers rapidly succumbed to heavy colds and influenza. It did not help that the army, in its own thoughtless way, sometimes failed to provide adequate shelter. In October 1942 some soldiers were quartered in sheep and cattle pens at the Hamilton Show Grounds, which predictably produced a near mutinous reaction. Others were obliged in live in tents or huts through which the cold winter winds blew. 35 Battalion's sick bay at Paerata consisted of a four-man hut without light, sink or running water.[1]

Apart from the units who had garrisoned Fiji, the units of 3NZ Division were almost conjured out of midair. The best men had already been sent to Freyberg's 2NZ Division and Barrowclough had to content himself with what he was given. Some men were volunteers. Others were conscripts. Very few thought that they would be sent to the South Pacific.

The army dredged its manpower reserves, sifting out those who were unfit or exempted. The formation of military units takes time but under the pressure of events the basic outline of 3NZ Division had begun to appear by early October 1942: a divisional headquarters, heavy artillery, field guns, anti-aircraft, anti-tank, engineers, signals, Army Service Corps, medical, dental, base units, ordnance and two infantry brigades. Soldiers had been recruited from the length and breadth of New Zealand and had been inducted into various army camps.

In terms of divisional staff, Barrowclough had Colonel John Brooke-White (Commander Royal Engineers) and Brigadier Charles Duff (Commander Royal Artillery), who had experience from the Desert War. Many of his other officers were First World War veterans, some physically unfit and most lacking recent combat experience. The division consisted initially of soldiers from 8 and 14 Brigade Groups, who were fit primarily for static warfare, together with hastily raised units that were generally ill-equipped and untrained. Those who had been in Fiji had received little or no training in operations larger than a battalion and there was almost no sense of unit cohesion, let alone divisional identity. Men had to be given uniforms, equipped, trained, inoculated and vaccinated, all under the pressure of time.

One of Barrowclough's major achievements was to make 3NZ Division capable of complex combat operations in a tropical environment. First, he purged the division of unfit, inadequate or elderly officers and promoted younger and more energetic men. This had a beneficial effect on morale but many of the purged senior officers were retained in New Zealand in administrative or staff positions and harboured no love for Barrowclough. Second, he ensured that his men were thoroughly trained. He devised a training exercise in the Kaimai Ranges for his two brigades ('the Battle of the Kaimais'), one defending and one attacking.

Barrowclough attempted to draw all of the elements of his division together in the Waikato. Efforts were made to harden the troops by marching them to their new campsites and bivouacking for the night. Their destination was a steep area thickly clad in bush, chosen because of its similarity to the jungle of Kokoda in Papua New Guinea, where the Australians had recently beaten off a Japanese thrust to Port Moresby. Barrowclough intended the 'Battle of the Kaimais' to be as realistic as possible and to give the infantry, engineers and supporting medical and logistical units a taste of operating in difficult terrain.

To his chagrin the script did not unfold as he had planned. The weather closed in and rain fell in bitterly cold torrents. The engineers found that the task of forming roads in the slush and close vegetation required superhuman effort. Advance patrols were so exhausted by the weather and terrain that they welcomed 'capture' and simply asked to be fed. The Army Service Corps performed prodigious feats of logistics, on some occasions passing supply containers from hand to hand in order to reach the soaking, cold, exhausted soldiers. Predictably radio sets failed and command and control broke down. RNZAF planes cast in the role of Japanese aircraft overflew 8 Brigade's positions, which were clearly delineated by campfires, and the soldiers waved at the passing planes. They in turn entered into the spirit of things by showering the watching troops with 'propaganda material' which on closer examination, to the delight of the young men, turned out to be 'cheap immoral publications'.

After three weary days with both groups floundering in the adverse weather conditions, Barrowclough decided to halt the exercise. A highly annoyed Barrowclough, in a post-exercise debriefing, accused his men of thinking that 'they were the Tararua Tramping Club making a road and packing in supplies'. He was concerned that they had not taken the exercise seriously. In particular they had concentrated on making themselves comfortable rather than setting up defences, and their attempts to camouflage their positions from aerial observation had been poor to non-existent. The exercise had yielded some benefits, however: its very adversity had helped the men bond together and the exercise had exposed deficiencies in terms of communications, anti-air precautions and traffic control. At its most basic, the exercise had exposed the soldiers to the close vegetation that they would soon encounter in the Solomon Islands. According to a captain with 30 Battalion, 'The jungle exercise was well conceived … and the mass route march to the base of the Kaimais in the Matamata area [led by Barrowclough] was an excellent boost to lead into the exercise proper. I think this exemplified Barrowclough's class in appreciating the need to lift morale and also to bring to all the new and old members of the force a sense of unity.'[2] Lessons were learned in air/ground co-operation, logistics and engineering, but above all consolidation of 3NZ Division was begun.

In the meantime events were happening that would clarify the division's role.

* * *

Ghormley remained unclear whether he had the New Zealand government's consent to use its troops, but a request from the New Zealand Supply Mission for anti-malarial drugs focused matters. These drugs could only be obtained from the US Navy. King advised Ghormley that Wellington had requested anti-malarial drugs for about 20,000 men and asked whether he intended to use New Zealand troops in the forward area immediately. Ghormley responded: 'Have as yet no permission from New Zealand Government to use its troops. In any case do not intend to use New Zealand troops in forward areas while situation remains critical.'[3] Indeed, while King favoured moving to offensive operations, Ghormley had become defensive-minded and consistently focused on the need to garrison bases, and this coloured his attitude towards New Zealand troops.

Prime Minister Peter Fraser (centre) leaving a US Naval Air Transport Service plane in Hawaii with Admiral Chester W. Nimitz and Rear Admiral Robert Lee Ghormley, COMSOPAC, c. 1943.

*(Alexander Turnbull Library, War History Collection DA-02002, photographer unknown)*

In early September 1942 Ghormley requested that New Zealand garrison Tonga and Norfolk Island,[4] although this adversely affected New Zealand's ability to have troops ready for deployment. Ghormley's response was that 'the flexible situation necessitates the employment of troops where and when they are available'.[5] In late September and October 1942 36 Battalion and 34 Battalion were detached to garrison Norfolk Island (N Force) and Tonga (T Force) respectively. Puttick supported Ghormley's request despite the havoc this played with creating a force for deployment overseas.[6] Norfolk Island was seen as important to New Zealand's security because of its cable station and airfield. Both battalions were eventually replaced with some difficulty and allowed to rejoin their comrades on New Caledonia.

Ghormley quickly followed up with a request for troops to reinforce New Caledonia,[7] thereby freeing up the Americal Division for operations on Guadalcanal following the withdrawal of 1st Marine Division. Ghormley had intended to use New Zealand troops there as follow-on units, allowing the Marines to return to New Zealand. He had anticipated that the New Zealanders would only have to deal with guerrillas and the New Zealand commander would assume overall command. However, the

Marines found themselves locked in combat and a full division was needed to relieve them. The War Cabinet seems to have contemplated sending a full division but Puttick recommended to Jones that Kiwi C should be made available immediately and be brought up to full strength as soon as possible. Puttick supported the dispatch overseas of an under-strength, under-trained force, but one likely to be only involved in garrison duty. The War Cabinet agreed to send approximately two brigades to New Caledonia as soon as transport could be arranged. Puttick advised the Americans that a depleted Kiwi C would be ready for embarkation by 7 November.

Belatedly, Puttick raised the issue of whether the force was really suitable for the task facing it, reminding the New Zealand government on 2 November of its responsibility to ensure 'that New Zealand forces are reasonably adequate to meet the conditions which may arise'. It had to have details of other forces involved, American plans to reinforce and support New Caledonia, and the overall US Navy plan so that Wellington could gauge the cover provided. Kiwi C lacked tanks, its field artillery was below strength, as were two infantry battalions. Puttick seemed to be offering Wellington a ready-made reason for not supplying troops. He rammed home his concerns by saying that 'New Zealand should at least make such preparations as would enable New Zealand troops [from home defence units] to be moved at short notice to the support of its forward troops if … necessary.' He also recommended that an armoured regiment be sent at the first opportunity.[8] The War Cabinet approved the dispatch of an armoured regiment on 5 November.

In October Ghormley, considered to be lacking in aggression, was replaced as COMSOPAC by Admiral William Frederick Halsey, an energetic, aggressive commander, who placed his battleships and carriers at risk in sea battles around Guadalcanal. Although suffering losses, he secured Allied naval dominance and then focused on taking the offensive.

In January 1943 Halsey visited New Zealand and made a favourable impression on Fraser. Subsequently, Halsey had a meeting with Admiral Nimitz in Noumea and discussed with him the changed directive that made him responsible for the defence of New Zealand via the NZCOS. Halsey complained that Wellington had not specified what was available for home defence and what was for use in the Pacific. Nimitz told him to 'make a specific request for forces you want and tell them how you are going to employ each unit. Then you can devise the command set up.'[9] The command of New Zealand forces was clarified in Halsey's directive of 25 February, with home defence forces being controlled through the NZCOS.

Barrowclough considered it most likely that his division would be called upon to relieve American units on Guadalcanal. However, two tasks had to be accomplished before it would be combat ready. The first was to flesh it out to make it capable of relieving an American division. The second was to train it to a suitable standard for combat and acclimatising it to tropical conditions.

Appreciating that the impedimenta of heavy artillery would limit the division's role and usefulness, Barrowclough argued instead for a normal British-style division based around infantry. He envisaged three brigades at full strength, together with supporting units, but the recently formed 15 Brigade lacked a third infantry battalion and consequently was not able to defend its allocated area, nor relieve the other two brigades. Puttick agreed with Barrowclough that 15 Brigade urgently needed filling out, probably from Home Defence Forces. Required as soon as possible were a Field Artillery Regiment, 15 Brigade Headquarters with its supporting Signal Section, a Defence Platoon and Light Aid Detachment, a further Infantry Battalion, a composite ASC Company, a Field Ambulance, a Field Company of Engineers, an Anti-Tank Battery and a Light Artillery Regiment. This meant the commitment of an additional 3000 men at a time of severe manpower shortage, but the experience of 2NZ Division had shown that a two-brigade division and two-battalion brigades were invitations to disaster.

Halsey, short of both assault and garrison troops, also pressed for the completion of the division. He told Gordon Coates, a senior New Zealand Member of Parliament, in Noumea on 24 February 1943 that he wanted this to be done as soon as possible and he welcomed the prospect of a Maori battalion.[10] On 11 June Halsey told Barrowclough that he wished to concentrate 3NZ Division in the Solomons about 15 August, 'preparatory to active combat employment'. He asked Barrowclough to present this proposal to Puttick and the War Cabinet. If they approved, a firm plan would be presented to Wellington.[11]

There had been a complete shift in attitude. New Zealand troops were no longer seen as solely for garrison duty. Halsey was displeased at the prospect of an under-strength two-brigade division – 'There is a hard fight ahead of us and we are relying upon the New Zealand Division to bear its share of the effort'[12] – but he did not make its completion any easier. He vetoed Wellington's suggestion that the division could be brought up to strength by incorporating Fijian troops, because American units would have to replace them and he would be deprived of the Fijian troops as scouts and raiders. Halsey grudgingly indicated that he would rather have a dual-brigade 3NZ Division. He agreed that a Fijian battalion be attached to the division for raiding and scouting and that a second-line New Zealand battalion would reinforce Fiji, on condition that the number of Fijian troops in the Solomons was not reduced. When the Fijian battalion did not become available, the War Cabinet authorised the reduction to a dual-brigade division and its use in combat, subject to Barrowclough's certifying that it was suitably trained and equipped. The Americans told Barrowclough that tasks allotted to the under-strength division would be 'proportionately reduced'.

On 26 July 1943 Halsey told General Millard Harmon, commander of the US Army Forces in the South Pacific, that once Barrowclough advised him that the division was ready for combat, Harmon was to issue orders for its movement to Guadalcanal ready for offensive operations. Halsey foresaw this happening by 15 September. Barrowclough advised the War Cabinet on 31 July that the division was combat ready subject to certain reinforcements, and informed Halsey that it was suitable, subject to ammunition being supplied and the addition of the tank squadron and other detachments.

At this point Fraser, perhaps realising the enormity of what was happening and fearful of casualties, began pulling back. Halsey was to be told that because New Zealand had manpower difficulties, Barrowclough would not receive reinforcements and that further agricultural production in New Zealand to supply the South Pacific would require withdrawing troops. Halsey was bluntly informed that the division would probably have to be withdrawn if New Zealand was to provide supplies for 50,000 men. Halsey still felt that the division should go into action, although he expressed his disappointment to Fraser that he was not only missing out on a full division but that it would not receive reinforcements.

Despite these concerns, Barrowclough and the Americans proceeded with plans for the movement of 3NZ Division to New Caledonia. The struggle for Guadalcanal was still raging fiercely and the battered 1st US Marine Division desperately needed replacement by the US Army units on New Caledonia. Because New Caledonia was still under threat of invasion, the soldiers of 3NZ Division would be given the task of garrisoning strategic areas of the island.

# 8 New Caledonia

## The land of the Niaouli trees

The time spent on New Caledonia was to be a critical phase in the division's history. It was on New Caledonia that the various parts of the division coalesced and combat training began in earnest. Base facilities were developed which were critical for later combat operations.

The movement of 13,383 soldiers of 3NZ Division and their equipment and supplies to New Caledonia was a massive undertaking. It was made more difficult by the acute shortages of shipping and escorts and the effects of the ongoing Battle for Guadalcanal. The division moved from New Zealand to New Caledonia in the period from November 1942 through to January 1943. Various ships were used with varying degrees of comfort. The two main vessels were the large American troop transports USS *President Monroe* and USS *West Point*.

On arriving at Noumea, the troops found that they had to be ferried ashore because of the inadequate wharves and the shipping waiting to be unloaded. There was little opportunity for the soldiers to tour Noumea. They were packed off by antiquated train or trucks to camps.

The New Zealanders were integrated in the American First Island Command under Lieutenant-General Rush B. Lincoln, and Barrowclough was given command of the northern part of the island on 17 December 1942, with the responsibility for defending airfields, radar installations and potential Japanese invasion beaches. The division's units were spread thinly. Communication and tactical mobility were limited by the inadequate road network. Roads which were often challenging, dusty and pot-holed could

# New Caledonia

showing final dispositions of 3NZ Division units

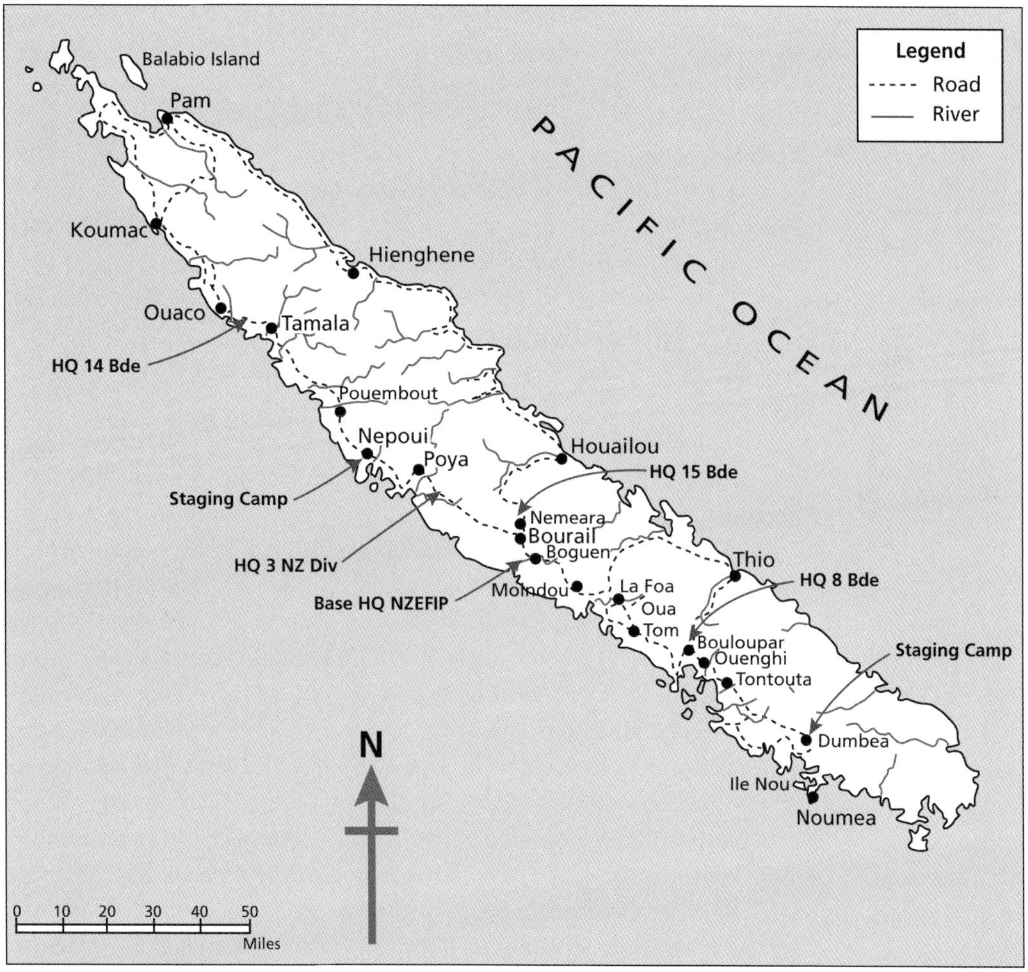


become impassible in adverse weather conditions. Barrowclough disposed of his units as best he could, with priority given to defending airfields and harbours.

The division had to establish its own facilities and often lacked necessary stores and equipment, as local resources were stretched. One of its major achievements was the creation of sophisticated base infrastructures such as 4NZ General Hospital at Dumbea.

From the time of their arrival, most of the troops lived in six-man Indian Pattern tents. They made full use of the local Niaouli tree for poles and makeshift furniture. Campsites were often isolated but sited close to water supplies. In time, the men began building sturdy bures in the local style and their living conditions became more sophisticated and comfortable.[1]

When they reached New Caledonia the New Zealanders were issued with ten days' supply of rations, most of which were in the form of tinned food, but some units were running short near the end of the designated period. Even worse was the change of diet. Used to solid meals of meat, vegetables and bread, the men found difficulty adapting to spicy, more liquid-based foods. Many suffered from stomach problems, and in January 1943 it was even suspected that a soldier from 29 Battalion had died from eating contaminated tinned food. Part of the problem was an initial lack of satisfactory storage and protection from sun and rain. After the first possible fatality the army became more vigilant. Thatched shelters were hurriedly erected and refrigeration facilities became available at Paita and Noumea.

With the shortage of fresh produce some soldiers took matters into their own hands and created vegetable gardens. The army approved of this and tried to obtain leases of land for growing food. The men also resorted to the time-honoured method of 'acquisition' to supplement their food supply. Much to the chagrin of local farmers their gardens were pillaged, and chickens and cattle lifted by hungry New Zealanders. Because of the threat to relations with the local community, which itself was feeling the pinch, the army made such thefts a court-martial offence. Generally, however, relations with the local French community were amicable.

A further torment endured by the troops as they set up their camps came from the swarms of salt-marsh mosquitoes (*Aedes vigilax*), which proved resistant to efforts to eliminate them. Attempts to spray kerosene or oil on their breeding grounds often resulted in the mosquitoes swarming to defend them. The problem seemed insuperable and at the very least the insects sapped morale and made the work of the troops much harder. In March 1943 dengue fever broke out, posing a serious risk to the health of the troops. A New Zealand Malaria Control Unit valiantly tried to battle the mosquitoes, aided by the expertise of an American lieutenant with knowledge of the diseases of the West Indies. This experience would stand the division in good stead when it moved to the Solomons.

Construction of infrastructure was the top priority and took up the time of the divisional engineers, to the detriment of their training for combat. They were engaged in what can only be described as heavy construction work, ranging from the design and construction of barracks, shelters and ration dumps to roading construction and maintenance. Non-engineer units also found themselves roped into building work, including the construction of hospital facilities. The preference was to use local timber and construction methods to create native-style huts to save on precious tents.

By the end of January 1943 the full division was in New Caledonia and widely dispersed. This placed a severe burden on logistical systems. Supplies had to be unloaded from the docks and hauled to the base supply depots, and from there distributed to units. Problems abounded. Bridges constantly had to be repaired, and with the roads in such poor condition the wear and tear on vehicles was significant. Flooding in the rainy season did not help, and sometimes traffic was held up for a couple of days until swollen streams subsided. Road maintenance was a particular problem: the red alluvial dust rose in choking clouds when the roads were dry but turned to glutinous mud in the rain. There was a constant flow of vehicles, some driven by Americans who were sleep deprived or just careless and who recklessly overtook other vehicles, failed to dip their lights at night or simply drove on the wrong side of the road. Accidents were inevitable and injuries mounted to serious levels.

The roads taxed even the best vehicles but spares and equipment were in short supply or simply non-existent. Soldiers attempting to service vehicles found themselves without overhead cover and three inches of mud underneath them.[2] Barrowclough sought heavy four-wheel-drive vehicles for the division, and although they were coming off the production lines, there were difficulties getting them to New Caledonia because of shipping shortages. Repair and maintenance facilities improved as the division settled in, and conditions eased. But the importance of logistics was rammed home to those in command.

The Army Service Corps trucks that were an integral part of the supply of 3NZ Division became a distinctive sight on the roads of New Caledonia. One vehicle had a pair of deer antlers on its hood, and others were inscribed with such names as 'Miss Carriage' and 'Dulcie from Waikuku'. The vehicles had the divisional insignia, a black kiwi, painted on them, which seemed to be a source of endless fascination to the Americans who puzzled over the significance of 'the Goddam Chicken' and who referred to it by such names as 'the Pregnant Duck', 'K one W one' and 'the Kaiwai'.[3]

The lessons of Fiji regarding the importance of hospital and medical facilities had been learned. Like everything else, however, it took time to set up infrastructure, and although the main party of 4 New Zealand General Hospital, including nurses, arrived in Noumea on New Year's Day 1943, the tented hospital did not open at Bougen until 8 March. The medical staff had been involved in the construction and had been hampered by wet weather and the ever-present mosquitoes. Furthermore, the basic equipment for the hospital did not arrive until early February 1943, and after landing at Nepoul had been left exposed to the elements. Precious medical supplies such as vaccines were rendered useless. In October the hospital was transferred to Dumbea, where it was housed in prefabricated wooden huts.

In the meantime, each batch of new arrivals seemed to succumb to diarrhoea as they arrived at their insufficiently fly-proofed camps. Only after proper sanitation measures were put in place and the troops acclimatised did the threat of a dysentery epidemic begin to abate. Much to the relief of medical staff, an outbreak of the tropical sores and ulcers that had been so prevalent in Fiji was avoided.

For the New Zealanders, New Caledonia, with its polyglot mixture of Kanaks, French, Vietnamese and Javanese peoples, the French architecture of its buildings and dominant French culture and language, was a strange and exotic place. Even the ubiquitous niaouli tree, with its multiple uses, seemed so different from the timbers of New Zealand. Contact with the local people was generally limited, if only by the isolation of the camps and language difficulties. When they did meet, relations with the French were usually cordial, sometimes helped by gifts of bully beef from the New Zealanders to the locals who were suffering from the rigours of food rationing.

3NZ Division had been sent to New Caledonia as garrison troops, but a Japanese invasion seemed to be in the offing. The engineers carried out surveys on how best to block roads and blow up bridges. Anti-aircraft guns had received priority because they were thought to be needed urgently for airfield defence. A battery of light and heavy AA guns was deployed to airfields at La Foa and Plaine de Gaiacs. The division was also laden with heavy coastal defence guns, which were placed to protect Noumea Harbour. Lacking AA guns for the division's own protection, the best Barrowclough could do was to retain two Bofors AA guns.

The gunners had one stroke of good fortune though: they inherited a supply of 25-pounder guns and stores of ammunition from 247th US Field Artillery Battalion. The guns had previously been owned by the Australian army and had been handed over to the Americans when they garrisoned New Caledonia. Third-hand they may have been, but the 25-pounders were a welcome addition to the Kiwi arsenal.

Troops were deployed to protect the airfields and harbours but the question still remained: would New Caledonia be a base or simply an advanced base for further deployment into the combat zone? For the moment the Kiwis concentrated on settling into their deployment areas and creating infrastructure.

Barrowclough was only too aware that if his troops were to fight they had to be properly trained. At the earliest opportunity he galvanised his men into route marches, river crossings and weapons training. The standard of rifle shooting across the division was found to be 'not high' and steps were taken to remedy this. In particular, Barrowclough wanted his men trained in 'jungle' warfare, 'always with an eye to combat in the Solomons', and directed that engineers, artillery, signals and ordnance personnel be trained with rifles and machine guns to deal with the expected Japanese infiltrators. If his men were to defend New Caledonia, they had to become familiar with the local terrain. 'Everyone trained ... There was no option since it was an instruction that all ranks of every branch and headquarters even the less conspicuous element such as cooks and batmen must undergo a fitness campaign and march certain distances.' Even the Army Service Corps (ASC) 'tramped many dusty miles normally dashed over by truck'.[4] The division discovered things the hard way: the necessity to streamline and lighten gear for jungle fighting, the amount of water to be carried by patrols and the absolute necessity of taking precautions against mosquitoes. The army also made the unsurprising discovery that the best way to revive the flagging spirits of exhausted soldiers was to provide them with tea.

'Everyone trained.' A 25-pounder gun crew training on New Caledonia, 1943.

*(Courtesy Lawrence Baldwin, author's collection)*

Troops from 3NZ Division undertaking amphibious training on cargo nets held up by timber frames in New Caledonia.

*(Alexander Turnbull Library, War History Collection, PA Coll 5547-039)*

Between early and mid-1943, the troops undertook Exercises *Styx*, *Scylla* and *Tonta*, which involved arduous river crossings, beach landings and mountain warfare. For the gloomily named Exercise *Styx*, carried out near the town of Pouembout in April 1943, the men were ordered to carry out an assault river crossing but had to spend the preceding night on the riverbank where they were assailed by masses of mosquitoes. One soldier 'tried everything including my respirator [gas mask] to escape them. I had a towel wrapped round my head and a jersey covered my face and neck. My hands were a problem. I tried putting them in my pockets, under my armpits, or wrapped in a ground sheet – all to no avail. At zero hour we crossed the river, formed up, then mopped up the "enemy" in the village and moved on.'[5] Exercise *Taniwha*, directed by Barrowclough, was intended to train signals personnel under field conditions. Lessons were learned – 'New Zealanders of 3 Division, for the first time in history preparing for jungle and island warfare, were practically writing their own text books as their training progressed.'[6] Operation *Cyclops* involved landing practice for 8 Brigade and Divisional Headquarters Staff. Training in embarkation and landing paid dividends later. Further training on the New Hebrides honed amphibious operations skills.

Exercise *Styx* with 14 Brigade Group at Pouembout River, New Caledonia. The folding boat and deck raft were constructed by No. 2 Platoon, 20 Field Company NZ Engineers, 28–29 April 1943.
*(Archives NZ WAII 7)*

35 Battalion Bren Carrier climbing out of the Pouembout riverbed after crossing the bridge.
*(Archives NZ WAII 7)*

Norman Harry Bonsell on amphibious training with the unit dog, 'Pooch'.

*(Alexander Turnbull Library, WH-0155)*

Barrowclough showed an interest even in tactical training. When visiting 15 Brigade, he noticed that their machine-gun pits were badly constructed, AA guns were misplaced and the laying of barbed wire was ineffective. He pointed this out to the brigadier and noted: 'On the whole the exercise should have proved of immense value as all arms saw a number of mistakes which it is hoped will not be repeated.'[7] Further training on Guadalcanal involved 3NZ Division Tank Squadron. Such training was not without its perils. A demonstration to Barrowclough of the indirect fire techniques of the tanks came to an abrupt halt when a misfire landed close to Barrowclough's group.[8]

Gun crews began doing live shoots. The previously unheard of amount of up to 20 rounds was allocated per gun. Proficiency in gun drills and camouflage increased significantly. ASC personnel were put through rifle training. Medical units trained for field operations. Infantry units previously hamstrung by the need to provide men for work parties and sentry duty were now provided with live ammunition and negotiated assault courses with targets scattered throughout the bush. Route marches with tight water discipline succeeded in hardening up the men. Weapons support units such as mortars and heavy machine guns were dismantled

'D' (Support) Company, 29 Infantry Battalion, with 3-inch mortars, climbing Mount Tonta, New Caledonia.

*(Archives NZ WAII 7)*

Sgt. R. Foster (left), No. 5 Platoon, A Company, 29 Infantry Battalion, fires a 2-inch mortar with an unidentified companion. This was during Exercise *Tonta*, New Caledonia, 19–20 May 1943.

*(Archives NZ WAII 7)*

and man-packed. Despite having to act periodically as wharf working parties and sentries at the airfields, the men found that their proficiency increased. Platoon training advanced to company level and companies undertook battle drills, attacking objectives on a three-platoon front. Specialised weapons training led to a steady improvement.

* * *

Brigadier General DeWitt Peck USMC, Admiral Halsey's War Plans Officer, told Barrowclough in February 1943 that the division would be required to train for amphibious operations. The 43rd US Division based in New Caledonia had already started such training. On 6 March the War Cabinet agreed to increase 3NZ Division from 14,400 to 17,637 and to give it priority in terms of reinforcements. Given the tremendous pressure on manpower, that expansion was a major commitment.

Barrowclough, annoyed at the uncertainty about the division's role and the lack of resources, wrote to Army Headquarters: 'I have to decide what should be the size of my base installations and what degree of permanence my building construction should take. This is naturally bound up with the possibilities of our returning here and the number of reinforcements which are likely to be retained as base.' He described his problems as 'almost overwhelming': large stocks of rations and ammunition deteriorating through exposure to the weather 'and only gradually are we being able to provide proper coverage for them'. Considerable supplies of both had been landed when Barrowclough 'had very few troops to handle them'. He complained that he was handicapped by a shortage of engineering equipment. The road-making tractors he had been sent were 'practically useless and in order to keep open access to my Brigade, I have to employ large numbers of men road making with nothing but picks and shovels ...'[9]

Frustrated at the lack of response to his requests in Wellington, he made representations to the United States Command, which consequently told Stewart of its concerns about the slow rate of reinforcement and stores to 3NZ Division. Wellington responded that the delay was due to unavailability of US shipping.[10]

The eventual decision to deploy 3NZ Division in combat was effectively made by the Americans. On 11 June Halsey told Barrowclough that he intended to move the New Zealanders to a forward base in the Solomons with a view to combat operations before the end of the year.[11] To fit in with other deployments, the division had to begin moving around 15 August. Barrowclough returned to New Zealand for a meeting with the War Cabinet on 15 June and produced Halsey's missive. Only a fortnight before, Rear Admiral Theodore S. Wilkinson had advised the War Cabinet that 3NZ Division was not required for active operations, and some were suspicious that Barrowclough had instigated the letter. A compromise of sorts was reached: Barrowclough recognised that his division might have a short existence, and would in the meantime have only two brigades. He was unhappy at what he considered 'shabby treatment',[12] but he had succeeded in getting the division over the start line.

Whether Barrowclough had encouraged Halsey to request the services of 3NZ Division is a moot point. However, Halsey would not have done so if the Kiwis were not needed. In 1943 there was a general shortage of trained combat troops in the South Pacific, and Halsey had been angry that 3NZ Division consisted of only two brigades. It is therefore likely that the suspicions regarding Barrowclough were unfounded, and his war diary supports this. He received a letter from Puttick concerning manpower difficulties and the possibility that the division would not be brought up to full strength. He noted that 'the matter is further complicated by confidential advice brought to me … from General Harmon's HQ. It appears that plans for the conduct of the war in the South Pacific until the remainder of the year 1943 contemplate the employment of 3NZ Div in an active role somewhere about the end of July.'[13]

Before the division could be sent into combat, Barrowclough had to certify to the government that it was suitably equipped, trained and ready for combat. This reflects how cautious Wellington had become and how sensitive it was to the risk of excessive casualties. On 27 June the War Cabinet gave its approval for the division to be deployed to the forward area, subject to Barrowclough's certificate that it was combat worthy.[14]

There was, however, a price to be paid. In the light of the parlous manpower situation, the War Cabinet formally recognised that 3NZ Division would have only two brigades and authorised a reorganisation. Both 2 and 3NZ Divisions would be maintained for as long as possible but be allowed to shrink in size. Further reinforcements for either division were to be suspended during 1943. 3NZ Division received final reinforcements, but other earmarked units were withheld. Barrowclough pressed for an additional engineering unit, more signals personnel and a field ambulance unit. He endorsed General Harmon's suggestion that only a squadron of tanks be sent, not the proposed battalion.[15] The issue of reinforcements continued to bedevil Barrowclough. 'I cannot face a situation,' he told Army HQ, 'where no reinforcements are behind me without running the risk of being unable to fulfill the role allotted to me ... As I have tried to emphasise on numerous occasions I feel it is absolutely essential to the morale of this Force that we should not decline the role that has been allotted to us.'[16]

15 Brigade had been sent to New Caledonia with the intention that it would be fully built up with units from New Zealand, but the demand for furlough replacements for long-serving 2NZ Division men and the expansion of the RNZAF meant that these were unavailable. Other sources of manpower such as Maori and Fijian soldiers were explored but did not materialise. Fijian soldiers would have been both a blessing and a curse for Barrowclough, since although they would have increased Barrowclough's force they would have required 'a considerable amount of training'.[17] Meanwhile it was contemplated that, in exchange, two of Barrowclough's trained battalions would be dispatched to the Middle East.

Wellington faced an acutely sensitive problem in dealing with Maori. Conflict and ill feeling over the appropriation of land and resources by European colonists continued to bedevil race relations. Consequently,

Maori were exempted from conscription and only volunteers would be accepted by the Army. 28 (Maori) Battalion served with distinction in Freyberg's 2NZ Division, but the issue was whether Maori volunteers would continue to go to 2NZ Division or could they form another Maori Battalion to serve with 3NZ Division? The matter was canvassed among Maori leaders and the unequivocal response was that Maori preferred to serve in the Mediterranean rather than in what was viewed as a secondary theatre, the Pacific.

Barrowclough also had concerns regarding American attitudes towards Maori, fearing they would be subjected to indignities they should not have to endure. He also feared that 'American relations with their Negro troops might be disturbed as a result of Negroes observing equality of status as between Maori and Pakeha'.[18]

Wellington, Barrowclough and Halsey reluctantly accepted the reality of a two-brigade 3NZ Division and on 1 July 1943 Barrowclough issued a formal order that 15 Brigade be disbanded and its men used to fill the ranks of the other two brigades and to act as a reinforcement pool.[19] Halsey told Fraser that he was greatly disappointed that New Zealand could not furnish a division with three full brigades.[20]

As Barrowclough reported to Fraser, 'it was necessary to adopt some very radical changes in the composition and organisation of 3NZ Division'. In addition to the disbandment of 15 Brigade, 33 Heavy Regiment and 28 Heavy AA Regiment were disbanded and the available troops were used to fill the ranks of the remaining units, to provide a reinforcement pool for the division and to satisfy a requirement to provide 400 men for the RNZAF. Barrowclough's reorganisation resulted in the division shedding much of its cumbersome heavy artillery, which was taken over by American forces or returned to New Zealand.[21] He was successful in retaining 26 Field Company because of the clear need for engineering support. This reorganisation radically altered the division's character, making it lighter, more easily deployed and more focused on its infantry elements. In late 1943 it had reached its apogee. It was clear that it would not receive further reinforcements and that it would retain a two-brigade structure. On that basis, it moved to Guadalcanal on the Solomon Islands in three groups on 27 August, 3 September and 14 September 1943 to await combat deployment.

# 9 To the Solomons

## Into the forward area

The move from New Caledonia was a huge logistical exercise. Gear and equipment had to be crated and moved to Noumea for embarkation. Camps were often left abandoned. Convoys of troops and supplies made trips at night and 'occasional groups of French stood in the darkness outside their isolated homes to swing lamps and shout farewell.'[1] At Noumea landing craft took the troops to waiting ships, where they had to climb some 30 feet up rope cargo nets slung over the sides of the vessels. The transports, loaded with up to 1500 men, remained in Noumea Harbour for several days, then sailed for Guadalcanal in three independent convoys. The troops leaving New Caledonia tended to view their sojourn as an interlude: 'somehow one was unmoved by the departure for there were "no ties that bind" and few could have regrent [*sic*]. Rather did it relieve that pent up feeling of frustration – a feeling few could have escaped having lived eight months in those back woods!'[2]

Bombardier Gordon Thomas found himself with 1300 soldiers on one of the large American attack transports, USS *President Adams*: 'It's a hell of a long way down to our sleeping quarters and it was a big job getting down with all equipment on!' The Kiwis were provided with plentiful food and, to Thomas's delight, tea. However, this was no pleasure cruise and the ventilation in the men's quarters was virtually nil. Thomas found the sweltering heat almost unbearable with the mess room's temperature hovering at 95 degrees all the time. Films such as *Wake Island* depicting the USMC's doomed attempt to defend the island in December 1941 were

## The Third Division's Area of Operations in The Solomon Islands 1943–44

showing 3NZ Division's long lines of communication and landing dates on Guadalcanal, Vella Lavella, the Treasury Islands and the Green Islands

*(adapted from the 3NZ Division Unofficial Histories)*

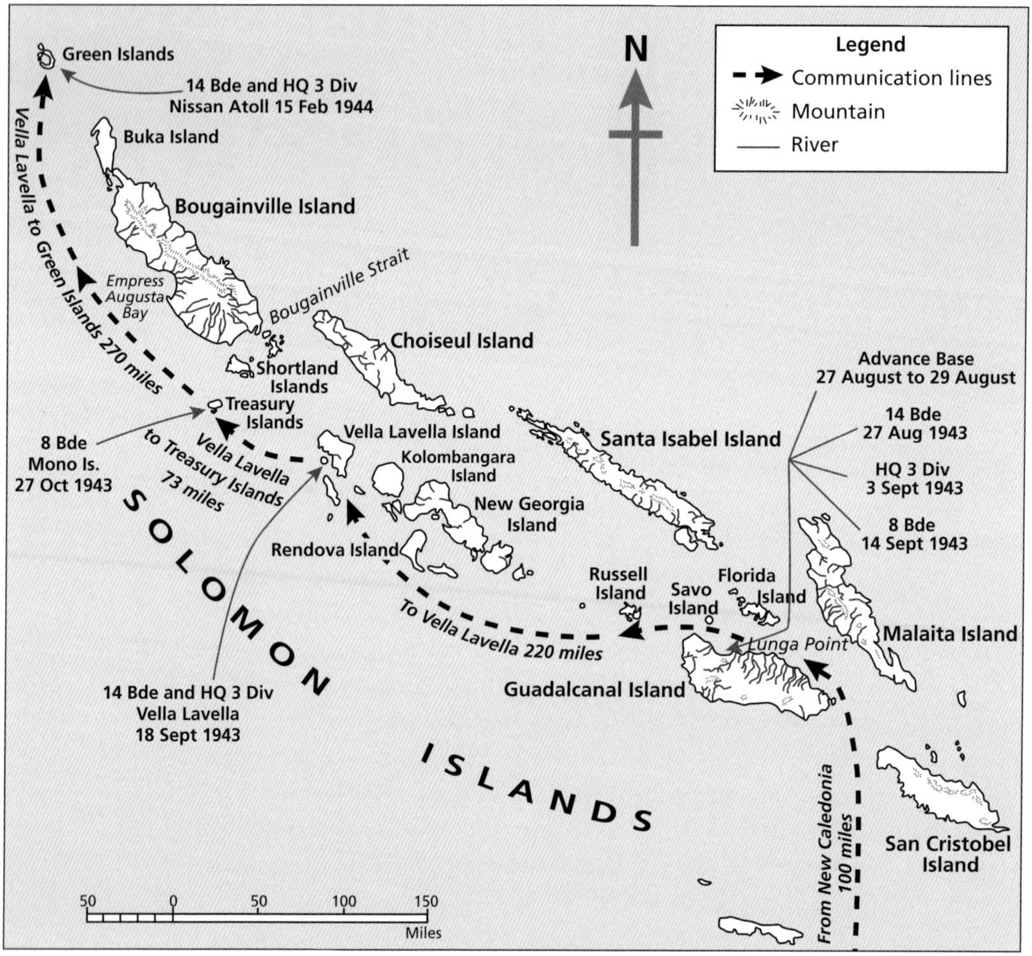


shown every night but even these were spoiled by the heat: 'the perspiration just runs off you all the time'.[3]

The troops were put through their paces with training on the rope nets, and doing practice landings. A day and a half after leaving Noumea the convoy arrived at Port Vila in the New Hebrides, where intensive amphibious landings were carried out as part of Operation *Efate*. Not everything went smoothly. Because of the sea conditions, several landing

craft were caught side on by the surf and control was lost. Nonetheless, the New Zealanders gained valuable experience. Having completed the training, the convoy arrived at Guadalcanal, 14 Brigade on 27 August 1943 and 8 Brigade 18 days later.

Soldiers of 8 Brigade on an LCVP training for amphibious operations, 1943.

*(Courtesy George Hodgson, author's collection)*

The New Zealanders went through the familiar routine of rapidly offloading their supplies and setting up camp. Guadalcanal still bore the scars of heavy fighting and, as Thomas observed, the dense jungle concealed corpses, frequently encountered by the Kiwis. In most cases only bones and boots were left. Care had to be taken because booby traps, live grenades and ordnance littered the area. Air raids were a regular nightly occurrence as the Japanese attacked Henderson Field, the American airfield on Guadalcanal and a major airbase. However, the Kiwis were in greater danger from shell splinters exploding overhead, fired by the Allied ack-ack gunners. When, in late September, a Japanese air raid was intercepted by a USAAF P-38 *Lightning* and enemy bombers shot down in spectacular fashion, the Kiwis yelled themselves hoarse with delight. The crew of the RNZAF *Hudson* bombers based on Guadalcanal became aware of the division's campsites and flew low over them on their return from operations. The troops entered into the spirit of things by forming a 'Huddy club' to cheer, wave and welcome back the returning aircraft.

Guadalcanal was the site of intense activity as supplies were cached and facilities developed. Many of the soldiers found themselves in working parties manhandling drums and cargo. The work, though tedious and unglamorous, was essential. Training on land and sea continued intensively. Guadalcanal would provide the advanced base from which 8 and 14 Brigades would move into the front line.

Soldiers undertaking boarding practice using rope nets.

*(Alexander Turnbull Library, WHC20441-1/4)*

* * *

The New Zealanders were an integral part of the plan to neutralise the Japanese strongpoint at Rabaul on New Britain, Papua New Guinea. Before the war Rabaul had been a significant port and administrative centre. It had an excellent harbour and potential as an air base. It also occupied a key position between the Japanese-held Caroline Islands, the Dutch East Indies and the Philippines. The Japanese seized Rabaul from the Australians on 23 January 1942, shipped in troops, aircraft and equipment, created extra airfields and dug fortifications into the surrounding hillsides. Protected by an arc of bases, Rabaul became the lynchpin of Japanese defences in the South Pacific, a formidable military, naval and air centre that, in Peter Stone's words, 'could have defended itself with bloody efficiency had the Allies invaded'. There were almost 98,000 men on Rabaul, many miles of tunnels and caves and a formidable array of weapons and ammunition.[4]

The key strategic problem for the Allies was that Rabaul dominated the South Pacific and posed a threat to any Allied offensive in the area. While the forces in Rabaul remained unsuppressed, MacArthur could not pursue his primary goal of a thrust into the Philippines. Conversely, for the Japanese Rabaul represented the key piece in a system of interlocking defensive positions critical to Japanese defence.

Allied strategists developed various plans for the elimination of Rabaul. Under the codename *Cartwheel* a series of complex operations was envisaged involving MacArthur's troops advancing northwards along the New Guinea coast while Halsey's forces advanced up the Solomon Islands chain. The two thrusts were to be mutually supporting and under cover of

Allied land-based air power. The ultimate aim was the capture of Rabaul, although this was later modified by the Joint Chiefs of Staff to bypass and isolate Rabaul using air and naval forces.[5] This was truly fortunate for the New Zealanders. They had been tagged with 2 USMC Division to assault Rabaul.[6] If this assault had gone ahead, the carnage would have made the slaughter on Tarawa look like a Sunday school picnic.

*Cartwheel* operations began on 21 June 1943 with American troops landing at Nassau Bay in New Guinea while Halsey's forces landed on Rendova in the New Georgia group. As part of the Solomon Islands prong of this dual thrust, New Zealand forces would find themselves fighting on an obscure island called Vella Lavella.

# 10 Fighting on Vella Lavella

## Initiation to battle

Vella Lavella. The name sits lightly on the tongue, evoking a Pacific paradise. For the men who fought there it would be a Green Hell. The Kiwis would experience their first land-based combat with the Japanese, involving semi-amphibious operations around the coast of Vella Lavella and provoking some of the fiercest fighting and the highest casualties 3NZ Division would suffer.

Vella Lavella is in the New Georgia Islands in the Western Province of the Solomon Islands. Forty miles long in a north-west to south-east direction, and 25 miles at its widest point, the centre of the island is dominated by hills that rise to 2650 feet. Streams and rivers flow from there to the sea. The island is covered in thick jungle and has several bays, some bounded by dangerous coral reefs. In short, the geography favoured the defenders and dictated how combat occurred.

The Japanese had intended to defeat the Americans on Kolombangara, but the Americans had wrong-footed them in the first South Pacific bypass and landed instead on the south of Vella Lavella, on 15 August 1943. 'Island hopping' is a strategy synonymous with the Pacific War, whereby the Allies bypassed strongly held Japanese islands and cut their supply lines, leaving them to wither on the vine. Whereas the Americans had previously seized islands with airfields, this time they seized an island without them. The airfields would be created by Seabees, the Naval Construction Battalions, performing incredible feats of construction

## Vella Lavella

showing the movement of the
35th and 37th Battalion Combat Teams, 14 Brigade

work.[1] In many ways Vella Lavella was a daring experiment and its success would set the pattern for future operations.

For the Americans the invasion of Vella Lavella ended the gruelling New Georgia campaign, which was notable for the considerable number of troops suffering from 'combat fatigue' or 'war neuroses'. By mid-1943 they faced an acute shortage of trained troops, as units needed time to recover. With strong Japanese forces still in the South Pacific, units were tied up in garrisons on Fiji, Tonga and Samoa. In all, SOPAC had only six divisions. 3NZ Division was available and it was decided that 14 Brigade would be used on Vella Lavella, while 8 Brigade was earmarked for operations on the Treasury Islands. This divided the division, with a main HQ on Vella Lavella and a rear HQ on Guadalcanal. Barrowclough had command responsibility not only for Allied forces on Vella Lavella, but also for the administrative tail stretching from Guadalcanal to New Caledonia back to Auckland. The operational handling of combat units on Vella Lavella fell to Brigadier Leslie Potter.

Barrowclough had been instructed 'to eliminate all Japanese forces on the island so that we could proceed with the erection of Radars on the

Brigadier Leslie Potter.

*(Alexander Turnbull Library, War History Collection, DA-00175-F, photographer unknown)*

North East and North West Coasts ...'. The establishment of these radar sites was of 'primary importance' because of their coverage of the enemy air bases on New Britain and Bougainville. The establishment of a Patrol Torpedo (PT) boat base at Horanui was a secondary factor. It was thought that the Japanese were 'anxious to avoid battle' and they would withdraw, resulting 'in a long and perhaps never ending chase'.[2] Personnel from 14 Brigade, three sergeants (one from each battalion) and Lieutenant D.G. Graham of Brigade HQ accompanied the South Seas Scouts on a stealthy reconnaissance of Vella Lavella.[3] They linked up with an American battalion and scouted for them, shooting two Japanese on 3 September in the first land combat involving soldiers from 3NZ Division.[4]

Superficially, 14 Brigade's task seemed simple: destroy a beaten enemy and secure the island. However, there were complications. Although some Japanese troops were reported 'short of food and in a weakened condition', it was feared that reinforcements were landing. Moreover, the Japanese had shown how determinedly they could defend and might retreat into the thick jungle of the interior. Another complication was that the Japanese dominated the skies and Allied air cover would be episodic. The nearest Allied airfield was to the south of Munda and Allied aircraft were restricted to irregular daylight patrols. Moreover, 14 Brigade was totally dependent on the Americans for sealift. The latter faced considerable calls on their shipping and the New Zealanders would be chronically short of the landing craft they needed.

The Allies believed that some 500–700 Japanese defenders, consisting of Imperial Japanese Army soldiers, Imperial Japanese Special Naval Landing Force troops and a mixture of shipwrecked sailors and shot-down aircrew, were left on the north of Vella Lavella.[5] They were being monitored by a detachment of the 1st Commando Fijian Guerrillas, including a coastwatcher, a lieutenant from 14 Brigade and some local islanders.[6] The Allies could use sea transport around the coast, albeit at the risk of being regularly bombed or strafed by Japanese planes. Potter had fourteen landing barges[7] crewed by Americans and he decided to transport infantry, artillery and heavy supplies in leaps – through openings in the reef – 'to feel forward with patrols and search the country and secure a base from which the next bound forward could be made.'[8] Potter decided to split his forces into two battalion combat teams, 35 Battalion Combat Team and 37 Battalion Combat Team, to hit the Japanese from the east and the west, push them against the northern coast and annihilate them. This split, Barrowclough felt, created the danger that the Japanese could concentrate on and defeat one of the pincers, but it was decided that the artillery component was capable of dealing with the threat. If the advance had been up one coast only, Barrowclough believed that the Japanese would simply have withdrawn steadily.

The mountainous terrain and dense jungle meant hauling artillery across land was impractical. Naval gunfire support was unavailable because US warships were fully committed elsewhere and would have been vulnerable to air attack in the limited sea-room around Vella Lavella. There was no close air support. If problems developed, Potter's troops would be on their own. The terrain also imposed difficulties in command and control. The division's wireless sets were unreliable in jungle conditions, owing to their fragility and the high humidity. Type 48 sets had to be abandoned because of their weight and antennae, but a Type 21 set was used satisfactorily.[9] It was also likely that there was jamming by the Japanese. On 8 October patrols planned for the Marquana area were almost shelled by 12 Battery as a result of a wireless communication breakdown. Fortunately, the barrage began before the infantry set out.

Jungle warfare tends to favour the defender because the attacker has to move forward and be exposed to enemy fire while the defender can set up killing zones and remain hidden. The Japanese proved masters at fortification and camouflage, with excellent fire discipline. Although driven out of their defences by the Americans, the Japanese had established supply dumps and further supplies were parachuted to them. On the positive side for the New Zealanders, Potter had coastwatchers who were able to supply intelligence on Japanese positions and friendly locals who provided pilots for the landing craft.

The combat teams were combined-arms units. The 37 Battalion Combat Team consisted of 37 Battalion, A Troop, 207th Light AA Battery, A Troop 53rd Anti-Tank Battery, a detachment of 20th Field Company, a detachment of 16th Motor Transport Company, HQ Company 22nd Field Ambulance and a detachment of signallers.[10] The 35 Battalion Combat Team was similar, with an infantry battalion, artillery battery, engineer section and ASC Section and a field ambulance company.[11]

Operations began on 21 September with reconnaissance parties in platoon strength taking Mundi Mundi and Paraso Bay unopposed. The 37 Combat Team then moved to take Boro. 35 Combat Team advanced in a series of bounds up the western coast. By 25 September Advanced HQ 14 Brigade was set up at Mundi Mundi, with 35 Combat Team to the north at Matu Soreto Bay and 37 Combat Team at Boro. When 35 Combat Team reached Timbala, reports suggested that there were approximately 300 Japanese soldiers between there and Marquana Bay. 35 Combat Team's commander, Lieutenant-Colonel C.F. Seaward, ordered two platoons to go to Marquana to stop them from retreating to Warambari Bay. One was

14 Platoon, commanded by 25-year-old Lieutenant Joseph W. Beaumont, who had been a regular soldier before the war. The other was the Carrier Platoon, a unit not normally used as infantry. The two patrols were told to take up positions to block the trails around Marquana. It was intended that a strong infantry force backed by artillery would then move forward and the Japanese would be caught in a vice. The plan soon fell apart: two survivors reached the New Zealand lines to report that the two platoons dispatched on 26 September had been ambushed. The advance of the main force had meanwhile stalled. The fate of the two isolated platoons remained unknown.

The second wave of New Zealand soldiers disembark from LCVPs at Barakoma on the morning of 18 September 1943. Note the mixture of lemon squeezer hats and tin helmets.

*(Archives NZ, WAII, 7, 3 Official Photograph Album, photographer unknown)*

Three companies of 35 Combat Team had concentrated around Timbala Bay. On 28 September, 12 Field Battery began firing at Japanese positions with fire control undertaken by forward observers with the infantry and on a boat.[12] Once the artillery barrage ceased, the infantry advanced, though torrential rain made progress extremely difficult.[13] B Company to the north of Timbala Bay encountered heavy resistance, called for reinforcements and dug in. Potter ordered 35 Combat Team to cease large-scale attacks until 37 Combat Team located the Japanese flank. On 1 October, 37 Combat Team established its artillery battery at Varuasi and both 35 Field Battery and 12 Field Battery were able to offer mutual support. The Japanese had only 'light mortars' and could not counter-battery, while their air attacks were largely ineffective because of the enveloping jungle. However, efforts to push north-west were stymied by cunningly sited Japanese machine guns. One position was nicknamed 'Machine Gun Gully'. The Japanese positioned riflemen on the flanks of the advancing New Zealand soldiers and encouraged them into the firelanes of skilfully hidden machine guns. The New Zealanders rapidly learned to respect the fieldcraft of their opponents.

The fate of the two missing platoons was revealed, by chance, on 1 October. The story of the missing men reveals much about the fighting qualities of the New Zealanders and also the vicious no-quarter-given nature of the war in the Solomons.

The two platoons had reached the area of Marquana Bay on 27 September. The men of 14 Platoon had been ambushed and the hunters had become the hunted. Beaumont took command and formed an oblong defensive perimeter. The Japanese attempted to unnerve the defenders by screaming abuse in English and Japanese. They attacked with machine guns, rifles and grenades during the day. By nightfall the defenders had suffered three killed and four wounded, including their signaller. To make matters worse, the wireless had been wrecked by machine-gun fire and their ability to communicate had been severed.

Beaumont was not equipped to withstand a siege. Most of the food, water and equipment had been lost in the Japanese ambush and Beaumont's force faced dehydration, hunger, fatigue and the prospect of annihilation. Nonetheless, the men held their perimeter for the next three days against determined Japanese attacks. Time was against Beaumont as his 51 men, six of them wounded, became progressively weaker. It was clear that they would be overwhelmed if they remained where they were. Beaumont made the decision to break through to the coast and, he hoped, help.

He later recalled what happened:

> At the bottom, still inside the Japanese positions, we hauled the stretcher wounded through mangrove swamps of black mud oozing deep to our knees. There wasn't a groan from them. We managed to collect a little water after we had formed our new perimeter on the fringe of the bush – enough from a hole scraped in the mud and from the hollow of a tree stump to fill three water bottles. Two were reserved

> for the wounded. One I handed around amongst the rest. … When the one bottle had been passed around its allotted 45 men and came back to me there was still water in it. That will show the spirit of the men.[14]

The Kiwis reached the coast with the Japanese close behind. Beaumont's position, on the edge of the shore, was very precarious. Then he and his men had an incredible stroke of good luck. An artillery officer in a barge cruising offshore looking for targets noticed a group of men on shore waving wildly. The barge attempted to come inshore but was prevented from landing by coral. One man swam out to the barge under Japanese fire.

On 2 October, two barges attempted to carry out a rescue, which rapidly went awry. Japanese fire killed an officer and four men trying to bring a cable to the shore. The rescue was abandoned. After dark a third attempt was made by volunteers who dragged a rubber dinghy and canoe to the shore. The wounded were the first taken off to a waiting barge, and then groups of a dozen men entered the water and swam to the boats. The defence perimeter shrank until there were only six men left. Mercifully, they withdrew without the enemy noticing.

The assumption that the Japanese were demoralised had been proven mistaken and their numbers had been grossly underestimated. However, the patrol remained cohesive and disciplined. Potter later commented that 'the action of this patrol in holding on to its position for that period [five days] was largely responsible for the success of the operation.' Yet it had been too weak to provide a blocking force, had been isolated for several days and had been rescued only by sheer luck and courage. The casualties were some of the heaviest in a 3NZ Division operation. The Japanese were not blocked but evacuated their forward positions and headed towards Warambari Bay.

35 Combat Team continued its advance by sending out patrols 200–300 yards ahead of the main body. Once the Japanese were found, the infantry attempted to encircle them. If they came across a fortified position which they could not take, they would pull back to allow artillery to bombard it.[15] By 5 October, Japanese resistance had melted away. On 8 October, Marquana Bay was found abandoned and soldiers from 35 Combat Team and 37 Combat Team linked up the following day between Marquana and Warambari bays. Patrols were sent inland to make sure that the Japanese had indeed left.[16]

37 Combat Team had a comparatively easier time, but mechanical breakdowns meant there was never sufficient shipping and their LCM, a larger, more useful craft, was only occasionally available.

New Zealand soldiers examine a captured Japanese Type 99 Nambu 7.7 mm machine gun on Vella Lavella, 1943.

*(Alexander Turnbull Library, War History Collection, Ref. 0237)*

On 21 September, a platoon landed at Paraso Bay, which one soldier described as 'an open bay fringed by coconut palms and a very shallow coastline. The platoon waded ashore expecting rifle fire and was pleasantly surprised when this did not eventuate. The soldiers did, however, take their first Japanese prisoner, who 'begged to be shot, pointing to our rifles and then to his forehead …'. The New Zealanders did not oblige.[17]

The platoon linked up with local scouts organised by Sub-Lieutenant Henry Josselyn, a coastwatcher and District Officer in the British Solomon Islands administration. As the reef at Paraso Bay prevented artillery being landed, it was decided to push on to Doveli. The company established a beachhead there on 22 September. They were joined by HQ, medical, signal and infantry units the following day. A jungle patrol was sent off in search of the Japanese, sometimes having to wade waist deep in fetid mangrove swamp mud. No contact was made with the Japanese but it was evident that they were close at hand and the unfortunate patrol had to spend a very uncomfortable night hunkered down in their foxholes.

37 Combat Team established itself at Boro on 25 September. Josselyn and teams of Solomon Islanders indicated that the Japanese were moving towards Warambari Bay. On 2 October, 35 Field Battery reached Varuasi and was able to provide fire support. Two days later 37 Combat Team reached Susulautolo Bay. Thinking that the Japanese were retreating, Potter ordered a landing on 5 October at Warambari Bay and allocated four barges from 35 Combat Team to assist. The landing met stiff resistance until artillery fire was brought to bear.[18] On 6 October, the Japanese area was again bombarded and B Company moved to clear the bay. A patrol commanded by Lieutenant D.J. Law came into contact with the enemy and suffered two killed and one wounded; four Japanese were believed killed. A patrol into the Japanese bivouac area developed into a firefight in which Lieutenant Owen Nicholls was killed. His soldiers retrieved his body under fire, a testament to the bond between troops and officers.

B Company reported that there were no Japanese between the perimeter and the head of Warambari Bay. On the night of 6–7 October the Japanese managed to evacuate their forces. In the process they triggered the naval battle of Vella Lavella. One Japanese and one American destroyer were sunk, but the Japanese evacuation was successful. The pincers of the two combat teams clanged shut, but to the disappointment of the soldiers the Japanese had gone.

Japanese casualties on Vella Lavella were estimated at 200–300. Four New Zealand officers and 28 other ranks were killed; one officer and 31 other ranks were wounded.[19]

As the Kiwis moved toward Warambari Bay, one of the participants recorded the fighting on Vella Lavella. [20] His account captures the tension and confusion of jungle fighting:

> Matters were warming up, and as we heard by radio about this time that the 35th had made contact on the other coast and were driving the Japs toward us, we began to feel that tautness of expectation which is the prelude to battle. I was like a wound-up spring, when, on October 5, it became the turn of my company to make the first hop, form the beach-head, and reconnoiter.
>
> No lovelier morning could be imagined as we chugged from the bay. The hour was about nine o'clock. The sea was glassy. Underneath were the fantastic shapes of the coral, overhead the vast blue belt of the sky, cloudless. It seemed as if we were making a pleasure cruise, only the rough ammunition in all my pockets, and the pile of equipment in

the barge, made me remember facts. We would probably have to fight – for our lives, and no one knew, or could guess, from where the bullet, the bomb, was going to come.

In the first of the three barges was myself and platoon, company headquarters, and signals. The plan was for my platoon to land, push in fifty yards, and then if we met no trouble, I would fire a green flare. The barges outside could land. We took with us rations for four meals (Rations K and C, with which we were just getting acquainted), and our armament was Brens, Tommys, rifles and grenades, plus an anti-tank rifle and a two-inch mortar. Our dress was green bush shirt and peaked hat like a jockey's. Faces were still light-hearted and smiling under those peaks as the ramp banged down and we scraped past the boxes of rations and gear, fanning out in three sections through the treacherous, evil-smelling swamp on the edge of the bay.

Soon my native guide was sniffing in the mud. Suddenly he stiffened. 'Jap here, okay,' he said. 'Here show foot.' I looked and yes, there in the mud were the prints, the unmistakeable prints of the one-toed Jap climbing boot. The print seemed fairly old. 'Long time?' I asked. 'Made – long time,' he replied after a further examination.

We scouted further till we were fifty yards from the water, and still there was nothing fresh. Having decided that all was clear, I jumped up on a rotting log, picked out a clear space in the canopy above, and through it fired my green flare, which finned up through the dark jungle air, then was gone in the brilliant sky. Immediately I heard the engines of the waiting barges boom into voice, heard them grounding with the rattling clank as their ramps hit the coral. Then came the knocking of equipment as one platoon went to our left and another to our right. I started to light a cigarette.

'Look! What's that over there?' I heard an excited whisper from the chap nearest me. I looked in the direction of his finger. Flitting through the undergrowth, like ghosts or moving shadows, I could see seven shapes in green, with peaked hats. Unconsciously we had both raised our rifles. 'Hold on,' I said, 'They may be our own blokes coming round from the right.' I passed the warning through my fan of men, and made my way in quick tree-to-tree rushes, back to the company commander. 'Are any of our patrols out on the right flank?' There were none. 'Then there are seven Japs at least working round to your left flank.' He agreed to send out a patrol to investigate and I went back to our position.

Nearly back to my log, I went into the mud like an arrow as a frantic burst of firing opened on the left – running commentary from the Brens, the jab of the Lee-Enfield, and occasionally, the lighter bark of the Nip rifle. I twisted round to look at my watch in the jungle twilight. It was eleven thirty – and we had to wait there, staring out in front trying to pick out the real from the unnatural shadows, sometimes drawing a bead and firing.

After half an hour a runner came with word to withdraw. D Company had arrived in response to a radio message, and a platoon would replace us, man for man, while we reformed towards the beach. We managed this without injury. Still a game!

Our next task was to test the Jap position on the left. This was no cake-walk. For the first time I was uneasy and wondered how we would get on. The Japs were invisible, well-placed, numerous, with several machine guns. And we had had nothing to eat.

I arranged with the platoon to advance in a shuttling system, two sections, one on each flank, to cover the centre section as it advanced ten yards: then vice versa. Some time after twelve we started, and I remember the comfort of seeing streams of tracer from the Brens, like a luminous wall on either side. We could never tell whether we were being shot at, owing to the din of our own ambuscade.

Sixty yards, and then I stopped. In front of me someone was shouting the words: 'Tojo, Tojo!' Then the voice became a scream: 'Moeji, Moeji! (The Japanese Emperor).' Finally it broke into song, and then started jabbering Japanese. A wounded Jap, ten yards ahead in the undergrowth, was making his peace with his Gods – and perhaps warning his mates of our position. Jim, one of my boys, said that he could see him. 'Finish him off,' I called. Jim, who had been kneeling behind a tree, now stood up to fire. I heard a crack and thought that he had fired. 'They've got me – across the back!' He slumped down into the hollow. The bullet had entered his shoulder and emerged from the back, cutting the V piece of the web, so that I saw it drop. I yelled to the platoon to give concentrated fire on the Jap position, while another chap hauled Jim back to the dressing station in the rear. This was done, and I was just sinking back thankfully into the mud when I felt a smack on the chin – put my hands up, and pulled out two wood splinters. There was a round hole in the tree-root six inches in front of my nose.

Now I knew the game was serious. Before this the platoon had been shouting gleefully about the wounded Jap: 'Get the swine, let him have it.' Now that one of us had been wounded, perhaps killed, it was different. Gone was the fun and games.

I decided to advance closer, and we managed another ten yards. But now the air was burnt with bullets. I learnt afterwards that a stream of chips was flying out from the log behind which I had flopped after the dash. Every time I spoke there was a grim whistle. Also, by the loud explosions, and clouds of mud, I knew that the Japs were using a knee-mortar [a 50-mm mortar] from the ridge behind. It was obvious that we were stuck, with machine guns left and right, and a mortar in front. I had decided to attack on the left, when a runner came up and said that another platoon was on that job, and that we were to stay until the battalion had formed its perimeter for the night.

The next three hours – Ah, the next three hours! May I never go through them again! I was face down in the mud, and had covered my face with it, so that it would be harder to pick up. I was lying in the V formed by two flanges of a tree-root. Round these I peered and fired when I saw any part of a man – that was all I ever saw. Gradually, as the slow minutes crept into slow hours, as my feet became numb in spite of my wiggling my toes in their boots, and my fingers became stiff, and as the jungle twilight darkened to the jungle night, I began to give up hope. Were we to be left there all night? If so the Japs would certainly get us, being isolated. Perhaps a sniper had a bead on me that moment, was waiting, finger on trigger. And still the minutes, the hours went by.

Perhaps at four, perhaps at five – I don't know, a runner came to say we were to withdraw to the main perimeter for the night. The best news I'd ever heard.

Back as we had gone up – in ten yard dashes, covered by flanking fire. I leap from tree to tree with new vigour as the blood comes back to feet and hands. Ten yards – wait and fire. Now they're all back – our turn again. I leap out from cover, run a couple of yards, slip on a root, stumble, fall into mud, waist high. The man on each side is the same. The bullets begin to churn up the mud around us – some of it goes up my nose. I shout to the sections to turn and fire while the others of my section haul two of us out. Dash for cover! I look around for the third man. He is still chest deep in mud, almost invisible, it is so dark. Two volunteers go to get him out. They drag him five yards when they stop in their tracks and shout: 'He's dead – back of his head's blown off.' 'Alright, come in,' I say tiredly.

A few more shots and we are back in the perimeter, our job done.

We had eaten nothing since eight o'clock that day, but now, sitting up to our ankles in mud, we could not eat. I managed a biscuit and a sip of water. Round us squelched the mangrove mud, soon complete blackout came down, and with it the mud, unceasing cacophony of the jungle night. Our first clash was over.

* * *

Despite their intense training, the Kiwi troops were green. This was to be their initiation into combat, but the shock of it was quickly overcome. The role of good leadership on the part of junior NCOs was critical to this success.[21]

The troops on Vella Lavella used 2- and 3-inch mortars, the latter proving the more useful. They also used the two-man Vickers machine gun for perimeter defence. Bren guns were particularly useful. Surprisingly, the Lee-Enfield rifle was little used because it was too heavy and the reloading process attracted enemy attention. Officers carried rifles but found they became too involved in reloading rather than commanding troops. The best weapons on patrol were the Thompson sub-machine gun and grenades. The long-barrelled Boys anti-tank rifle was apparently the worst because of its weight and bulkiness. For both combat teams artillery was critical to dislodging the Japanese, as small-arms fire proved ineffective against fortified positions. A total of 3338 rounds was fired by 12 and 35 Batteries.[22]

Intelligence played a limited role. It was hard to pinpoint the Japanese, and their numbers fluctuated as they were reinforced by barge and by shipwrecked naval personnel and shot-down aircrew. The coastwatchers and South Seas Scouts could only estimate their numbers and whereabouts. The withdrawal of the exhausted Scouts meant that the New Zealanders were reliant upon their own patrols and local islanders. The difficulties faced by Beaumont and his men arose partly from the fog of war and from a misunderstanding of Japanese intentions and capabilities.

Because one tree looked much the same as the next, it was difficult for artillery to plot targets or assess damage. Photo reconnaissance material was distributed, but there were few accurate maps. The local transport network consisted of trails on which motorised units became bogged. The jungle canopy made the fall of shot difficult to observe and set off artillery rounds above ground, so artillery had to be specially fused, while heat, humidity and rain affected the artillery pieces and their accuracy. Forward observers were located with infantry units or on native craft at sea, but this was dangerous because speech could draw Japanese fire. The Japanese largely controlled the skies. Their airfields were only minutes' flying time away. The nearest Allied airfield was to the south of Munda, so Allied aircraft were initially restricted to irregular daylight patrols.[23]

Troops on Vella Lavella wore US-made cotton twill green camouflage clothing and cloth caps. Steel helmets were found to be too heavy, and also uncomfortable to wear in the jungle; gas masks were discarded. Each soldier had two days' rations plus an emergency chocolate ration. Drinking water was at a premium and was frequently supplied with rations. The men carried chlorinating tablets.[24] Logistical arrangements were very successful, with 16 Motor Transport Company maintaining five days of rations to the front-line units despite the shortage of craft. Supplies were usually moved by barge to beachheads and then dispensed by carrying parties.

Vella Lavella provided 3NZ Division with its first combat experience. Overall, the 14 Brigade soldiers functioned well; they adapted quickly and learned to overcome Japanese defences with artillery and infantry attacks. They were victorious with relatively light casualties, compared with the US Army experience on New Georgia. Vella Lavella also gave 14 Brigade expertise that it was able to use in Operation *Squarepeg* in the Green Islands. Casualties did not end with the Japanese withdrawal. Japanese planes bombed New Zealand positions and Allied ships. As Barrowclough noted, 'the whole operation cost us 47 killed and 36 wounded. A conservative estimate of enemy casualties was two hundred killed.'[25]

An unconventional aspect of the operation was the capture of a Japanese barge and its use to support 14 Brigade. Because of their loss of merchant vessels, the Japanese began producing Daihatsu wooden

HMS *Confident*, the captured Japanese barge converted to use by New Zealand soldiers.

*(Archives NZ, WAII, 7, 3 Official Photograph Album, photographer unknown)*

motorised craft to deliver supplies to their garrisons. On 27 September, a patrol of 37 Combat Team saw one entering Tambama Bay. The Japanese went ashore and the New Zealanders took over the barge. When the Japanese returned they were called upon to surrender but a vicious firefight broke out and the Japanese were killed. The barge was renamed HMS *Confident*, a singularly inappropriate choice. The diesel engines had to be heated with blow lamps before they could be started,[26] and were difficult to maintain. Nonetheless, the vessel proved useful for hauling equipment, men and supplies. Because of the mechanical difficulties that plagued the American landing craft and the need to refuel, 37 Combat Team had only four barges available from 28 September to 3 October. This meant lengthy delays in moving it from Boro to Tambama Bay. On 5 October only two craft were available. *Confident*, crewed by five New Zealanders,[27] became the flagship of 37 Combat Team. Three wrecked Japanese barges were also put into service. Boro became so busy that Lieutenant R.A. Stokes became harbourmaster.[28] The willingness to press enemy equipment into service illustrates the adaptability of 3NZ Division's soldiers.

General Robert B. McClure of the US Marine Corps 'believed that the Vella Lavella operation could have been shortened and the defenders wiped out.' He maintained that 'had sufficient landing craft been available I could

Troops of 3 NZ Division on Vella Lavella Island during World War II.

*(Alexander Turnbull Library, War History Collection, Ref. WH-0213)*

have cut off Jap forces on Vella with small local amphibious operations.'[29] That was precisely what Potter was attempting; lack of landing craft prevented his success. He did not stop the Japanese withdrawing by sea, but neither did the United States Navy. The New Zealanders had carried out their primary mission, which was to eliminate the Japanese defenders on Vella Lavella.

## Behind-the-lines operation: Choiseul

3NZ Division personnel were also involved in a behind-the-lines mission from 30 September to 12 October 1943. American planners lacked accurate maps, so specialists were sent to the Japanese-held island of Choiseul to gather astronomical data. Sergeant G.G. McLeod from 29 Battalion led four New Zealand soldiers to protect four American specialists. They travelled by LST and seaplane to Choiseul, where they landed in canoes. Local help was key in avoiding the 4000–5000 Japanese on the island.[30] Peter Carey, a Solomon Islander, guided the Kiwis, while friendly locals also warned the patrol of Japanese activity, provided crews for the canoes and supplied shelter and food. The patrol 'carried food, clothing and tobacco, gifts for the natives, who had been deprived of such commodities since the advent of the Japanese.' The patrol reached Samasana and then returned to Nanano Island. The New Zealanders were flown back to Rendova for debriefing and on to Tulagi to rejoin 8 Brigade.[31] It is noteworthy that this patrol was commanded by a sergeant (as were the later Cowan patrols on the Treasury Islands) and that it relied on stealth, being small and lightly armed. It was also hugely reliant on the local population. It is significant that the Americans entrusted four specialists to New Zealand protection.

# The Treasury Islands 11

## Operation *Goodtime* – a diversionary operation

The division's second major military operation, Operation *Goodtime*, on the Treasury Islands, presented even more complex challenges than Vella Lavella and involved working intensively with American planners and fighting alongside American units. In many ways *Goodtime* epitomises New Zealand's land war in the South Pacific: limited numbers involved, a desire to limit casualties and a complete reliance on the Americans for sealift and naval support, supplies and even choice of objective. *Goodtime* was undertaken at brigade level because 3NZ Division was under strength and the operation was tailored to the capabilities of 8 Brigade. It assisted, but was not vital to, American success in Operation *Cherryblossom*, the later invasion of Bougainville. New Zealand soldiers were used because it suited the Americans, who were short of combat troops.

The Treasury Islands consist of two main islands – Mono and Stirling. Mono is four miles north to south and six miles east to west, with three peaks up to 1050 feet, thick forest and few suitable landing beaches. Stirling, four miles long and up to a mile wide, is to the south, separated by Blanche Harbour. It had the best potential for an airfield because of its flatness and thinner forest. It also had a basic road system. Blanche Harbour has a number of small islets, including Watson, Wilson and Savo. Missionary influence was strong and the islands' population was pro-Allies. Before the Allied invasion, locals had sheltered seven American aircrew and an RNZAF pilot. In September 1943, the Japanese had 213 troops manning a radio station and lookout, but the main threat lay with

A view from the heights of Mono Island across Blanche Harbour to Stirling Island.

*(Alexander Turnbull Library, War History Collection, F-44769-1/2)*

their possible reinforcement from the Shortland Islands, eight miles to the north. 14 Brigade garrisoned Vella Lavella, 60 miles to the south-east, but there was little hope of reinforcement from there. The Japanese on Mono were progressively developing their defences and the garrison was being reinforced.

In the USMC official history, Operation *Goodtime* is lumped in with the Marine landing on Choiseul as 'Diversionary Assaults' associated with the attack on Bougainville.[1] This accurately sums up the purpose of *Goodtime*, but does not lessen its importance, nor the benefits that flowed from it. In this operation, 8 Brigade was to assault a Japanese-held island amphibiously, eliminate its defenders and establish radar stations to cover Bougainville and provide early warning of enemy aerial activity, and most importantly to draw Japanese attention away from Empress Augusta Bay, where the American invasion was to take place. This made *Goodtime* doubly risky: if the New Zealanders succeeded in distracting the Japanese there was the possibility of an overwhelming counter-attack.[2] Barrowclough had real concerns about this, as well as the uncertainty of USN protection, the extent of air cover after the first day of the invasion and doubtful fighter control. 'We are bound to have a good deal of air opposition and I am

## The Treasury Islands

showing the movement of 8 Brigade Group, 3NZ Division, on 27 October 1943

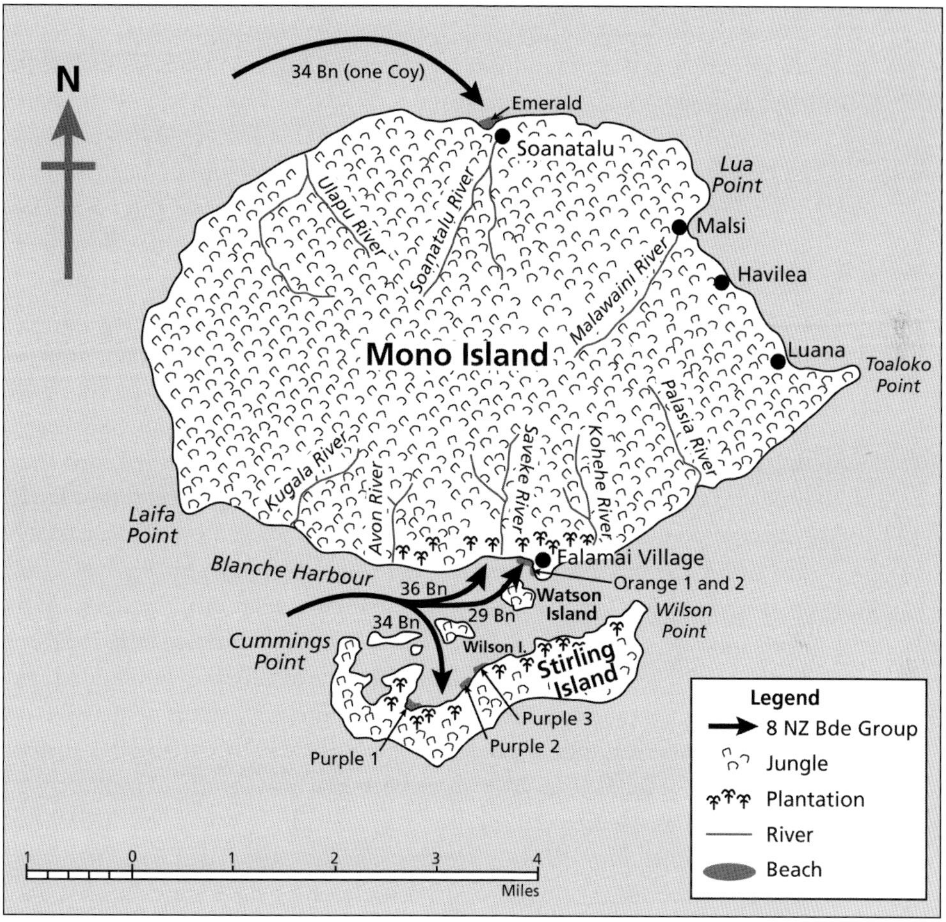


afraid we must expect not inconsiderable casualties during the landing operations, and the few days following until the 3 Marine Division effect their landing on Bougainville ...'. Moreover, the lack of landing craft meant that only a limited number of troops could land in the first wave.

Rear Admiral Theodore Wilkinson, USN, an experienced amphibious warfare practitioner, oversaw the operation. However, Rear Admiral George Fort USN and his staff were most closely involved in planning with the New Zealanders. Brigadier Robert Row was designated landing force commander and 8 Brigade would supply most of the troops. The whole operation was American-controlled though their troops were theoretically support rather than fighting personnel. The 'Seabees' (named after the acronym of their name, the Naval Construction Battalion – NCB) who took part in *Goodtime* had the proud motto 'We build, we fight', and on the Treasury Islands they fought shoulder to shoulder with the Kiwis.

Brigadier Row first learned of the projected seizure of the Treasury Islands from Barrowclough on 14 September. He was told that 8 Brigade would come under the command of First Marine Amphibious Corps (1MAC) and that the invasion date was 1 November.[3] Row met with the commander of 1MAC, Major General Charles D. Barrett, on 28 September and learned that the plan was for a simultaneous assault on Empress Augusta Bay and the Treasury Islands. This was later amended so that 8 Brigade would assault the Treasury Islands initially six days, and then only five days, before the American landing on Bougainville.[4] On 29 September, Row received instructions that set out the 'tentative task of the Brigade' as the seizure of the islands, and the establishment of long-range radars and a landing-craft staging-point. The forces involved would be 8 Brigade Group and various US naval units. Tentatively, eight fast troop-carrying destroyers (APDs), two huge Landing Ship Tanks (LSTs) and eight Landing Craft Infantry (LCIs) were allocated for the first echelon with two Landing Craft Tanks (LCTs) and four LCIs for each succeeding echelon.[5]

The planners of *Goodtime* were competing for resources with *Cherryblossom*, which was to begin a mere four days later, not enough time to redeploy shipping and other assets. Limited numbers of landing craft in particular had a considerable influence on planning, as did the need for a Combat Air Patrol over the shipping and beachheads. The fighter aircraft would have limited time over the area and would have to be rotated, so shipping would need to be unloaded quickly. The memory of the debacle at Guadalcanal was relatively fresh, when Japanese naval and air threats meant the transport ships departed unexpectedly, leaving the US Marines unsupplied. LSTs especially were in chronically short supply and too valuable to expose to air or naval attack unnecessarily.

Row and Fort, given only basic information, began planning in general terms. The decision about where to land was facilitated by an earlier reconnaissance team landed from the submarine USS *Greenling* and excellent low-level reconnaissance photos.[6] They decided that the main landing should be at Falamai on Mono, which had beaches suitable for LSTs. Stirling would be captured simultaneously, and New Zealand artillery established there in case the Japanese resistance proved too effective, or there was a counter-attack. A major consideration was the timing of the establishment of the north-facing long-range radars. On

Brigadier-General Neal C. Johnson, United States Army, and Brigadier R. A. Row, New Zealand Army, Vella Lavella, Solomon Islands, 1943.

*(Alexander Turnbull Library, Ref. WH-0178-F)*

18 October, the 8 Brigade plan was altered 'to permit the early placement of long range and surface warning sets'. To establish these radars an APD was allocated to transport 'an infantry rifle company, a section of MG's, a section of twenty CB's, and sixty radar personnel' to Soanatalu on the northern coast shortly before the Falamai landing. Brooke-White hoped that these radars would be operational a day after landing.[7]

Row was constantly aware of the limited shipping available and friction arose over the space allocated for the radar units. He complained to Barrowclough that originally no priority had been given to a radar station. Now two radar units were considered – light and heavy – with the heavy radar in operation five days before the landing at Empress Augusta Bay. Row wanted the whole of 30 Battalion to protect the radar, but needed an LST and an APD for transport. This was refused and Row had to make do. Row was aware that heavy equipment, including a bulldozer, had to be landed. It would take 12 hours to set the radar up and another one to two days to get it functional. If the Japanese attacked in overwhelming strength, the radar could be destroyed and the force could 'retire by the West Coast'. AA protection was 'unsatisfactory' and Row sought four 20-mm AA guns from the Seabees, but this was 'washed out' because the Seabees had no trained personnel. Barrowclough indicated that he might be able to provide a battery of 37-mm AA guns in the second echelon: 'The problem is one of shipping and the value placed on the radar. If it is of first importance then sufficient shipping should be provided to land radar, AA, Seabees and a sufficient force to guard the installation.'[8]

Barrowclough had real concerns about the risks to 8 Brigade, principally because of the limited number of troops that could be landed in the first wave at Soanatalu, the beach most exposed to a Japanese counter-thrust. On 22 October, Barrowclough asked Row why a full battalion could not be landed, emphasising 'the advisability of strengthening the small detachment as soon as you get an opportunity'. He went on: 'I realise that I am much more concerned over your venture than I would be if I were at hand with the rest of the Division to come to your assistance. Many of my fears may prove groundless but you must forgive my not unnatural anxiety over this operation.'[9]

For their first opposed amphibious landing since Gallipoli, the New Zealanders were fortunate to be under the command of the masters in such operations, the US Marine Corps and the US Navy. Row moved his headquarters closer to Wilkinson's, but he experienced problems during the planning because the headquarters of the amphibious force for Task Force 31 and the headquarters MAC were located twenty miles away from 8 Brigade, 'and the roads were, to say the least of them, NOT in the nature of speedways'. In addition, there was no satisfactory telephone line from Corps to Row's headquarters. In his after-action report, Row would record that 'much time was lost. Information and decisions could NOT be obtained quickly just when they were most needed. ... It was NOT possible for me to move my own HQ for had I done so I would have been out of contact with my own units.'[10]

Operation *Goodtime* was put together hurriedly and the start date was advanced, resulting in some friction. Row recorded that some American units under his command reported after 28 September but were unable to give him precise details of numbers of personnel and their equipment. Still other units did not report until later and one Seabee unit had to be brought from the Russell Islands to substitute for one that had not arrived at Guadalcanal in time. The American officers were helpful but often had 'very sketchy orders'.[11] Another example of haste was the late arrival of Fort, who left Auckland on 26 October. He was in charge of the naval aspects and his absence during planning must have caused problems. Initially an essential ingredient had been the unloading of an LST at Stirling, until the US Navy declared this was impractical. Similarly, loading plans on the basis of maximum capacity had to be amended when the US Navy Commander rejected them. Unlike 3NZ Division's previous amphibious exercises, *Goodtime* did not involve large attack transports, but rather 31 ships of varying size, function and capability, which meant devising more detailed plans that had to be finalised at least ten days before the operation.

Each item had to be assessed carefully because of the acute space shortage, and combat loading was absolutely critical. The weapons and equipment likely to be used in combat would be loaded onto the vessels last so they could be taken off first. AA guns, bulldozers, tractors, radar and communication vehicles and, most importantly, vehicles for unloading the landing craft, had to be available immediately. As it was, the ships in the first echelon had to carry 7500 men when they only had capacity for 3795 men and 1785 tons of cargo. Consequently one infantry battalion was reduced from 729 to 600 men and only one battery of the Field Artillery Regiment could be transported. The Tank Squadron was left behind, though its usefulness was doubtful, given the jungle and hills of Mono Island. The move from New Caledonia to Guadalcanal had given 3NZ Division staff valuable experience in working out loading tables for its equipment, supplies and personnel, but 'it was determined that supplies and equipment would be cut to the barest minimum and that only about 50-60% of the troops could be taken in the first echelon'.[12] Planning was also complicated by the fact that not only New Zealand units were involved, but also those of the US Navy, US Marine Corps, US Army (including United States Army Air Force) and the RNZAF. All had different cultures, terminology, doctrines and experience.

Amphibious operations are immensely complex and unforgiving of errors. It was important for the planners to take into consideration such factors as tidal height and the slope of the beach in deciding where and when landing craft could be beached. Other factors considered were the ability of naval forces to provide support, shelter from unfavourable sea and weather, the size, draught, manoeuvrability and beaching characteristics of the assault ships and landing craft, offshore water depth and bottom configuration, the extent of mineable water (any depth less than 600 feet was considered mineable), conditions that might affect the enemy's ability to defeat mine clearance efforts, and facilities for unloading shipping.

The area around the Treasury Islands was not mined,[13] but the beach-heads were adjacent to Blanche Channel, with coral reefs and restricted sea-room, unsuitable for large ships. The US destroyers USS *Pringle* and *Philip* would therefore provide fire support. Additional fire was provided for the first time by LCI(L)s, LCI(G) craft equipped with two 20-mm, three 40-mm and five .50-calibre machine guns. They 'required much larger crews and sacrificed most of their troop carrying function, but … proved to be the answer to prayer for fire support of assault troops delivered close to shore'.[14] In addition, PT boats were to set up a picket line from the Shortland Islands to Choiseul to screen the convoy[15] and prevent a counter-attack on Mono Island. A short beach close to Falamai was the only one suitable for beaching LSTs and had areas close by where supply dumps could be established. Hence the main thrust of the invasion would be made there. Stirling was the only place where field artillery and AA guns could be quickly sited, but LSTs could not beach there until engineering work was carried out.[16] Likewise, when it was decided to place a radar station on the north of Mono, a suitable beach had to be located. A small beach capable of accommodating an LCT was discovered at Soanatalu, but it would be exposed to a counter-thrust from the Shortlands and would be in the path of Japanese retreating off the island.

Once the task of taking the Treasury Islands was established, the Intelligence Section of 8 Brigade HQ constructed a sand-table model of the islands.[17] Daily low-level reconnaissance flights obtained excellent photos of the proposed landing sites. Intelligence gleaned from radio intercepts, code-breaking and other sources was available to American planners, but not necessarily to Barrowclough or Row. The latest information, dated 8 September, indicated that there were 130 Japanese on the island, but it was possible that the garrison had been reinforced from the Shortlands or from units retreating from Vella Lavella or New Georgia. Barrowclough ordered that a reconnaissance patrol be sent to Mono, despite the risk that its members might be captured and disclose the invasion plans.[18]

* * *

The patrol was led by Sergeant William Albert ('Bert') Cowan, a New Zealand bushman who had taught bushcraft to coastwatchers on Guadalcanal. His colleagues were Corporal Frank Nash, who had previously been a communications specialist in the US Army but who had inveigled himself into the coastwatchers, Frank Wickham, whose family had long been traders in the Solomons, and Sergeant David Ilala. Wickham and Ilala belonged to the Solomon Islands Defence Force (SIDF). After being transported to the area by PT boat and canoe two days before the scheduled invasion, they were given 24 hours to reconnoitre the island and to ascertain troop numbers. Luckily they established contact with friendly locals who hid them and provided intelligence on Japanese numbers and positions. Cowan also rescued three downed American aircrew. Back on Guadalcanal, Cowan reported there were 225 Japanese on Mono and none on Stirling. The Japanese had machine guns and two 40-mm AA guns, and the local population was pro-Allies. Cowan persuaded a reluctant Barrowclough that he should return to Mono to cut telephone wires linking the Japanese outpost at Laifa Point with their headquarters near the Saveke River, to mobilise the local population as scouts, guides and information gatherers, and to report any last-minute Japanese reinforcements.[19] He also wanted to warn the locals of the impending invasion[20] and the Allied naval bombardment.

This patrol, consisting of Cowan, Wickham, Ilala, Corporal W.M. Gilfillan, Private C.M. Rusden and Private J.B. Lempriere of 29 Battalion, travelled from Guadalcanal by plane, then by PT boat to Mono, landing by canoe.[21] On 27 October they cut the telephone wire linking Laifa Point to the Japanese headquarters at Saveke. Cowan experienced great difficulties with radio communication. The set initially malfunctioned, then an incorrect message was sent indicating that the Japanese had been reinforced, causing Barrowclough considerable anxiety.[22] Subsequently the members of the patrol linked up with 8 Brigade following its landings. Cowan again made effective use of the local population, sending out groups of between 10 and 16 scouts, referred to as 'blokes', to gather information. They brought in a number of Japanese prisoners.

Sgt W. A. (Bert) Cowan, DCM, 1944.

*(Archives NZ, WA, 1, Treasury Islands Photos, D1 #190, official photographer)*

From aerial reconnaissance, rescued aircrew and the first Cowan patrol, planners knew that the 225 Japanese on Mono had their headquarters west of the Saveke River. They had artillery on both sides of the Falamai Peninsula and machine guns covering its beaches. Despite this, Row considered that 'provided that the enemy could be subdued by support fire during the approach of the landing craft, a landing at Falamai was also the best way of getting at the enemy quickly.'[23] He was clearly counting on naval gunfire suppressing the Japanese defences. The invasion sites consisted of two 'Orange' beaches near Falamai, two 'Purple' on the north central area of Stirling and one 'Emerald' near Soanatalu. These were small stony or sandy beaches with a tree line close to the water.

The USN made four APDs and LCIs available, and from 14 to 17 October 8 Brigade practised loading and unloading, and embarkation and disembarkation.[24] Great importance was placed on the rapid unloading of the invasion craft and getting vital stores into dumps hidden from attack. Working parties for the unloading were organised, as were beachmasters. Each company was allocated space, but this was often filled with non-essential items such as bed rolls, spare boots and hot boxes, which could have been on follow-up shipping. Unloading this superfluous cargo may have resulted in casualties during air raids.

There were four phases to the loading and embarkation. One group of

LCTs loaded up and embarked for the Treasury Islands on 23 October, staging through the Russell Islands and Rendova; a second group of LSTs loaded on 24 October and sailed in company with LCMs on 25 October; a third group of LCIs embarked personnel and sailed on 26 October; and a fourth group loaded personnel on to APDs which sailed on 25 October. The ships were divided into three groups according to their speed and roles. Each had to sail at a carefully regulated speed to arrive at the same time. This worked relatively well and the force arrived together off the Treasury Islands in the early hours of 27 October, though H-Hour [the designated time for the operation to begin] was delayed because the APDs were twenty minutes late.[25]

A Japanese plane detected the force during the night, but the enemy response was sluggish. The 8th Fleet Commander was uncertain where the blow would fall until the garrison on Mono reported enemy landings. He then ordered his forces to concentrate on the Solomons rather than New Guinea and to make air attacks on vessels off Mono. He also instructed the Japanese submarine RO-105 there, and began assembling a naval force to launch a night-time raid against the Allied ships. Despite Allied radar, the Japanese Type 93 *Long Lance* torpedo could have made such an attack force extremely potent. Fortunately, the attack was cancelled when aerial reconnaissance early on 28 October reported no sign of Allied activity.

Two dead Allied soldiers on the beach at Falamai, 27 October 1943. Note the LCI in the background.

*(Alexander Turnbull Library, War History Collection, F-41854-1/2)*

The Japanese commander then refocused his forces on New Guinea until the landings on Bougainville on 1 November diverted Japanese air and naval power there.[26]

The American naval bombardment of Mono on 27 October was initially thought to be largely ineffective. Most shells overshot the island; *Philip*'s gunfire in particular was 'disappointing in accuracy, timing and quantity'.[27] The vegetation hid Japanese positions and Blanche Harbour was overcast with heavy rain, while a spotting plane experienced radio failure. Furthermore, the narrow waters of Blanche Harbour prevented the destroyers getting in close. They ceased fire four minutes before the first assault was due to land, but LCI(G) gunboats continued to fire. *Pringle* then patrolled to the west of Blanche Harbour while *Philip* patrolled to the south of Stirling. However, a group of recently arrived Japanese reinforcements found themselves in the area plastered by the destroyers' fire and were in disarray. It also seemed that the destroyers' fire had been effective in suppressing Japanese defences.[28]

The first transport group anchored in Blanche Harbour and began disgorging their assault troops down nets into the smaller landing craft. Training proved its value and the process was orderly. The landing craft then formed up and moved towards the designated beaches. To get to Falamai they had to travel two miles into Blanche Harbour. As the first wave passed Stirling Island, fire from a machine-gun position not detected by the Cowan patrol hit the LCIs and five personnel and eight New Zealand soldiers were wounded,[29] one officer mortally. The later waves of troops landing on Stirling found it deserted; the Japanese had probably returned to Mono.

The LCI(L) gunboats proved manoeuvrable and packed a considerable punch.[30] As one rounded Watson Island, it succeeded in knocking out a 40-mm twin-mount gun.[31] Conversely, supporting fire from an Allied gunboat held up the advance of 36 Battalion. Nevertheless, Row commented that 'the close support rendered by the LCI gunboats undoubtedly kept down casualties during the assault. These boats protected the left flank of the first wave, and in addition shot at opportunity targets. One of them proceeded past Falamai Peninsula and raked that area with fire just prior to the landing (of the) 29th Battalion'.[32]

An opposed amphibious assault is by its very nature an exercise in controlled chaos:

> an unholy orchestra made up of the crack of rifle fire and the stutter of machine guns; the crunch of exploding mortar bombs and the angrier bursts of artillery shells. Bullets hiss and spit, fragments of shell ping

and whine; the regular beat of moving vehicles and machinery and the throbbing engines of the landing craft are almost lost in the confusion. Still, the men in camouflaged jungle dress continue to disembark and the emptied landing craft leave the beaches to make way for those following them. Movement is swift and continuous as each man accomplishes his appointed task. No one has time to see the waves gently and regularly removing footprints hurriedly trodden in the sand.[33]

For the New Zealanders landing on Mono, there were extra challenges. Packed into too few landing craft, they could not take cover behind the shield of the ramp and were subjected to a rain of rifle, machine-gun, mortar and mountain-gun fire. As Robert Dunlop, a Private in 'A' Company, 36 Battalion recalled, 'We were under fire as we came in, and I can remember looking around and thinking it was quite interesting until I looked at the side of the LCI, and like a sewing machine, splinters started flying off the side of the LCI. I got down and was almost at the same level of the keel after that'.[34] The beach near Falamai was an obvious landing site and the Japanese had machine-gun positions there, but initial opposition was comparatively light, probably as the Japanese had pulled back during the naval bombardment. Unfortunately, movement in the tree line by the first wave of troops attracted the attention of a trigger-happy American machine gunner who proceeded to machine gun the troops until stopped.[35] At about 0735 hrs a well-concealed Japanese machine-gun position opened fire on the follow-up wave, forcing LST 399 to raise its loading ramp. The anti-aircraft guns on the bow could not be depressed sufficiently to reply. In an action later celebrated in the John Wayne movie, *The Fighting Seabees*, Seabee Aurelio Tassone lowered the blade of his bulldozer and, using it as a shield, advanced on the Japanese position, crushing the defenders.[36]

An AA gunner, Frank Cooze, recalled his introduction to Mono:

With its guns firing into the bush our barge crept in between two islands to be met by a stream of tracer which streaked in front of us. I had visions of being cut off in my prime, but a few well directed shots silenced the Jap – much to my relief.

The barge grounded on Mono Island and the ramps clanked on the sand. We streamed off at the double to cries of 'Let's go … Come on. Let's go!' from the barge crew who were anxious to unload and depart before the Jap bombers became too inquisitive.

The infantry made their way into the jungle while we dropped our packs and returned to the barge. We filed up one ramp, grabbed a box and scurried down the opposite beach in Unit dumps.[37]

A Japanese gun sited a short distance along the beach began to cause concern. A group from Les Taylor's Carriers Platoon were ordered to board an LCI and deal with it. His diary records: 'As we charged in from the sea we grounded on a coral reef about two hundred metres out and looking straight down the barrel of the mountain gun in its fortified position. It was our lucky day as the Japs had fled and it took us some twenty minutes before we got free and captured the gun which we dismantled and brought back to Falamai.'[38] 8 Brigade Recce Company's Bren gun carriers were landed to cut off the Japanese retreat. A mangrove swamp prevented this, no doubt to the relief of the soldiers, who would have faced lethal grenade attacks and rifle fire from Japanese in the trees. Open-decked Bren gun carriers were sitting ducks, as the Australians had found at Buna. The carriers were used instead, hauling ammunition and cargo up to front-line units.[39]

Two Japanese 75-mm mountain guns and a 90-mm mortar on the hills above Falamai rained down shells on the beachhead at about 0735 hrs, coinciding with the arrival of the LSTs. Two LSTs were hit, men were killed and wounded and unloading was held up. Disembarking troops also came under fire from concealed machine-gun, mortar and artillery positions. Damage from Japanese artillery consisted of one 90-mm AA gun destroyed, one 25-pounder gun damaged, a Bofors AA gun, ammunition and medical stores destroyed. Around noon, soldiers from 36 Battalion stormed the Japanese mountain-gun positions and continued uphill to destroy a 90-mm mortar. The destruction of the Japanese artillery effectively ended their ability to dispute the beachhead. Meanwhile troops from 34 Battalion landed unopposed on Stirling. The HQ of 8 Brigade and Artillery units joined them.[40]

The Japanese were still capable of surprising the Kiwis. On Mono, Robert Dunlop and his comrades

> had to dig a perimeter around what was the Japanese headquarters, which was pretty empty by that time except for the ones that had been killed. There was a big marquee – a big tent. After I dug my foxhole, I thought I would have a look around inside for a few souvenirs, because the Americans were good at buying souvenirs, and they always had more money than what we did. I ended up with a big clock, a Japanese flag, a Japanese rifle, a bottle of sake, and a Japanese water bottle with Japanese writing on it.

> When I came out through the tent flap, a Japanese ran outside beside me. He fired a shot into the air, all our fellows dropped to the ground and the Jap ran straight through them and into the jungle. I would like to think he is alive today.
>
> I was grateful to him, really. He must have had a bead on me [in the tent], and he could have shot me so easily, but if he had he would have alerted all the rest of the men – the rest of our company – and he wouldn't have got away.[41]

By the end of the first day it was clear that the invasion had been a success. The troops had landed in good order on all beaches, artillery positions had been set up on Stirling and casualties had been relatively light. The enemy reaction had been sluggish and disjointed. On the night of 27–28 October the Japanese infantry used 50-mm mortars and harassing rifle fire, probing the New Zealand perimeter. On 29 October patrols made no contact and Row correctly concluded that the Japanese were withdrawing northwards.[42]

The fight at Soanatalu on the northern coast of Mono turned out to be one of the most intense and vicious of the Treasury Islands operation. It would involve two groups of desperate men battling for their survival and showing their foe no quarter. It began innocently enough with the landing on 27 October of American Seabees, radar specialists and their New Zealand protectors, Loganforce, under the command of Major Gordon Logan. The landing was unopposed and Logan and his men set about establishing a defensive perimeter. A bulldozer was landed and used to clear a site for the radar. The quiet was not to last long. About 80 of the Japanese who had fought in the south of Mono had decided to retreat to the north of the island, seize a Japanese landing barge and escape from an island which had become a death trap. Their destination was Soanatalu.

Logan became increasingly worried as Japanese soldiers began to probe his defences. However, he knew that he had the support of the artillery and that his troops were reasonably well dug in.

On the night of 1–2 November, the Japanese force of 80 desperate men attempted to overrun Logan's perimeter. They attacked in the early hours of the morning, so the darkness negated Logan's advantage of artillery. On the other hand, the darkness and the rough terrain soon destroyed Japanese plans and their attack became disorganised. The blockhouse held by the Seabees and New Zealanders on the beach near the Japanese barge became the centre of Japanese efforts. The defenders, six New Zealanders and three Seabees, began to take casualties. Captain Les Kirk and Staff Sergeant D.O. Hannifin were killed, and command passed to Private

C.H. Sherson who was then wounded. Private Joe Smith, the cook, then led the defenders in repulsing fierce Japanese assaults. The beleaguered defenders considered whether they should make a break for it. They decided, however, to hold on. Just when the Japanese seemed to be on the verge of success, their attack faded away. In the morning light the defenders were able to survey the carnage. Over 50 Japanese soldiers had been killed, with two of them falling close to the landing barge. Private Joe Smith was discovered making breakfast at the blockhouse. He was awarded the Military Medal.[43]

Second wave troops of 29 Battalion land from an LCI at Beach Orange 1, Mono Island, 27 October 1943.

*(Alexander Turnbull Library, War History Collection, F44798-1/2)*

The fight for Soanatalu had cost five dead and nine wounded. It did, however, break the back of Japanese organised resistance. Thereafter, only small groups of desperate, ill, starving Japanese would be encountered.

On 2 November, three New Zealanders encountered a Japanese soldier who approached them shouting, 'Don't shoot'. On getting close enough he armed and threw a grenade, which wounded one of the soldiers. The Japanese soldier was promptly killed.[44] Patrols combed the island, sometimes encountering Japanese soldiers. Although eight prisoners were taken, they had all either been badly wounded or had surrendered to the islanders. The Japanese were not inclined to surrender.

By 12 November, the island was secure and was made even more so by the successful landing of American forces at Empress Augusta Bay, which had occurred on 1 November. Row implemented his plan for holding the Treasury Islands and the New Zealand forces went into garrison mode.[45] This would be the end of combat operations for the men of 8 Brigade, but not the end of danger. The Treasury Islands were regularly subjected to Japanese air raids.

The apparent ease with which *Goodtime* took place and the comparatively light casualties disguise just how risky the operation was. Good luck, and the efforts of New Zealand and American personnel, combined to make it a success.

In one respect *Goodtime* was not a complete success. One of its objectives had been to divert Japanese attention away from the planned American landing at Empress Augusta Bay, Bougainville. If *Goodtime* had been completely successful, the Japanese would have launched a counter-invasion from the nearby Shortland Islands. If this had occurred, the New Zealanders would have been at the centre of intense fighting and the outcome could have been very costly.

As it was, *Goodtime* paid dividends – radar stations were set up, airstrips created and a naval base established which was able to provide safe haven for any ships damaged in the invasion of Bougainville. Again, it proved that the New Zealanders could be relied upon by their American allies.

# The Green Islands 12

## Operation *Squarepeg*

Operation *Squarepeg*, the taking of the Green Islands, was the final major military action of 3NZ Division. It involved 14 Brigade, Divisional HQ and support troops, and was the largest amphibious operation carried out by New Zealand troops in World War II. It was extremely successful, with limited casualties, and featured the first use of tanks by New Zealanders in combat in the Pacific war.

As always in the Pacific war, the key aim of seizing territory was to establish an airfield. Halsey saw *Squarepeg* as a step towards taking Kavieng, providing an airfield from which fighters could cover bomber strikes. However, he thought the seizure of Kavieng could not take place for some time, leaving a hiatus in major operations that he feared 'would kill the momentum of the South Pacific Drive'. Nimitz wanted 'some intermediate operation … to retain the initiative and to provoke enemy reactions which would enable us to engage his forces.' The Green Islands fitted 'the geometric requirements': they were close enough to Kavieng for fighter operations but also within fighter coverage of the Allied airfields at Torokina. The seizure of Emirau was considered as an alternative to Kavieng and it was thought the Green Islands operation would assist this as well.[1] Furthermore, establishing a PT boat base would enable attacks on the Japanese supply network of barges between New Ireland and Bougainville.

Nissan, the main coral atoll of the Green Islands group, is 37 miles north-north-west of Bougainville and 55 miles from the south-eastern end of New Britain. Nine miles north to south and five miles east to west, it has an opening in the north-west allowing access to a lagoon. There are two small islands, Barahun and Sirot, just above sea level and covered in thick vegetation and coconut plantations. Although aerial photos indicated the practicability of building an airfield, there was no certainty. Nor was it certain that large landing craft could be beached.

What made the Green Islands attractive to American planners made the operation hazardous. With the main Japanese base at Rabaul only 115 miles away, and Japanese-held Buka 36 miles to the south-east, a vigorous response was likely, especially as the Green Islands were an important link in the Japanese supply system from Rabaul to Buka. As at Vella Lavella and the Treasury Islands, there was substantial risk, with Japanese forces on New Ireland, New Britain, Bougainville and Buka. Although the Green Islands could have been invaded by 15 January 1944, the target date was set for 15 February, to allow time for the 'partial neutralisation of the powerful enemy air base at Rabaul'.[2] 3NZ Division was given the task of invading the Green Islands. As Commander of Task Force 31, Admiral Wilkinson became the overall commander, with Barrowclough resuming tactical command of the landing.[3] Consequently, the headquarters of 3NZ Division shifted from Vella Lavella to Guadalcanal on 5 January.

14 Brigade had continued regular patrols around Vella Lavella, and 30 Battalion was selected for further amphibious training on Barga Island on 1–3 December 1943. The rest of the brigade did further specialist jungle training, involving fire and movement exercises. The brigade was ready for further combat operations by December.

Barrowclough decided to strengthen his force 'by the inclusion of the 144 Ind Bty and the Tank Squadron, though it might not be possible to get the latter organisation into the island until the second or third echelon.'[4]

As Coastwatchers had been unable to operate in the area, a 'commando raid' was sent in to discover beach information and the enemy's strength. As with the Cowan patrols, there was a risk of alerting the Japanese to the invasion. This time, Barrowclough noted, COMSOPAC decided that because Green Island was 'very small and ha[d] a native population of fifteen hundred, most of whom were thought to be Japanese sympathisers ... it would be impracticable to send a secret reconnaissance party.' Barrowclough planned to use men from 30 Battalion, 'which is the only infantry unit in my command which has not yet had battle experience. They are all keen to undertake it.' Calling it a 'commando raid' added a certain glamour to the operation. As he explained:

# The Green Islands

showing the movement of 14 Brigade, February 1944

*(adapted from 3NZ Division Unofficial Histories)*

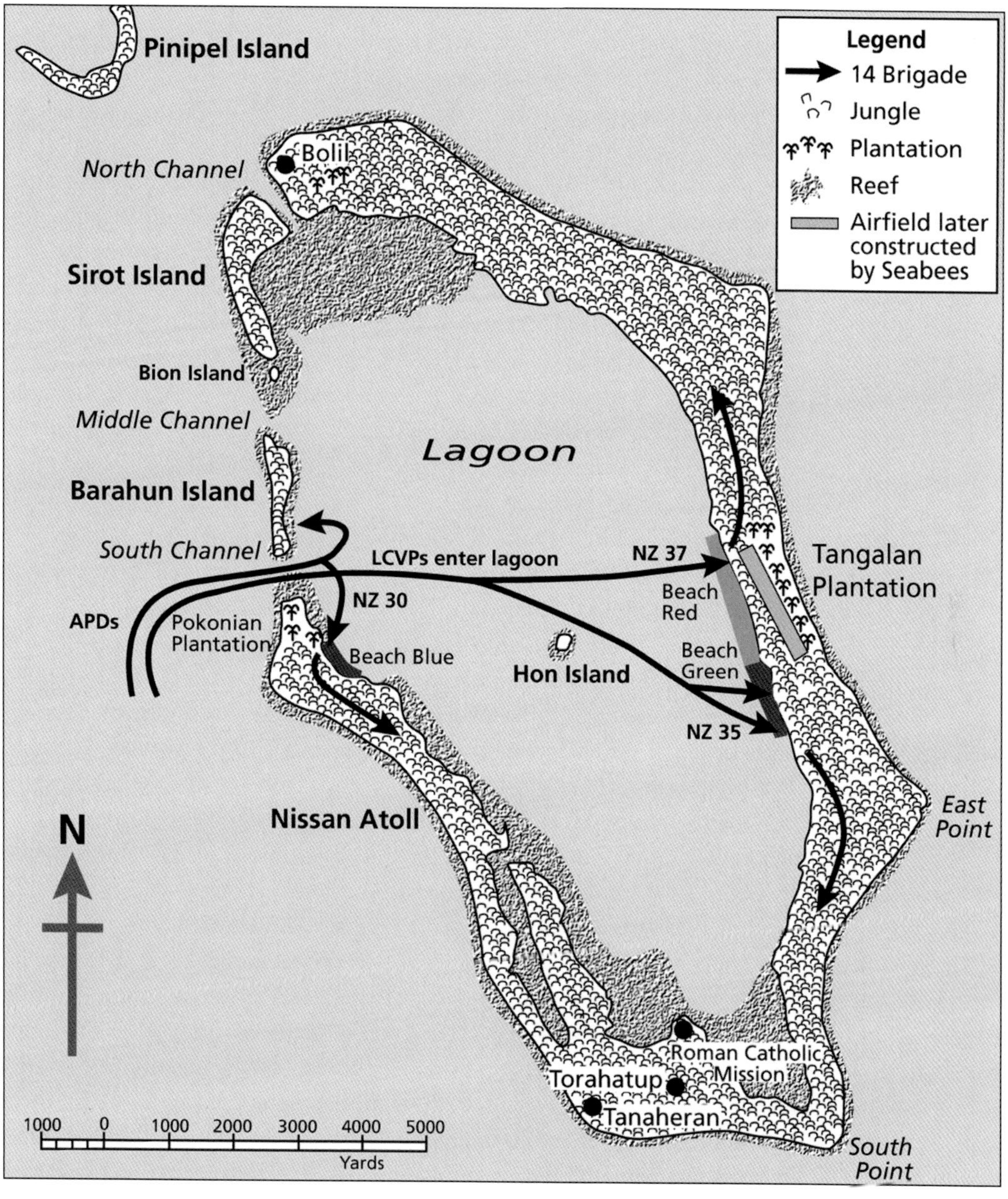

We shall probably contrive to leave behind under as realistic circumstances as possible a bogus order for the operation describing it as a commando raid directing the troops to destroy any equipment used in the barge staging operations which the Japanese are carrying out. I shall instruct them to patrol at length inland with the object of finding and destroying any dumps of oil, fuel, etc. The real object, of course, will be to investigate the ground with a view to ascertaining its suitability for airfield construction and also to undertake certain hydrographic surveys that are requisite if we are to ascertain that we can effect landings at the points we desire.[5]

The 300 chosen men consisted of A, D and C Companies, 1 Platoon from B Company, mortar sections, a reconnaissance section, intelligence personnel, signals personnel, a medical officer and orderlies and the battalion padre.[6] Attached to the unit were 30 USN intelligence, communication, airfield, landing craft and beach specialists, mainly from Admiral Wilkinson's HQ but including New Zealand Artillery, Engineer and ASC officers. A former plantation owner, Lieutenant F.P. Archer, attached to the British Solomon Islands Administration, provided expertise in pidgin. The primary role of the New Zealand troops was to protect these specialists.[7] The raid illustrates the complex nature of amphibious operations. The force was commanded by Captain Ralph Earle, USN, the New Zealand troops by Lieutenant-Colonel F.C. Cornwall and the naval unit by Commander J.D. Smith, USN.

The force sailed from Vella Lavella at first light on 30 January 1944 in three Assault Personnel Destroyers (APD) with four destroyer escorts; two PT boats later joined the convoy. On the stroke of midnight, the landing craft from the APDs passed through the entrance to the lagoon, shrouded in a night so dark it might have been prepared for such an undertaking.

Rough seas made the transfer to LCVPs difficult: seasickness was rife.[8] When the tide was right, a PT boat led a column of 12 landing craft through the gap between Barahun and Nissan and into the lagoon. As Lieutenant Frank Rennie commented, 'it would have been disastrous if we had been fired upon from high ground as the … barges went through the gap'.[9] The Allied personnel landed on Nissan and the ships returned to the Treasury Islands to be out of the reach of Japanese aircraft before daylight. The following day patrols examined Barahun. Two companies were sent across the lagoon to Tangalan Plantation on the eastern side. As their landing craft surged across the lagoon, an RNZAF *Ventura* Bomber came in low and attempted to communicate by Aldis lamp, eventually dropping a roll of toilet paper on the beach. Rennie recovered the roll thinking it

Soldiers of 30 Battalion apply camouflage paint to each other's faces in preparation for the Commando Raid, 30 January 1944.

*(Alexander Turnbull Library, War History Collection, WH-0808, photographer unknown)*

New Zealand troops on Nissan Atoll, Green Islands, firing mortar shells at Japanese barges, 30 January 1944.

*(Alexander Turnbull Library, War History Collection, Ref. PA Coll 5547-026)*

was simply a raw joke on the part of the RNZAF, and shook his fist at the disappearing plane. No message was found in the roll. In fact, the pilot was attempting to warn the troops that a large Japanese barge had landed on the seaward side of the atoll.[10]

Three other parties in barges explored the beaches around the lagoon and the Mission Station to the south. Archer made contact with friendly locals who provided information on the Japanese. While returning, a Japanese barge was discovered moored in a small bay under trees. Commander Smith could not detect any Japanese, but as a landing craft neared the barge, another well-camouflaged barge was discovered alongside and rifle and heavy machine-gun fire broke out from the coral cliff above the beach. Unfortunately, the Allied force's eagerness to close with the Japanese meant the muzzles of their machine guns were knocked skywards by tree branches and they could not return fire. The landing craft coxswain and a gunner were hit, as were two men who tried to take their places, and 23-year-old Lieutenant Patrick O'Dowd, the senior New Zealand officer, was killed. Fortunately, another landing craft opened Bren gunfire on the Japanese, enabling the first to withdraw. Smith wanted to return to destroy the Japanese, but the New Zealand commander insisted that the reconnaissance missions be finished first. Afterwards an assault was launched on the Japanese positions, but half a dozen *Zero* Fighters appeared and began bombing and strafing the Allied landing craft. One of these beached and disgorged two platoons, who found themselves with Japanese troops in front and strafing *Zeros* to their rear. One American was killed and one wounded. The scene is described in *Pacific Kiwis*:

> 'It will be our turn soon,' everybody thought as they lay in fox holes in the plantations. Some in their eagerness scooped sand out of their trenches with their hands, others with arms like flails shoveled deeper into their slit trenches to get more protection. The barges were still being strafed while one badly aimed bomb fell somewhere on the seaward side of the coast. Why the Zeros failed to make another run and strafe the beaches is a mystery, for had they done so, casualties would have been certain.[11]

Rennie agreed. 'The combined fire power of the barges must have kept the Japanese from coming too low, but with the advantage they had, why they didn't press this home will always be a mystery. Our barges were peppered with holes including the one carrying the explosives. We would have been very badly placed had the Japanese concentrated on the barges – and on us.'[12]

Landing craft on Nissan. Troops of 30 Battalion pulling out from Pokonian to move into the lee of Barahun Island on 30 January 1944. The troops had been strafed by Japanese aircraft 45 minutes before this photo was taken.

*(Archives NZ WAII 7)*

The air attack was sufficient to deter further offensive action and as it was getting dark the two platoons reboarded and headed for Barahun. There they waited until midnight for the return of APDs. A receding tide and darkness hampered the withdrawal. At one point a landing craft became grounded and had to be manhandled into deeper water. Sea conditions outside the lagoon were rough but the troops were able to re-embark, albeit perilously, and return to Vella Lavella.[13]

Much valuable information was obtained, including details of the suitability of landing beaches and the effects of tides. Locals said there were roughly 100 Japanese to the south of Nissan. Positions were marked out for the placement of artillery. A mystery was also resolved. Aerial photographs had shown small clearings at regular intervals around the coast, apparently made by the Japanese. However, the Allied force established that the work had been done by a local cargo cult.[14]

The lack of air cover almost proved catastrophic. Allied fighter aircraft would have been near the limit of their operational range, but missions against Rabaul, which was much further away, were being routinely undertaken. There were airfields on Bougainville, including the RNZAF Base at Torokina. US night fighters may actually have been in the vicinity, as the troops heard engines in the distance as they awaited evacuation at midnight. The official history, *The Pacific*, records that No. 18 Fighter

Squadron RNZAF was given the task of providing fighter cover. For whatever reason, it was ineffective.[15]

The composition of the force was also odd – not small enough to be stealthy, nor big enough to deal with substantial opposition. Arguably a small group would have been preferable. Furthermore, it is curious why the US Marine Corps had not used its specialist reconnaissance teams to investigate the Green Islands. Two American PT boats had already surveyed the two lagoon entrances undetected, so they could presumably have landed a specialist team. A well-camouflaged PT boat would have been much less noticeable than 12 LCVPs. The answer probably lies in the fact that the Americans knew the Green Islands were used as a staging point for barge traffic, and Japanese were 'present in light strength'[16] and contact was anticipated. Barrowclough thought that a large force had the advantage that the specialist teams could carry out their work more effectively because they did not need to be stealthy. Yet such a large force would only alert the Japanese to the planned invasion. Indeed, the raid was set for 31 January, which was considered the latest time at which information could be used to assist in the 15 February attack without giving the Japanese enough time to reinforce the garrison.

When a report from a Japanese lookout was received on 31 January, the commander of the South East Area immediately ordered an aerial reconnaissance and a fighter bomber strike. The attacking pilots reported the presence of six motor torpedo boats. Japanese forces on the Green Islands signalled that they were being attacked, had incurred heavy losses and were going to destroy their code books. They requested reinforcements, which left Rabaul on 1 February and landed 77 men in the Green Islands. Meanwhile some of the original Japanese garrison returned on 5 February.[17] The net effect of the commando raid had been to increase potential opposition. Furthermore, the idea that the Green Islanders were pro-Japanese proved to be flawed: the Allied forces 'found the Green Islands to be inhabited by some twelve hundred Melanesians who were so friendly to us and so hostile to the Japanese ...'.[18]

## Operation *Squarepeg*: Invasion 15 February 1944

Meticulous planning began for the main landings. Lieutenant M.A. McKenzie, who had been involved with the commando raid, helped construct a sand-table model of the terrain based on aerial photos. Every man in the battalion was expected to study it. On 3 February intelligence officer Lieutenant Dean lectured company commanders on terrain and Lieutenant-Colonel A.H.L. Sugden outlined the brigade plan whereby

30 Battalion would secure the entrance, followed by 35 and 37 Battalions landing in the vicinity of Tangalan. Lieutenant Zivaneth, the US Naval Gunfire Officer, and a naval gunfire observation party consisting of Lieutenant Kelly, USMC and seven Marines were attached to 37 Battalion. Captain Brooker of the 3NZ Division Tank Squadron lectured on infantry–tank co-operation and Lieutenant Bartos was sent to 14 Brigade as Liaison Officer and Air Support Control officer.[19]

In 3NZ Division's previous operations the amphibious force had left from Guadalcanal, but now separate groups came from Guadalcanal and Vella Lavella, the slowest ships sailing first so everyone would arrive off the Green Islands at the same time. The force consisted of eight APDs, thirteen LCIs, seven LSTs and six LCTs. Two task forces of destroyers and cruisers were to act as protective screens around the Green Islands. The Allied convoy was so large that it was inevitably detected by the Japanese on the morning of 14 February 1944. In an all-out night attack by 32 Japanese aircraft, 12 were shot down. The USS *St Louis* was hit and severely damaged with the loss of 23 sailors and another 20 wounded. RNZAF No. 14 and No. 18 Squadrons were designated to provide fighter cover and managed to keep eight aircraft over the Green Islands in conjunction with US Marine Corps fighters.[20]

No amphibious operation proceeds perfectly. On 15 February 1944 the minesweepers arrived late and it was fortunate that no mines had been laid. Nor had the Japanese sited artillery at the entrance to the lagoon. To avoid endangering the co-operative locals, the usual preparatory naval and aerial bombardment was dispensed with.

US fighters and anti-aircraft fire drove off the Japanese so that 'by the time the New Zealanders came on the station the attack was over and they saw no enemy aircraft during the day'.[21] Many larger landing craft flew barrage balloons to deter low-level attacks.

At 0641 hrs the first wave of assault boats left the line of departure. Assault troops from 30 Battalion landed from the lagoon side of Pokonian Plantation and a follow-up wave from 35 and 37 Battalions landed at Tangalan at 0740 hrs. For Ron Tucker the approach to Nissan was particularly tense as his landing craft surged into the lagoon through a gap in the coral. Tucker felt that he and his comrades were sitting ducks. As soon as the ramp of his landing craft hit the beach they worked frantically to offload their guns and their gear.[22] Altogether, 4344 tons of supplies were landed on the first day.[23] Patrols fanning out from the landing sites encountered no resistance. The headquarters for 3NZ Division was located at Pokonian, and the advanced headquarters of 14 Brigade was at Tangalan. Fire from a Japanese barge to the south-east of Pokonian was rapidly dealt with by two LCI gunboats.[24] A more substantial Japanese response was an air raid on the night of 15–16 February, when 20 bombs were dropped from high altitude and five locals were wounded.

## Skirmish at Sirot: 17 February 1944

On 17 February the process of patrolling and probing for the elusive Japanese enemy continued. The Islanders told the New Zealanders that a number of Japanese had fled to the densely wooded island of Sirot, at the entrance to the lagoon. A reinforced Company of 30 Battalion, 14 Brigade was given the task of eliminating the defenders.

An intense seven-minute artillery barrage preceded the attackers. They discovered that the Japanese were no pushover – the defenders had taken full advantage of the jungle, set up machine guns and were prepared to fight to the death. The New Zealanders found themselves fighting against a near-invisible enemy of unknown strength. They pushed forward but it was a bitter and costly close-quarters fight. Five New Zealanders were killed and three wounded. Some 21 Japanese defenders were killed. Barrowclough summed it up in his war diary: 'It was quite a desperate fight as the Japs were cornered and fought to the last man.'[25]

## Tanks and infantry at Tanaheran: 20 February 1944

The first real combat use of armour by 3NZ Division came during *Squarepeg*. Its Tank Squadron was equipped with *Valentine* Mark III Tanks and Mark III Close Support Tanks, which had proven extremely vulnerable in the Desert War but were considered adequate against the Japanese in the Solomons, who were not likely to have any tanks. Barrowclough had had reservations about accepting tanks in lieu of an additional infantry brigade, but did so when it was clear that he was saddled with a two-infantry brigade division.

It was decided to use the Tank Squadron in *Squarepeg*, even though 14 Brigade had not trained with them, as 8 Brigade had done, and shipping limitations meant only eight tanks could be deployed initially, with the remainder to follow five days later. Unloading was completed by mid-morning on 15 February. The next few days were spent carrying out probes in concert with infantry. There was no contact with the enemy, and squadron members were 'browned off' that they were not going to be involved in combat.[26] However, on 20 February Japanese were encountered at Tanaheran and Captain Stronach of the Carrier Platoon requested help. The Japanese were concealed by the dense jungle and it was impossible to

gauge their strength. Rifle fire was causing casualties. Major Rutherford, commander of the Tank Squadron, ordered two tanks to accompany him to Tanaheran. They met accurate sniper fire, one losing five periscopes to Japanese snipers, but succeeded in recovering a wounded soldier. When the remaining tanks arrived, they laid down general area fire intended to suppress the Japanese. Conditions for tank warfare were terrible: the close jungle made movement difficult, and with the Japanese so well hidden the tanks were reduced to firing blindly. Major Arthur Bullen of 30 Battalion was unwilling to attempt a tank–infantry assault because his men had not trained for it. With darkness falling he knew he had to act quickly to avoid the Japanese escaping. He began a set-piece attack with mortar fire followed up by an infantry assault. The soldiers threw grenades and fired as they ran forward. Fifty-one dead Japanese were counted. New Zealand casualties were five dead and seven wounded.[27]

*Valentine* Tanks offloaded from an LST at Nissan Atoll, Green Islands, February 1944.

*(Alexander Turnbull Library, War History Collection, Ref. 1/2-044755-F)*

The flavour of the action at Tanaheran was captured by the Third Division unofficial history, *Tanks, MMGs and Ordnance.*

There was an hour of hectic 'busyness' – feverish swinging of periscopes, fire orders not according to the book, the thrill of the first shell fired at the enemy, straining of eyes desperately searching for an enemy who kept pouring a stream of bullets at you from a few yards away, and who infuriatingly remained invisible and kept his bullets going from the very spot, seemingly, where a moment ago you had planted a shell. There were the racket of the *Besa* and the pungent fumes that came back from it, the bellowing of the engine, and the crackle of the earphones, the flickering of the leaves where the Jap bullets came through and the tack-hammering on the turret where they struck. There was the view of leaves and vines and trucks that in an instant burst into a silver-splintered nothingness, when a bullet hit the periscope prism. In the hot reeking security of the turret there were the recoiling gun, the gunner who turned to grin when his shell smacked an indicated target and the cheerful shirtless loader who worked heroically at the heavy shells and the refractory *Besa*. There was the backing and filling as your tank manoeuvred amid closely spaced coconut palms, scraping ominously over the hard coral as it heaved around, and the anxiety lest you break a track in there where you could least afford to break it. And there was the sickening fascination of that close range view of a wounded Kiwi climbing painfully on to an adjacent tank a few short feet from the Jap position, the slow suspense as the tank backed away to safety, the relief when he made it. There was a period while the tanks were reloading and the ground troops had a go. Machine-gunners moved closer in, infantrymen sniped from the doubtful shelter of coconut palms and mortars barked viciously. Jap .25 bullets cracked sharply about, and positions previously thought safe became untenable as concealed tree-top snipers opened up. You became confused and a little fearful as they seemed to be all round you. You stared as our dead and wounded came trickling back.

Eventually it was over, the tempo had slackened as the enemy strength dribbled away. The infantry had gone in with grenade and bayonet and the remaining Japs had been scuppered. We rode our *Vals* back to the leaguer area, examined our battle scars and talked excitedly far into the night. Next day there was the visit to the scene of operations where the contorted and mutilated bodies lay everywhere – big, evil-looking men who had fought till they were wounded, patched themselves up with field dressings and gone on fighting till they were killed or until there was no more ammunition, only one grenade, which pressed tightly against the chest, sent them violently into eternity. You did not stay long in that macabre spot.[28]

*Valentine* Tanks at Tanaheran, Nissan Atoll, Green Islands, 20 February 1944.

(Alexander Turnbull Library, War History Collection, PA Coll 5547-030, photographer unknown)

## Pinipel and Sau

Nissan Island may have been cleared, but a reconnaissance patrol found evidence of a Japanese bivouac on Sau, a small island island west of Pinipel, on 21 February 1944. Two days later, soldiers from 37 Battalion landed on Pinipel and using it as a base laid down a mortar barrage on Sau and raked it with machine-gun fire. A company of soldiers then landed on Sau and encountered a small group of Japanese equipped with a light machine gun and grenades. The New Zealanders killed eight of the defenders, but their luck was not to last. A further group of six Japanese were found and killed, but this time four New Zealanders were injured by Japanese grenades.

Further patrols established that there was a Japanese position on Sau, and on 23 February an infantry company of 37 Battalion was landed and destroyed a small group of Japanese soldiers. Organised resistance ended and the New Zealand units went into defensive positions. For several days afterward occasional stray enemy were found and one prisoner taken. Meanwhile Seabees began to create airstrips, roads and other facilities. A mere eighteen days after the troops arrived, an Allied aircraft was able to make an emergency landing. By 7 March, staging aircraft were using the airfield on their way to bomb Rabaul. Naval base facilities were also established, and by 17 February a PT boat squadron was patrolling from the Green Islands.

Further mopping-up operations took place to eliminate small groups of Japanese. By 28 February 1944, the Green Islands were considered secured and orders were issued defining defensive zones to be held by the garrison. There remained the possibility of a Japanese counter-attack or an attack from Japanese units retreating from Buka, so the New Zealanders had to remain on alert. Nightly air raids remained a source of stress. An American Seabee, Bob Conner, noted in his diary: 'Tokyo Ann has announced for the second time we have been here that The Green Islands have been bombed into oblivion.'[29]

Despite these perils, the Americans and New Zealanders worked hard building infrastructure so that the air and naval bases could be used to their full potential in isolating the Japanese base at Rabaul.

Once more the New Zealanders had accomplished the mission entrusted to them and at low cost. By this stage, both brigades had experienced combat and had developed considerable expertise in amphibious operations and jungle warfare. The seizure of the Green Islands completed the encirclement of Rabaul, and Allied air and sea power then neutralised it.

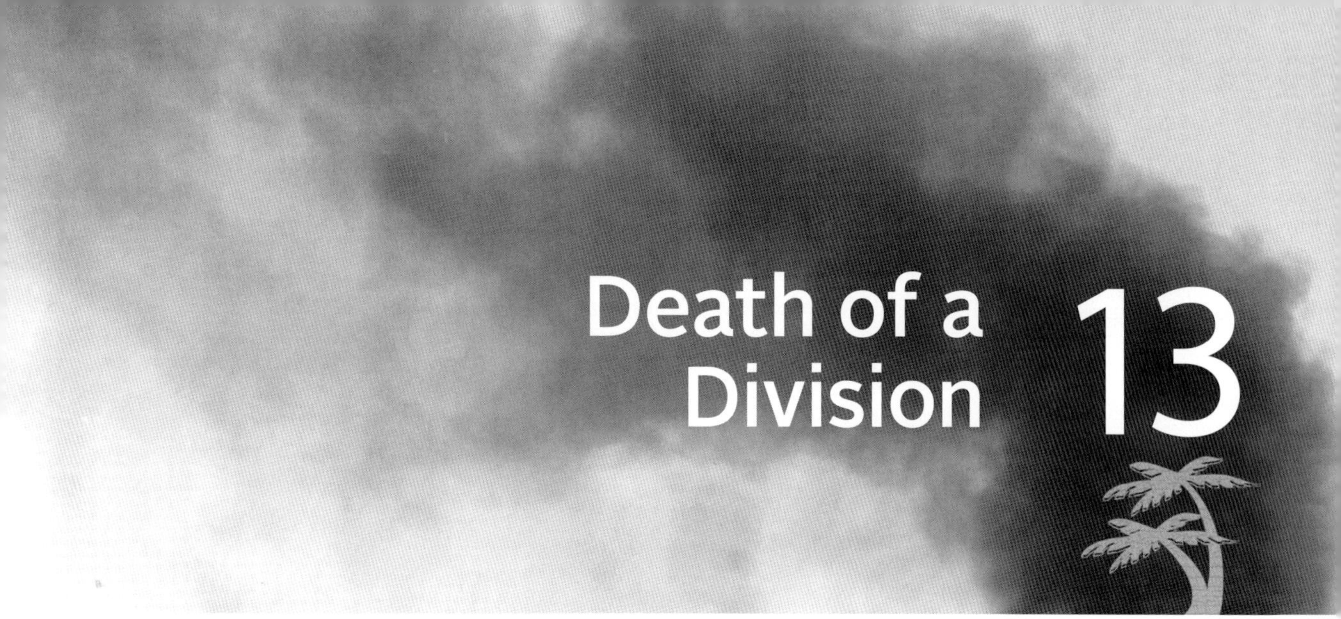

# Death of a Division 13

The death of 3NZ Division was as complex and convoluted as its birth. 3NZ Division was disbanded after it had gained the respect of American commanders, built up a good working relationship with US forces, become adequately equipped and achieved victories. It was dismantled despite strong opposition from Barrowclough and despite the support of the Chief of Imperial General Staff. The decision was taken at a high political level and after much debate, characterised by Wellington's reluctance to forgo strategic options by losing one of its divisions. Ultimately, the issue was where New Zealand's limited resources could best be deployed. The survival of 2NZ Division and the demise of 3NZ Division in part demonstrate the importance Wellington attached to its Commonwealth ties and the fact that, by 1944, New Zealand was safe from invasion and consequently the American connection was less important. The disbandment was not completed until 20 October 1944. Even so, there were suggestions of a Pacific Division being reconstituted in 1945.

From its inception, 3NZ Division was starved of manpower, with personnel taken from it to bolster 2NZ Division. Whereas the latter's creation and development was deliberate and methodical, 3NZ Division was an afterthought, a reaction to a strategic need. Once that need had been met by blunting the Japanese drive south, the existence of the division was open for debate. That debate centred on where New Zealand could best contribute to the victory of the British Commonwealth: with 2NZ Division in Europe, with 3NZ Division in the Pacific, or producing food and manufactured goods for the Allies. Indeed, the decision to send 3NZ Division overseas had been critically influenced by the fact that there had been a good harvest in 1942.[1]

As the war progressed, there were increasing demands on New Zealand's limited pool of manpower for service in the two overseas divisions, the Royal New Zealand Navy, the RNZAF, the RAF, the British Merchant Marine, the Home Defence Forces (especially in 1942), and agriculture and industry. New Zealand struggled to cope by introducing conscription and directing its population into essential industries. It rapidly became clear that the deployment of two divisions overseas could not be sustained: one or both divisions would have to shrink in size or one would have to be disbanded to bolster the other.

In 1940 2NZ Division had been created and deployed overseas under British command. It was recognised that if Britain fell, New Zealand's future as an independent country was in jeopardy. Its best option appeared to be to contribute to British victory in Europe while maintaining some degree of local defence. With Japan's entry into the war, Wellington was obliged to give more thought to homeland defence, and for a brief period soldiers were sent to bolster 3NZ Division at the expense of 2NZ Division, and mobilisation of home defence forces reached a peak. It was clear that New Zealand could not defend itself with the forces available, and the prospect arose of withdrawing 2NZ Division from the Mediterranean. The deciding factor was the American agreement to send troops to New Zealand in exchange for New Zealand troops remaining in the Middle East.

Despite American victories at the Coral Sea and Midway in May–June 1942, the Japanese still posed a considerable threat in the South Pacific. On the basis of Puttick's advice in early August of that year, the War Cabinet approved the enlargement of 3NZ Division and this was offered to the Americans. Wellington bound itself to the ultimately untenable task of sustaining two separate divisions in different theatres.

In mid-1942, 2NZ Division sustained heavy casualties and narrowly avoided annihilation. Freyberg reported that it had to be reinforced by October 1942, and Fraser agreed, but the reinforcement pool in New Zealand was insufficient to meet the needs of 2NZ Division fully. This was addressed by creating a tank battalion to lessen casualties and by providing 5500 reinforcements. Puttick warned that 'any serious deterioration in the Pacific situation in the meantime would of course affect the whole question.'[2] The need to reinforce 2NZ Division continued as it became involved in the battles for Egypt, but with victory at El Alamein in November, its continued presence in the Middle East seemed unnecessary.

On 19 November 1942 Fraser requested its return, given the Anglo-American build-up in North Africa, the increased danger from Japan and the need to 'launch a counter-offensive at the earliest possible date.' Fraser declared that '2nd NZ Division's place should be in the Pacific' because New Zealand's manpower had reached 'straining point' and it was no longer possible to have two overseas divisions and maintain its commitments.[3] Churchill opposed the removal of 2NZ Division, pointing out that it was easier for American troops to move into the Pacific than for Australasian troops to be withdrawn from the Middle East. Shipping difficulties were paramount. Influenced by Churchill and General George C. Marshall,[4] Fraser agreed to support 2NZ Division remaining in the Middle East. At a secret session of Parliament on 3 December 1942, it was decided to maintain the status quo.[5]

However, the critical manpower shortage remained and the size of the Armed Forces peaked at 157,000 men in September 1942.[6] The diversion of so many men from New Zealand's agriculture and industry impacted on the economy at a time when there were increased demands for production. Despite this, Fraser was wary of a Japanese resurgence. He recognised that New Zealand was a Pacific nation and that it was 'of overwhelming importance' that New Zealand should not be accused of shirking its responsibilities in the Pacific.[7] The decision taken by the War Cabinet on 6 March 1943 to expand 3NZ Division to 17,637 men is a manifestation of this. There was general parliamentary support for a Pacific focus, but the needs of 2NZ Division could not be ignored. As Fraser commented, 'we must take a share in the Pacific Battle and we must keep the division for the time being in the very stern battle for Tunisia.'[8]

With the end of the Tunisian Campaign, Churchill pressed for 2NZ Division to be used in the invasion of Sicily, but Fraser declined to commit to this and eventually the British proceeded without 2NZ Division.[9] Fraser confided to Freyberg: 'The simple fact is that we no longer have the Grade A men to maintain two divisions abroad, and within a few months the question must be determined which division is to be used to reinforce the other.'[10] He told Churchill the same thing and urged him to make an appeal on symbolic, historical and military grounds for the retention of 2NZ Division. Fraser had swung towards the European commitment, but also stressed the importance for the post-war world of British participation in the Pacific War.[11] This duality of position would prolong the life of 3NZ Division. Churchill duly despatched an impassioned plea for the retention of 2NZ Division, also indicating that Roosevelt supported him.[12] Again, shortage of shipping was cited as the key reason to leave the division in place. The vast distances of the Pacific strained New Zealand's slender maritime resources. Consequently, 3NZ Division was virtually dependent on the Americans for its shipping needs.

Meanwhile arrangements had been made for the return to New Zealand of long-serving members of 2NZ Division. This 'furlough scheme' had a huge impact. The sudden need to find 9000 replacements triggered a crisis: the only viable source of manpower was 3NZ Division. A senior civil servant observed that Fraser's 'personal position is both difficult and delicate. In the first place he does not know which is the right thing to do – to sacrifice the Pacific Division or the Middle East Division – because clearly we cannot maintain both plus this Frankenstein of an air force and the semblance of a home defence force, the maintenance of which is dictated by Politics.' He also noted the 'division in the War Cabinet, probably four-fifths opposition in Cabinet and an equal proportion of opponents in Caucus when it comes to leaving the division in the Middle East.' However, opinion in the War Cabinet 'veered around to the retention of the division in the Middle East'.[13]

Fraser was well aware of the strong feeling in Canberra that New Zealand troops should return to the Pacific. Australian troops were heavily engaged in New Guinea and the Solomons, and the Australian perception was that their sister Dominion should be the first one to be called upon for assistance. There was also a feeling that Wellington was far too acquiescent towards Britain's demands.

In terms of maintaining a significant contribution in the Pacific, New Zealand had already developed an alternative to 3NZ Division in the form of the RNZAF squadrons and, to a lesser extent, naval units. Indeed, the rapid expansion of the RNZAF during 1942 and 1943 to seventeen squadrons for the Pacific contributed greatly to the manpower crisis of mid-1943. Between September 1942 and September 1943 the RNZAF's strength in the Pacific rose from 1341 to 3667 (while personnel in New Zealand went from 19,300 to 30,700).[14] Puttick acknowledged that men were to be withdrawn from 3NZ Division 'for Air Force which Army must assist in its large expansion'.[15] That expansion was based on the agreement from Admiral King in August 1942 for 500 aircraft to be supplied to the RNZAF from USN stocks. Hence it was equipped with US-designed aircraft, albeit sometimes of obsolete design: *Kittyhawks, Corsairs, Hudsons, Avengers, Dauntlesses* and *Catalinas*. The fuel, munitions and equipment were all inter-operable with US air units, posing far fewer logistical problems than the almost entirely British-equipped 3NZ Division. New Zealand air power in the Pacific had a number of advantages: it was easier to deploy aircraft from airfield to airfield than to ship soldiers with their associated impedimenta; it was cheap in terms of both money and lives; it arguably offered the Americans greater offensive and defensive capability than a ground unit; and it would have fewer problems with sickness. For an army commander, Puttick was very air-minded. By 1943 he strongly preferred New Zealand air power to land forces in the South Pacific, for the above reasons and because, with only 4696 Air Force and 404 Navy personnel in the Pacific on 31 December 1943, the immediate cost of those commitments in manpower was significantly less than the 19,649 in 3NZ Division. Much more labour for the Home Front could be released by running down or disbanding the latter.

To exacerbate matters, the British were requesting more agricultural products,[16] while the increasing numbers of American forces in New Zealand and the South Pacific were demanding more food under reciprocal lend lease. (The United States–New Zealand Mutual Aid Agreement (or 'Lend Lease') had been signed on 3 September 1942.) Wellington found itself facing growing criticism from the Americans that its war effort was misdirected: it had a tremendous army in proportion to its population, but vital industries were under-utilised due to lack of labour. It was felt 'that New Zealand's contribution to the war should be economic rather than military' and that although New Zealand was supplying food to American forces, 'the present contribution is minor indeed when compared to the Dominion's potentialities'.[17] In June 1943, Puttick warned that 'the seasonal demand for labour will be particularly difficult this year.' He considered that 12,000 men were required for harvesting and 18,000 for food-processing industries. He noted that 'the PM has emphasised that the harvest must be gathered, regardless of anything else'.[18] Dairy production reached its nadir for a decade and meat production was also significantly down.[19] A crisis was looming.

Wellington struggled to cope by reducing its Home Defence forces, but this was insufficient. But for its involvement in combat operations in late 1943, 3NZ Division would probably have been reduced. In December Nash cabled Halsey that there was 'a most serious crisis, particularly in regard to the production of foodstuffs … Unless men in the Pacific can be made available for employment in the freezing works before the peak of the season in January, it will not be possible to fulfil the commitments in respect of meat either for the United States Forces in the Pacific or for the urgent needs of the United Kingdom.'[20] Nash asked for the release of garrison troops in Tonga and Fiji and for shipping to be made available.

However, there was also strong support for 3NZ Division in Wellington. Carl Berendsen, the Secretary to the War Cabinet and from March 1943 New Zealand's High Commissioner to Australia, considered that New Zealand troops should have returned to the Pacific even though the threat to New Zealand had evaporated. He thought that 'our Forces should be fighting in our own geographic area where our post war interests would be'. Barrowclough's arguments for concentration on the Pacific carried considerable weight with Fraser, who on the whole considered 'it was preferable for our main effort to be in the Pacific theatre'.[21] As Chief of General Staff, Puttick viewed 3NZ Division as simply filling the gap until American forces could arrive. In the early years of the Pacific War he considered that 'NZ's Armed Forces, being more or less on the spot, are of very special value during this period, much more so than when in the future larger forces are available from other sources.'[22] Later Puttick admitted 'we gambled a bit on the operational timetable, hoping by the time the manpower situation became critical, operations in the South Pacific might be over.'[23] That gamble had paid off, but had been complicated by Fraser's desire for 3NZ Division to take part in offensive operations.

By keeping 3NZ Division below strength and using Home Defence forces for reinforcements, Wellington was able to keep both divisions in the field during 1943. However, in August Barrowclough and the Americans were told that 3NZ Division would be receiving no further reinforcements and only limited replacements.[24] In response to Halsey's protestations about the inadequate manning of 3NZ Division, Fraser told him that once the reinforcement pool for 2NZ Division had been exhausted in New Zealand, reinforcements would be drawn from the South Pacific.[25] Matters worsened as 2NZ Division became involved in the Italian Campaign. The Battle for the Sangro River and Orsogna between 12 November 1943 and 10 April 1944 resulted in 1507 casualties, who had to be replaced to maintain combat efficiency. Complicating the situation further, from February to April 1944 2NZ Division became involved in costly operations at Cassino.

Fraser told Nash to sound out Roosevelt and Churchill on whether the Pacific or Europe should be given priority,[26] but he received no clear answer. There was also a financial factor: Wellington would have preferred its soldiers to be growing pumpkins rather than fighting because of the cost of Lend-Lease. As American aircraft were supplied to the RNZAF, the cost to New Zealand skyrocketed. One way of offsetting the nightmare of potentially owing the United States £40–50 million[27] was to supply American forces in the South Pacific with 'Reciprocal Aid' in the form of food.

At a critical juncture New Zealand lost the support of one of its chief American supporters, Admiral Ernest King. He became incensed at the Canberra Pact in January 1944 in which Australia and New Zealand proclaimed their defence interest in the South Pacific. King saw this as an Australasian attempt to play power politics and he took the view that Australasian forces should not be used for further operations in the Central Pacific for fear that this would bolster Australasian demands to be consulted in the post-war world.[28]

Barrowclough vigorously resisted the destruction of his command, stating that 'it will be impossible to withdraw the Division before the end of June (1944) as it will be actually engaged with the enemy and I do not see any other Divisions in this theatre in the near future who could undertake our relief.' He then pointed out that to ask for the relief of the division 'before the end of June would considerably embarrass Admiral Halsey'. Barrowclough thought that Wellington supported his division and that these arguments 'would strengthen the Government's hand'.[29]

After setting out all the pros and cons in detail, Puttick recommended to the government that 2NZ Division be retained abroad and that 3NZ Division be returned to New Zealand. This view was endorsed by the New Zealand Chiefs of Staff. Puttick structured his arguments to favour 2NZ Division, but given his knowledge of wartime conditions and the likely progress of the war against Japan, his conclusions were reasonable.[30] He subsequently reiterated his views.[31] He traversed the New Zealand Army's commitments, highlighting the problems of shipping 2NZ Division home ('this movement would probably be slow, leading to the NZ troops being held in base camps overseas for a lengthy period, thus causing discontent and waste of manpower resources'), manpower wastage ('it would take six months to return 2NZ Division to New Zealand with a consequent loss of manpower resources to either the fighting or production forces') and sentiment ('bitterness amongst the troops and NZ public at 2NZ Division being deprived of the spectacular and easy final stages of the campaign').

Furthermore, Britain's food requirements soared as preparations were made for D-Day. In February 1944, British Minister of Food John Llewellin informed Nash that 'if New Zealand's production declines below the present level I do not see how we can possibly maintain our present standards of feeding in this country.'[32]

Parliament decided that 11,000 men from 3NZ Division – over half its strength – should be returned to New Zealand by October 1944. But the dissolution was not a clean one. In line with the suggestion from the British Chiefs of Staff, a cadre was retained on New Caledonia to be 'a nucleus for a reconstituted division which was hoped could be provided for operations in the Pacific in 1945.'[33]

Barrowclough was informed by Wellington on 7 March that the division was to be withdrawn from the Solomons. He returned to New Zealand on 24 March and attended Cabinet meetings on the next two days. Despite his vigorous opposition, arrangements were made for 7000 soldiers to be returned to New Zealand by 1 July and 11,000 by October.[34] The rest of the division was to withdraw to New Caledonia.

Another chance that 2NZ Division might return to New Zealand came after Rome fell on 4–5 June. 2NZ Division was suffering from battlefield fatigue and needed rest and reorganisation.[35] Wellington agreed on 1 July to send Freyberg 2000 reinforcements.[36] Realistically there was only one source for these men: 3NZ Division. In comparison with the sweeping events in Europe, the Solomon Islands campaign had become secondary and Japanese forces on Rabaul had been effectively neutralised by February 1944.

The dismemberment of the division began on 24 April 1944 when 1850 men from the Green Islands garrison were sent to New Zealand. This was followed by further withdrawals from the Treasury Islands and the Green Islands. The last Treasury Islands troops were withdrawn by 15 May. The command of Green Islands was handed over to the Americans by Barrowclough on 30 May and the remnants were returned to New Zealand by 12 July 1944.

Barrowclough re-established his command in New Caledonia in early June but found his work was bedevilled by requests for personnel for industry at home and for 2NZ Division and South-East Asia Command.[37] There was an absence of clear policy from Wellington regarding the future of 3NZ Division, and units were progressively run down. While retaining full stores and equipment, some sub-units were 'reduced in strength to less than a football team'.[38] Barrowclough still hoped to retain a cadre so that the division could be resurrected. On 26 June, he alluded to 'the wish of the War Cabinet ... to retain this Division in such shape that it will be capable of re-expansion.' He considered this was possible provided that it did not fall below 6000 soldiers, and he was concerned about the loss of technical specialists and key personnel:

> if the decision was made to focus the Army's efforts in the Pacific, it will take a long time to re-build this Division and even in the most favourable circumstances I cannot see it being ready for action before March of next year [1945] at the earliest. Indeed, as far as I can see, it would have to be built up largely by raw recruits from New Zealand as any men who are likely to be available from the Middle East are not likely to be back, finish their leave and transferred to me until after March next.[39]

As late as October, Barrowclough discussed with Nimitz a possible assault on Ocean and Nauru Islands.[40] Both were British territories and Nauru in particular had been a major supplier of phosphate for New Zealand and Australian agriculture. Nimitz, however, firmly indicated that he could not spare shipping for such an operation.

Although he acknowledged the value of 3NZ Division's cadres, Puttick considered that the delays before they could be expanded to a full fighting force and the pressures to release troops to civilian life dissipated any advantages. He recommended that 2NZ Division be retained in Europe until the German surrender, that the cadres of 3NZ Division be disbanded and that officers, NCOs and technical personnel be provided to Fijian and Tongan forces, British forces and India.[41]

Barrowclough set up Divisional Headquarters in New Zealand in August 1944, and the division's strength fell to 6000 men. Yet even now Wellington deferred making a final decision, awaiting a further recommendation of the British Chiefs of Staff. This never arrived. On 11 September the War Cabinet approved the disbandment of 3NZ Division and use of its personnel to reinforce 2NZ Division. Fraser made the announcement in Parliament on 21 September. By the time Barrowclough issued his final order disbanding the division on 20 October, there were only a few headquarters and base staff to read it.[42]

As a veteran observed:

> That the ranks of 3 Division slowly eroded piecemeal, until in October 1944 the Division was no more, must have brought varied reactions. For those already back in civilian life, the event would have gone unnoticed. Back in the islands in the closing months there had been rumblings of frustration and disillusionment. Disgruntled soldiers uninformed about their future wondered whether it had all been worthwhile. That battalion camaraderie and esprit de corps built up over a few years had gone never to return.[43]

With the end of the war in Europe, attention focused on the Pacific. It was a common theme in military and political circles in 1944 that the return of 3NZ Division was only as a temporary withdrawal from the Pacific and that a division would be fielded in 1945 against Japan.[44] There were limits to New Zealand's resources and the population was war weary. Nevertheless, on 21 June 1945 the War Cabinet approved the creation of a two-brigade division for the Pacific, composed of 2NZ Division veterans and troops from New Zealand. This unit would be additional to RNZAF and RNZN units, and was to form part of what Churchill shortly afterwards referred to as 'a British Commonwealth force of some three to five divisions, carried in British shipping and supported by British naval forces and a small tactical air component. The whole force would be placed under United States command.'[45] However, the deployment of such a contingent was forestalled by the Japanese surrender.

The pressures on New Zealand's manpower remained constant right up until August 1945. Had there been a series of bloody, attritional, amphibious assaults on Japan, the only group of New Zealand soldiers who had practical experience of American amphibious doctrine and the idiosyncrasies of the USN were the veterans of 3NZ Division. The experience they had so dearly bought may have come into its own on the beaches of Japan. Fortunately for all concerned, that invasion did not take place.

# 14 'Mud, Mosquitos and Monotony'

## The hard slog

### A South Seas adventure

In the years leading up to World War II the popular image of the South Pacific had been largely shaped by Hollywood in a genre featuring romantic South Seas adventures such as *Aloma of the South Seas*, starring Dorothy Lamour. For the Allied soldiers deployed to the Solomon Islands, there was a huge gap between what they expected and what they found. Illusions of a lush, sun-drenched paradise evaporated on contact with what historian Eric Bergerud has described as 'nature's killing machine'[1] and the reality of emaciated, diseased islanders, the stench of rotting jungle and flora and fauna intent on killing or disabling the unprepared, the unlucky or the unwary.

Not that they did not have warning. Writing about the Solomon Islands in the early twentieth century in his book *South Seas Tales*, the American novelist Jack London had referred to 'the terrible Solomon Islands', commenting that 'It is true that fever and dysentery are perpetually on the walk about, that loathsome skin diseases abound, that the air is saturated with a poison that bites into every pore, cut or abrasion and plants malignant ulcers, and that many strong men who escape dying there return as wrecks to their own countries.'[2] The men of 3NZ Division would come to appreciate the truth of London's words.

## The killing ground

The Solomon Islands, with its malignant, disease-ridden environment, high precipitation, humid temperatures and dense jungle, is one of the worst places on earth for a modern industrialised army to fight. The following description of Vella Lavella, published in the official New Zealand Army history, could apply to all of the Solomon Islands:

> The jungle is the most difficult and pestilential country in which to wage war. Visibility ends only a few yards away in a barrier of thick, fleshy leaves, writhing vines and creepers, shrubs and tree trunks as this mass of vegetation fights upwards to the sun. Large trees, whose massive trunks sprawl out like flying buttresses several feet above the ground, are matted together with stout vines and a horrible variety of climbing palm which has nasty barbed fronds, the whole forming an impenetrable canopy overhead. Only a few tired rays of sunshine filter through to rich earth which is never dry and never free from the heavy odour of decay. The moist, warm atmosphere produces a crop of mildew overnight on anything damp. Growth is so swift that a rain of leaves falls continuously though the trees are all evergreens. By day the jungle is comparatively quiet except for the chatter of parrots and parakeets and the harsh grating of myriads of cicadas, one variety of which makes a piercing noise like a small but particularly busy sawmill. These insects, as though working to a signal, begin and end their crude orchestra in a flash. One moment the air is vibrating with their shrill din; the next all is silent. But when night falls, as it does swiftly with the setting sun, the jungle comes to life and bedlam reigns until dawn. The noise is incredible. Millions of frogs, one resembling a tiny brown leaf, croak and whistle; night birds chatter and screech; the cicadas maintain their incessant chirping and rasping.
>
> Among dead and dying leaves underfoot the jungle seethes with insect life. Every creeping and crawling thing finds a home there, from crabs, millipedes and myriads of ants of various sizes and colours to bright green, blue, and brown lizards, including one fellow some feet in length rather like a prehistoric dragon in miniature. By day brilliant butterflies with inches of wing-spread hover among the trees like large snippets of coloured paper; spiders, swinging their strong webs among the undergrowth, are almost as brightly decorated. At night fireflies flicker like tiny street lamps in the velvet gloom, and the phosphorescent light from chips of one particular tree is so strong that a newspaper may be read in its glow. To this exotic land thunderstorms of

> great violence bring frequent torrents of rain, adding to the discomfort and depression which are born of a feeling of imprisonment under a canopy of leafy growth. In the plantation areas, of course, there is more freedom and space, though fallen nuts have taken root and grown in thickets to a height of several feet during the war years.[3]

From a military point of view, the jungle terrain of the Solomons presented formidable challenges. The dense jungle restricted visibility and limited movement. Allied with the torpor-inducing heat and humidity, it was extremely hard for commanders to keep control of their units. The use of infantry support with weapons such as artillery and mortars was also restricted. Decentralisation, effective small-unit tactics and above all good leadership at a lower command level were critical to success.

The night-time environment was especially challenging to inexperienced troops: in addition to a natural fear of the enemy, the pitch blackness and unfamiliar sounds of birds and animals combined to encourage soldiers to fire wildly and risk fratricide. Barrowclough commented 'that the nocturnal noises had to be heard to be believed' and drowned 'every other sound except gunfire'. Relatively quiet during the day, the jungle came alive at nightfall with 'every kind of bird or insect or reptile that clicks or scuffles, whistles or hiccups, mockingly or threateningly.'[4] On Mono, Robert Dunlop of 36 Battalion found that 'there were these fireflies that would fly around at night and they seemed to circle your head. They seemed like they were illuminating your head, to give a good shot for the Japs.'[5]

In jungle warfare the rules of linear warfare do not apply and defences have to cover 360 degrees. Digging foxholes or defensive positions was often difficult owing to rock-hard coral just below the surface and tangled tree roots. Foxholes were apt to fill with water and mud, which 'smelt of sweat, excrement and death'. One veteran on Mono remarked that when you were lying at the bottom of the foxhole 'the heat is oppressive; there is no position of comfort and it is difficult to sleep …'.[6] Adding to the discomfort were the Japanese, who were especially adept at jungle warfare and infiltration. One fear that haunted the New Zealand troops on Mono was having their throats cut:

> A South Island Corporal now knows what it feels like to have his steel helmet lifted slowly back while he slept in his foxhole. He awoke to semi-consciousness one night as his hat was being pulled gently upwards. Not realising what was happening he drowsily pulled it back on his head. The next moment a hand jerked it up again, and the truth dawned on the corporal. Someone was trying to lift his chin up to

Divisional Signals Radio Operator in the jungle on Vella Lavella, using a Set Number 11, 1943.

*(Archives NZ, WAII, 7, 3 Official Photograph Album, photographer US Signal Corps)*

> expose his throat. The corporal did not doze anymore. He lashed out with his fists and a dark form slid off in a hurry. Rumour has it that the corporal slept no more that night, nor the night after.[7]

Because of the difficulties of fighting at night and the risk of killing their own men, New Zealand and Allied units in the Pacific dug in at night and ceded the initiative to the Japanese. Anything that moved in the darkness was considered to be hostile and fired upon. In a number of instances this resulted in deaths from 'friendly' fire.

The New Zealanders with no experience of jungle warfare had to undertake the same learning curve as their Australian and American counterparts. The New Zealand Army had to learn on the job and adapt to the challenges of tropical warfare. For example, the humidity of jungle conditions and geography often rendered radio sets inoperable and communications were reduced to laid field telephone cable or runners carrying messages. Fortunately, the experience of route marches and training exercises on relatively benign New Caledonia helped prepare the Kiwis for the rigours of tropical warfare.

In the Solomons there were no safe areas, even for units considered to be non-combatant. The Post Office unit on Stirling Island was hit by a bomb that struck the coconut trees above, shattering the tent and sorting cases and ripping letters to shreds. Luckily no one was wounded and in a couple of days the office was operating again. When asked if they wanted to be relieved, the men's answer was a decided 'No, we'll stick it out'.[8]

The New Zealanders were fortunate to have been given time to train for jungle warfare and to be acclimatised at the advance base at Guadalcanal before being committed to combat. They were also fortunate to have superb logistical and medical support, and it was to their advantage that they faced limited numbers of Japanese who were often considerably outnumbered by their Allied opponents. These elements of good fortune were the outcome of careful planning and consideration and in no way detract from the New Zealanders' success in combat operations in the Solomons.

The injuries the soldiers suffered reflected the close-quarter nature of jungle warfare: bullet, bayonet and grenade wounds. Limb wounds occurred in half the casualties handled by medical units; head wounds accounted for a quarter; chest and back wounds for the rest.[9] Rifle wounds comprised 40% of injuries, grenades 18% and mortar rounds 24%.[10] Eighty-five members of the division were killed in action, 12 later died of wounds and 189 were wounded.[11]

Evacuating the wounded from Purple 2 Beach, Stirling Island, October 1943.

*(Archives NZ, WAII, 1, Treasury Islands Photos D1 #28, official photographer)*

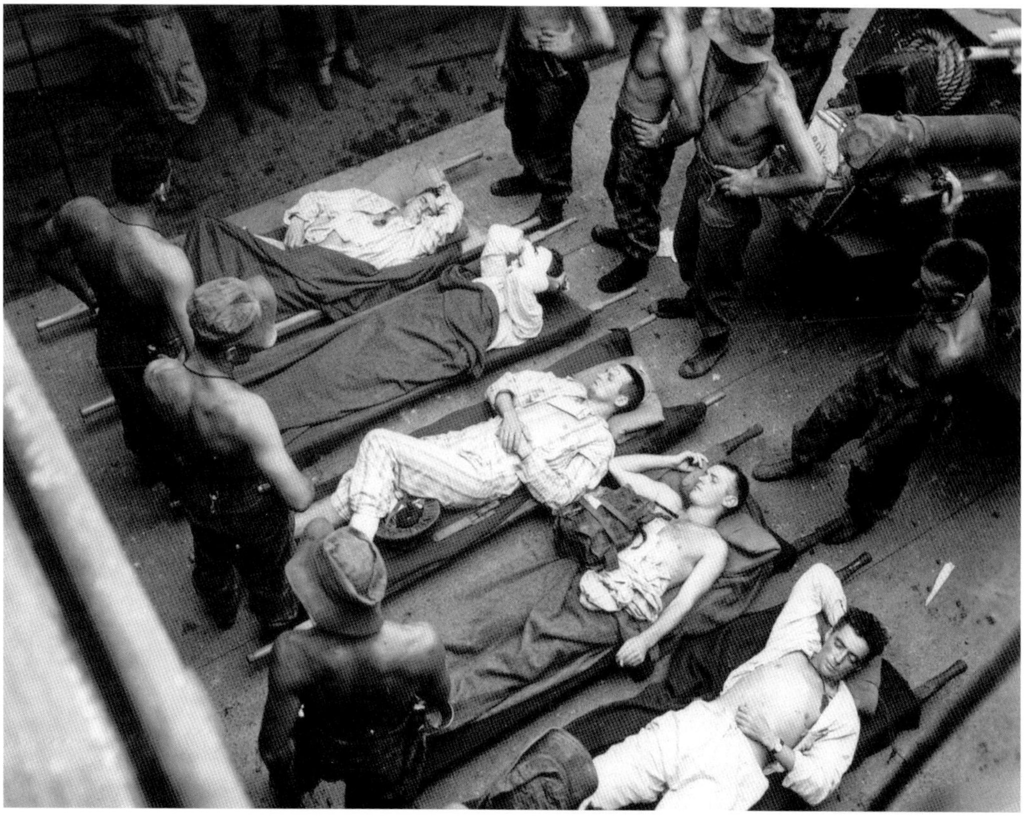

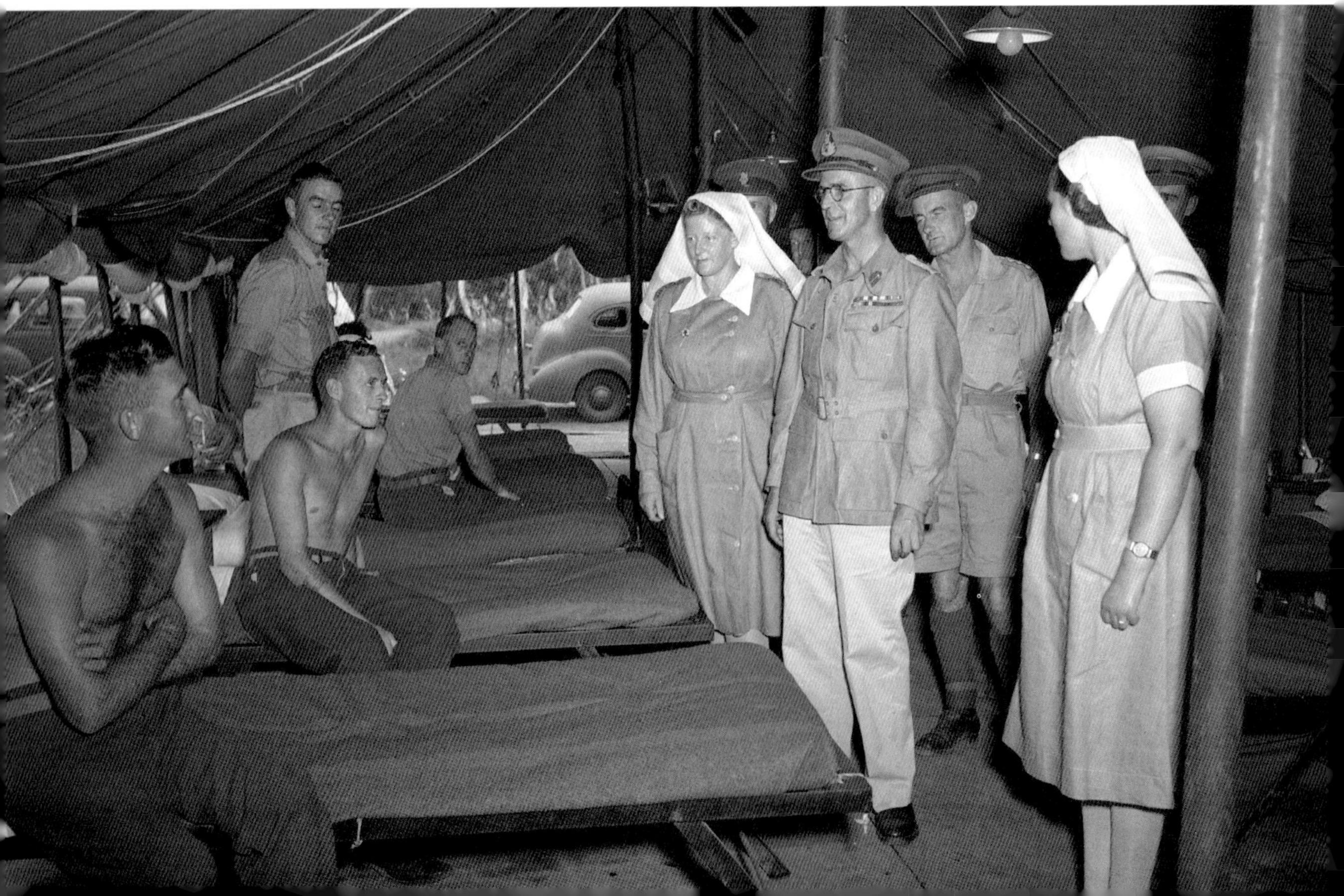

Those who saw their comrades killed or maimed no doubt suffered the after-effects in their civilian lives. Post-war New Zealand unfortunately had little to offer those suffering what would later be described as post-traumatic stress disorder.

The recovery rate for the wounded was high, a testament to the excellent medical services provided. Medical units in the Solomons faced challenges different from those in Europe. Generally there was an absence of wheeled transport, and units had to adapt planes, ships, barges and hand transport for casualties. The practice was to establish hospitals within hours of an invasion. In the Treasury Islands, field surgical units landed at 0700 hrs, shortly after the first wave of troops, and provided prompt surgical facilities. This played a considerable role in limiting fatalities.

## Hard labour

Poor or non-existent port facilities meant hard, dangerous, physical labour for the men of 3NZ Division as they loaded and unloaded heavy, bulky supplies including everything from food to petrol drums. By mid-1943, Guadalcanal had been developed into a major supply base. Labour to handle cargo was always chronically short, and it was both inevitable and unavoidable that New Zealanders would have to do such work. There was some resentment at being used as 'wharfies for the Yanks' rather than fighting. The work, for which they had not been trained, was dangerous, arduous and boringly repetitive. On Guadalcanal the Kiwis were also required to handle the disposal of chemical warfare ammunition which had become hazardous. The ammunition was loaded onto barges and then dumped at sea.[12] In the forward areas of the Solomons the need for labour was just as chronic.

Sometimes the hard work had its benefits. The 37th Battalion historian recorded its experience on the Green Islands:

> March 12–14. Unloading parties which worked in relays from dawn until late at night, kept many of us occupied during the next few days. It was hard work, particularly for those handling petrol drums, but there was some compensation when working at ration dumps. No objection was made to the men eating and drinking as much as they liked, provided they did not take the rations away with them – of course no one did that ...[13]

Men from infantry units were used for cargo handling but the units most heavily involved were the engineers. On New Caledonia they had

**Opposite above**

Medics working on a wounded soldier.

*(Alexander Turnbull Library, War History Collection, Ref. F-4159-1/2)*

**Opposite below**

Major General H. E. Barrowclough, Commander 3 NZ Division visiting wounded soldiers.

*(Alexander Turnbull Library, War History Collection, Ref. F.41530-1/2)*

to unload the division's equipment quickly because only one boat could dock at Nepoul at a time.[14] On Vella Lavella, New Zealand soldiers constructed a wharf to utilise a captured Japanese barge, which entailed blowing up underwater coral. They also built docks on Nissan. Cranes and specialised equipment were in short supply. American officers, observing the construction of dock facilities at Halis on the Green Islands, were amazed that the logs for cribbing 'were handled not by cranes but by submersible sappers'.[15] The engineers' role of course also encompassed road construction, water supply, fortifications and accommodation, generally under trying and uncomfortable conditions.

As American air and naval bases were developed, the New Zealanders often ended up handling live ammunition and bombs, tasks for which they had received no training. On the Treasury Islands in January 1944, Lt. Colonel W.A. Bryden of 38 NZ Field Regiment lamented:

> A case has been reported of the rough handling of bombs. These bombs were dumped from a dump truck in a position where some of them were later run over and damaged by a bulldozer. In both those instances it must be considered extremely fortunate that a serious explosion did not result. It will be necessary for unskilled personnel to

New Zealand and US forces unload cargo from LST-485, Purple 2 Beach, Stirling Island, October 1943.

*(Archives NZ, WAII, 1, Treasury Islands Photographs, D1 #26, official photographer)*

handle air bombs and ammunition and it must be firmly impressed on all ranks that all types of ammunition but particularly air bombs must be handled with the greatest care.[16]

## Military discipline

To be effective, a military unit must have cohesion and discipline. On the whole, 3NZ Division was a well-disciplined unit. The men were, with rare exceptions, not professional soldiers but rather civilians prepared to be soldiers for the duration of the war. Before the outbreak of the Pacific War, when the soldiers were employed in a static garrison role in Fiji which seemed to lack purpose, it was doubly hard to maintain discipline. Officers struggled to instil both discipline and morale. Difficulties with discipline became evident early on: Cunningham complained about soldiers failing to salute officers, officers and men fraternising informally, drunkenness and lack of smartness with uniforms. Once the Pacific War started the sense of purposelessness evaporated.

Insubordination in the combat zone can be extremely corrosive of unit morale. Bill Ashton recounts an incident on Vella Lavella immediately after combat had ceased, when a soldier in his battery refused an officer's order to clean his rifle. The response resulted in a charge of refusing to obey an order and using insulting language to an officer. An armed trooper was detailed to guard the miscreant. The staff sergeant-major attempted to get the soldier to clear a track using a grubber but his order was defied. 'And how did it end? When a trooper refuses to obey any order out in the bush like that, what can "they" do? Nothing. He was taken back to his rest area where he was guarded and eventually it fizzled out and he merged back into his normal duties.'[17]

There were, however, sanctions that the Army could apply and some were unpleasant. Barrowclough had to remonstrate with his officers and urge them to impose only humane punishments on offenders. He had been disturbed at the sight of soldiers incarcerated in wire cages.[18] In addition, military prisons operated on New Caledonia where soldiers could be sentenced to hard labour.[19] Commanding officers had the power to award up to 28 days' detention and/or forfeiture of pay. If matters were really serious, they could apply for a court martial of the offender.

According to Gordon Campbell Davie, a veteran of both 2 and 3NZ Divisions, 'The discipline in 3 Division was strict. We respected our officers and referred to them by their rank. This contrasted sharply with 2 Division where it was a free for all and officers were referred to by their Christian names.'[20]

The soldiers of 3NZ Division were overwhelmingly civilians who reflected New Zealand's contemporary values. Very few of them were involved in criminal activity or rejected army discipline, as the files relating to discipline and court martials in 3NZ Division reveal. Most offences were minor. Soldiers were charged with such offences as being 'improperly dressed' for church parade or when out and about, such as in Bourail. This often meant having sleeves rolled up, shirts unbuttoned and wearing shorts. In one embarrassing instance, a sloppily turned-out soldier happened to be at the Noumea Wharves when an official party, including the New Zealand Minister of Defence, arrived. Other offences included improperly wearing a US uniform, insubordinate language, using violence to a superior officer (throwing sauce), being grossly intoxicated, petty thefts and being absent without leave.[21] One soldier deserted from New Caledonia simply by boarding an American ship and travelling to Auckland, but such instances of desertion were rare. Some New Zealanders became involved in criminal activity with American soldiers on New Caledonia, much of it alcohol based.

## Weapons and equipment

As the first into combat, the men of 14 Brigade were given priority for American-designed twill 'jungle suits'. With their light, relatively comfortable, green clothing and forage caps, they were distinguishable from their less fortunate brethren in 8 Brigade who had khaki drill uniforms, painted camouflage and steel helmets covered with green hessian. This was immensely uncomfortable: 'The thick jungle uniform coated with green paint and further proofed against the air with its new coating of mud, is a very different affair from the ducks and silk shirts of traditional tropical wear. Your clothes are continuously soaked in sweat and when you lie down at night in your little hole in the ground, you sweat again.'[22]

It was a similar situation, initially at least, with weaponry. In 1940, New Zealand faced a chronic shortage ranging from small arms through to anti-aircraft guns. Rifles for Cunningham's Brigade Group were not issued until the men had been in camp a month and machine guns were swapped among units for training purposes.[23] The troops' introduction to basic weapons training was often with First World War weapons such as the Lee-Enfield rifle, the Vickers machine gun or the Lewis gun. Weapons instructors were few and training often inadequate. Ammunition shortages meant opportunities for live shoots were rare for artillery units. Grenade training was often done with wooden mock-ups. The shortages of weapons

Lance Corporal Brewster and Private Walker behind a Vicker's machine gun at Marquana Bay, Vella Lavella.

*(Archives NZ, WAII, 7, 3 Official Photo Album)*

and ammunition were alleviated as Australian and British supplies became available. By the time the division was deployed to the Solomons, it was adequately equipped with weaponry.

New Zealand soldiers, particularly the engineers, adapted themselves to conditions and tried to overcome equipment shortages. Vehicles, especially bulldozers, were repaired and kept going long after they would have been junked by an American unit. The 37th Field Park worked hard to prepare D-4 bulldozers for the invasion of the Treasury Islands:

> A large gasket was required in the hydraulic circuit and nothing suitable was to be found. Finally, however, an old fire extinguisher was straight ended, cut, annealed and fitted with the result that the dozer did its job in the landings until knocked out by mortar fire.
>
> Similarly by salvaging materials from American dumps and using bits and pieces, the 37th Field Park created a makeshift workshop before a fully equipped workshop lorry was sent from New Zealand. By using welded bits of metal, wood and other items ingenious pulleys and other equipment were created.

By far the greatest testament to Kiwi ingenuity was the restoration of a captured Japanese barge on Vella Lavella which was overhauled and pressed into service.[24]

## Living conditions and tropical diseases

Living conditions were often primitive. The first soldiers deployed to Fiji faced testing conditions that only gradually improved. Allied troops sent to the Solomons had to deal with a range of deadly tropical diseases, of which malaria was one of the most potent. Malaria causes debilitating fevers, headaches and vomiting, reduces energy and if left untreated can result in death. When combined with other diseases such as typhus, the victim's resistance is severely diminished. Fortunately, 3NZ Division did not experience malaria in Fiji or New Caledonia, but it was prevalent in the New Hebrides and the Solomons. Allied medical services coped with the challenge, whereas the Japanese medical services collapsed.

The success of 3NZ Division entailed ensuring that anti-malarial precautions were followed. It had learned bitter lessons from its exposure to tropical diseases on Fiji and it was appreciated that anti-malarial drugs needed to be available before the troops were sent overseas. Sources of quinine had been seized by the Japanese, but a synthetic malarial suppressant drug, Atabrine, was available from American sources. Getting the troops to practise anti-malarial precautions such as wearing long-sleeved shirts and trousers, and using insect repellent, anti-mosquito nets and Atabrine tablets proved to be difficult. A rumour among American troops that Atabrine resulted in impotence or sterility (false) and turned the user's skin yellow (true) meant that their troops had to be forced to take the drug.[25] The correct dosage was unknown, and there was uncertainty regarding its safety or efficacy. Atabrine tasted bitter and 'sometimes caused headaches, nausea and vomiting, and in a few cases it produced a temporary psychosis'.[26] The New Zealanders had somewhat more success in administering Atabrine, if only because their soldiers were strictly monitored. David Williams, an officer with 36 Battalion found that:

> Our battalion accepted the need and the officers had no problem with it. Atabrine was administered on parade and you watched each man swallow it. We started with a dose of four tablets a week (1/2 daily & none on Sunday) rising to six (1 a day, none on Sunday). When in action we had to rely on buttoning up clothing and putting repellent on exposed skin. When in tents and mosquito nets arrived we used them.[27]

3NZ Division had a Malaria Control Unit consisting of a headquarters unit and three Field Malaria Control Sections. It trained in conjunction with the USMCU,[28] and its duties were to survey malarial areas, plan control measures and implement them. Unit officers described the malaria discipline in the division as 'average to poor' and ascribed malaria casualties to 'gross carelessness, poor discipline, the failure to use repellent, mosquito nets and Atabrine'. The units on Vella Lavella were described as having an apathetic and fatalistic attitude to malaria.[29] They had been involved in close-quarter jungle fighting and had let anti-malarial precautions lapse. The discipline of 8 Brigade was described as 'poor',[30] and on Stirling Island New Zealanders and Americans habitually bathed in the evening and failed to wear long-sleeved shirts and trousers. It was difficult when Americans failed to practise anti-malarial measures and there were New Zealand soldiers living alongside them. There were no easy answers. When orders were given that no short trousers were to be worn in the malarial zone, the troops simply took to wearing their underpants.[31] Ultimately, anti-malaria discipline rested with the officers, but it took time for them to be educated and to enforce the necessary preventative measures.

Although it was in a malaria-prone area, 3NZ Division had a comparatively low rate of infection.[32] However, it was lucky in that much of its time there was outside the malaria season of February to June. Of the 120 malaria cases from September 1943 to June 1944, 43 were from Guadalcanal, 44 from Vella Lavella, 11 from the Treasury Islands and 22 from the Green Islands. This reflects the greater degree of control of malaria as the war progressed. Ironically, a Field Park Company based on Guadalcanal had the division's highest rate of malaria due to its proximity to a mosquito breeding area, followed by a battalion involved in fighting on Vella Lavella where malaria discipline broke down.[33] Arguably, if the division had been deployed to Guadalcanal in August 1942, it would have suffered the same high malaria rate as American units. Luck and timing played a role.

Many other tropical diseases and medical problems afflicted the soldiers of 3NZ Division. These varied from the uncomfortable to the lethal, and included sunburn, bronchial problems, hookworm, septic sores, dengue fever, typhoid, dysentery and hepatitis. When the division went to New Caledonia in 1943 there was an outbreak of dengue fever and Bourail and Noumea were placed out of bounds. Mosquitoes breeding in the coastal marshes were impossible to eliminate and the best the men could do was use mosquito nets. Dysentery was particularly common. Outbreaks occurred when B-Force deployed to Fiji in 1941, and this was repeated as new camps were set up. On New Caledonia, timber and flyproofing materials were scarce. Disinfectant was in short supply. Inability to provide fly-proof latrines, cookhouses and sleeping areas meant that infection spread until these facilities became established.[34] Poor sanitary practices and lack of discipline contributed to the problem. Dysentery had no respect for rank. Brigadier Cunningham was hospitalised with it and returned to New Zealand.[35]

Skin diseases plagued the soldiers from the start. On Fiji the soldiers suffered skin irritations and eczema. Minor cuts had to be treated or would turn septic, due to sweat, inadequate washing facilities, larval mites, fungoid infection and sodden clothing.[36] Fungal infections picked the most sensitive areas to make raw, invading the armpits and getting between the toes, into the groin and between the buttocks.[37] A small mite caused havoc on Stirling Island, biting around waistlines and boot tops. Bad ankle rashes were alleviated by clearing the camps of undergrowth.[38] On the Green Islands, dermatitis and septic sores were prevalent. A furry caterpillar which produced an irritating secretion afflicted the soldiers with skin problems.[39] At one stage the Minister of Defence reported that 2NZ Division had heard about conditions in New Guinea and the Solomons, and while he felt sure that they would serve where required, 'the majority given the option would prefer the healthier Middle Eastern theatre'.[40]

## Water

Clean drinking water was essential to avoid typhoid, other waterborne diseases and dehydration. On New Caledonia one of the chief problems was a supply of good water. In spite of abundant rain and many rivers on the mineral-rich island, the mineral content of the water rendered it undrinkable. Supplies had to be brought in using water carts, which only the dental section had. Supplies of water on Guadalcanal were limited and required co-operation from American units. Combat units on Vella Lavella had to practise water discipline, while those on Mono had access to streams. On the Green Islands, however, water had to be imported or distilled, as David Williams recalled:

> On this coral atoll there were no streams and there were a number of condensers, petrol driven, and converting sea water to 'fresh'. The many vehicles had first claim for their radiators and each man had a ration of a water bottle (I think). It rained heavily every morning and we would use it for a shower. It usually stopped just as you had soaped up! Bamboo guttering for our tents and empty petrol drums helped.[41]

Sgt G. Irvine of 'A' Company, 29 Infantry Battalion has a welcome drink, Mount Tonta, New Caledonia, 19–20 May 1943. Water conservation was a vital skill in tropical warfare.

*(Archives NZ WAII 7)*

The experience of 37 Battalion was typical. 'Water was still on the scarce list and we were still washing ourselves and our clothes in the sea or brackish water. We must have developed quite a distinctive aroma, but as we all smelt the same none of us noticed anything wrong. The engineers gave us very valuable help in constructing several wells and with the usual ingenuity of the average New Zealand soldier we rigged up showers – very brackish, but very welcome, nonetheless'.[42]

## Food

The New Zealand Army realised that in order to sustain a fighting force in the tropics it needed to ensure that its soldiers were adequately fed. Problems arose with monotony of food, scarcity of fresh vegetables, reliance on dried food and resistance to food that differed markedly from what the soldiers were used to. Food tended to spoil rapidly in the tropics. The Americans were able to supply Allied troops with canned goods, but there was 'consumer resistance' to things like chili con carne, which was heartily detested. The American 'C' and 'K' rations supplied to New Zealand troops in the forward zone received mixed reviews. On New Caledonia there were complaints about New Zealand soldiers stealing from local gardens, helping themselves to chickens and shooting cattle.[43] Generally, the diet of the troops was unpopular, but it was high in protein and did them no discernible harm.[44]

## A sexual paradise?

Those who believed that the South Pacific was a sexual paradise populated by dusky maidens and Dorothy Lamour lookalikes soon received a rude awakening.

3NZ Division had the lowest VD rate of New Zealand land forces deployed overseas.[45] The reasons are obvious. There were few opportunities for fraternising with women in the South Pacific, and the army discouraged contact with the local population. There were few European women, and after the Americans entered the war there was also competition from the better-paid and better-dressed American troops. In Fiji the Army limited contact with the local Fijian population. The soldiers of 3NZ Division were predominantly young men in their sexual prime. The lack of sexual outlets undoubtedly made their South Pacific experience more uncomfortable.

Members of the Kiwi Concert Party (Pacific). In the middle is Ralph Dyer in women's attire. His drag routine was very popular. Left to right: Sayers, Tansley, Dyer, Burns and Davidson.

*(Alexander Turnbull Library, War History Collection, WH-0291)*

Homosexual activity at the time was not only disapproved of by the society of the time, but was also an offence punishable by imprisonment. The New Zealand Army mirrored the attitudes of civilian society. Any homosexual activity was therefore kept hidden from official eyes.

The Kiwi Concert Party (Pacific) toured the Pacific, putting on over a hundred shows.[46] The female impersonators in particular were immensely popular with New Zealand and American units.[47] A veteran recalled that they were shows done in good taste, unlike American USO shows which were smutty.[48] The New Zealanders did, however, get to see American movies. 'It needed only one pair of chorus girl legs on the screen to create bedlam in the audience. Pathetic cries of "Take me home" could be distinguished from other inarticulate groans.'[49] On New Caledonia 'picture shows were long a great want'. When the 16-mm sets arrived they were found to be faulty and repairs had to be improvised.[50] Films were almost always popular, even if they were years old. The one exception was any film that 'portrayed the idyllic life of the South Seas Islands'. 'Strongest exception was taken to anything that purported to show tropic life as an endless round of romance and beauty.'[51] Films allowed the troops to let off steam: 'The usual rules of decorum did not apply, and any man who differed from the views expressed on the screen said so, loudly and clearly.'[52]

Ralph Dyer performing for the troops in the Pacific in women's clothing.

*(Alexander Turnbull Library, War History Collection, Ref. F-41567-1/2)*

The delicate issue of race relations was raised at a Brigade Conference in Fiji in 1941 by the RNZAF Commander who complained that New Zealand troops had been 'consorting with native women, giving New Zealand forces a bad name'. He wanted orders issued to ban fraternisation. Cunningham did not want the Army accused of having raised the colour question. He instructed his commanders to discuss the matter with their troops and explain why they were not allowed to fraternise freely with the natives.[53] When a 21-year-old private wanted to marry a local half-caste Fijian woman who was 'exceptionally dark', his CO and other soldiers tried unsuccessfully to dissuade him. Two days before the marriage ceremony he was sent back to New Zealand.[54] A soldier of 30 Battalion in Fiji in 1941 recalls an officer being paraded before the troops, having his epaulettes torn off and being sent home to New Zealand in disgrace. His offence was that he had been found in the native women's quarters.[55]

On Guadalcanal and Vella Lavella opportunities to interact with the native populations were severely limited. The inhabitants of Mono Island kept their women away from the soldiers.[56] In the Green Islands, too, there was little interaction. The troops most likely to have had sexual activity were the units in Fiji and New Caledonia, where prostitution existed, but even then their chances would have been limited. A New Zealand sergeant reporting on his visit to Houailou, New Caledonia, advised that the local policeman had arrested eight indigenous women on a charge of prostitution with Allied soldiers. The women were described as 'a repulsive looking lot' and 'all syphilitic'.[57]

## Kiwi Company and the WAACs

3NZ Division did field a female unit of base support staff, Kiwi Company. There is no evidence of illicit sexual activity and the WAACs – members of the Women's Army Auxiliary Corps – were well disciplined and useful.[58] WAACs were employed as nurses, clerks, batwomen, telephone operators, laundry personnel, waitresses, cashiers and cooks. Most were attached to 4th General Hospital and 2nd New Zealand Convalescent Depot and Hospital at Kalavere. Others were attached to Base Training Depot and

Members of Kiwi Company on New Caledonia enjoying some recreational downtime, 1943.

*(Alexander Turnbull Library, F-41533-1/2)*

the Kiwi Club at Bourail. The WAACs shared the privations of their male counterparts: a trying climate, monotonous routine, uncomfortable tents, unpalatable food, mosquitoes and bugs. At 2 NZ Convalescent Depot one of the WAACs found that a deadly black widow spider and its young had taken residence in the sleeves of her greatcoat. The practice of shaking and examining garments before putting them on became routine.[59] The work was often hard – the laundry staff handled 4000 items per week using petrol-driven washing machines and irons,[60] and the staff of the Kiwi Club served 200 cooked meals daily.[61] The WAACs 'danced thousands of miles with men who could dance, couldn't dance and who hadn't seen a white woman for twelve months'.[62] They also shared many of the risks and challenges faced by the men. On 30 January 1944, 23-year-old Marcel Hartnett, a WAAC with 2 NZ Convalescent Depot, was killed in a road accident one mile north of Plaine des Gaiacs.[63]

## Alcohol

In 20th-century New Zealand society, alcohol played an important role and consumption of it in large quantities was reckoned as a mark of manliness. For the soldiers of 3NZ Division, the problem with alcohol was generally a lack of it, particularly in the forward area. Beer was part of the ration while the men were in the base camps on New Caledonia, and McLeod notes that 'many of the liquor problems focused on the New Zealand Forces Club [at Bourail]. There were repeated drunken brawls, but at least it did keep the soldiers away from the less reputable areas.'[64] Barrowclough noted that 'consignments have not been very frequent. Such beer as we have received has been very carefully apportioned.' He also commented that one brand, *Cascade*, was so bad that the men 'have been heard to say that they would rather go without than drink that particular brand'.[65] The usual beer ration in the Solomons was one can per week.[66]

Inventive solutions were tried. 'Up Voh and Temala Way it was necessary during long droughts to try various substitutes. Raisins, sugar and yeast with the help of cook house staff were a useful line and when supplemented by fruit juice had astounding effects.'[67] There was a 'roaring trade in private stills and the problem of how to get the dollars back to New Zealand'[68] challenged Kiwi ingenuity. In March 1944, 2 Platoon, 4 NZ Motor Transport Company, based in the Treasury Islands, created an illicit still using drums and copper wiring. The product was either consumed or sold to neighbouring American units, but the latter proved to be the New Zealanders' undoing when American soldiers suffered the side-effects and their officers located the still. Worse was to follow as a

New Zealand court of inquiry discovered a number of other stills in the area.[69]

On New Caledonia the Army and French authorities had grave concerns about the sale of adulterated liquor to New Zealand soldiers. It was believed that local people were selling liquor with methylated spirits added.[70] Harry Bioletti, a New Zealand infantry officer with 14 Brigade, said that 'those who came to know "butterfly" brandy or "Marie Louise" gin or so called pernod were reminded of it for days afterward.' Drunkenness underpinned most disciplinary problems on New Caledonia.[71]

## Monotony and boredom

Arguably, the most serious morale problem for 3NZ Division was the absence of facilities and entertainment. On Vella Lavella after combat, 30 Battalion went into garrison mode. 'If you didn't play cards, write, read or "mag" you devoted your time to resting – the most popular pastime in the Third Division, irrespective of rank, commonly called "cot bashing", "Maori PT", "ceiling inspection", or "spinal exercise" – all sooner or later succumbed to its wiles'.[72] After combat ended on the Green Islands, the battalion settled into 'another one of those dreary waiting periods which men of the 3rd Division had come to know so well.'

> You looked at the well-handled photo of the wife on the ration-box dressing table and thought, 'it won't be long soon'. When not on working parties over at the other side of the lagoon the boys squelched round the muddy area in underpants and boots, the almost uniform dress of officers and men alike, dropping into tents to hear the latest rumours or hiving off down to the YMCA tent for a cup of stewed tea. Cards – cribbage and bridge – occupied leisure hours and the reading of well thumbed magazines and out of date newspapers.[73]

Frank Cooze described his sojourn on New Caledonia with his anti-aircraft unit as 'ten months of soul destroying boredom' on that Pacific paradise – one-time French penal settlement. His unit travelled to Mono Island and 'settled down gradually to the usual humdrum island existence'.[74]

Commanders organised sporting activities such as boxing and swimming. Barrowclough reported that on New Caledonia 'the recreational facilities are not ideal ... All formations have held sports meetings including all athletic events and swimming sports as well as cricket and football matches.'[75] He instituted 'The Barrowclough Cup' for rugby between the division's units.

Leave in the South Pacific was limited. It was one of the greatest problems on New Caledonia because, in Barrowclough's words, 'there is no single village which offers any attraction to the soldier. Noumea itself has little of interest or entertainment ...'[76] The men of 2NZ Division were able to explore cities such as Cairo and see the sights, but there was virtually nothing of tourist interest in the South Pacific. Leave to New Zealand was granted only on compassionate grounds.

Time away from family and friends, cut off from the world, was often barely tolerable. One veteran commented: 'The only sour note in my relationship with the Americans was when we were sailing a boat we had put together in the Blanche Channel. An American sailor on board one of the ships leaned over the rail and spat into the water and said "you guys don't want the war to end do you?".'[77] Nothing could have been further from the truth.

## Mail: the link with home

Troops could write home but their mail was censored, generally by their unit's officers, who excised information regarding location and unit movements. For many of the officers, this intrusion into their men's lives was a matter of some delicacy. For some of the men censorship caused resentment, one believing that 'it is one of the most crooked things in the Army'.[78] There was also the difficulty of what to write about. There was little point in telling their families of the awfulness of their conditions. As one officer observed, there were restrictions on what one could write; when there was time to write there was often very little of interest to write about; and when something really interesting occurred, one was not permitted to write about it till months afterwards.[79]

The army recognised the value of regular mail for sustaining morale and made efforts to ensure that troops in the combat zone received mail. Not all correspondence was welcome – from time to time 'Dear John' letters arrived, informing the recipient that the sender was now with someone else. One soldier from 36 Battalion received such a letter telling him his fiancée in New Zealand had formed a relationship with an American. Totally bereft, the man committed suicide.[80]

Although mail arrived on virtually a weekly basis, parcel delivery was less frequent owing to shortage of shipping space. The further the soldiers moved from their base areas, the more infrequent the arrival of parcels became. Not all offerings were suitable: much to the amusement of his tent mates, one soldier sweltering in the tropical heat received a woollen pullover.[81] Care parcels were also sent by the National Patriotic

J. Allen of 8 Brigade handling mail on Mono Island, 1943.

*(Alexander Turnbull Library, War History Collection, PA Coll 5547-025)*

Fund Board. In 1943–44 the Auckland Patriotic Committee prepared some 36,734 parcels, 12,000 of which were intended for the soldiers in the Pacific. Shipping space was always chronically short and it is doubtful that the men of 3NZ Division received anything like that number. The packages contained a variety of items ranging from cigarettes to jams and socks. To the men's bemusement, they sometimes received canned pineapple, a luxury in New Zealand but commonplace in the Islands.

## The Nat Pat and the YMCA secretaries

Of all the soldiers of 3NZ Division, some of the least warlike but probably the most appreciated and most important for maintaining morale were the YMCA secretaries. These soldiers (technically civilians but granted the right to follow the Army and given a commissioned rank) were representatives of the YMCA and were charged with assisting the troops by providing non-alcoholic beverages, comforts and care packages. These were sent from New Zealand by the National Patriotic Fund (the 'Nat

Pat'), an umbrella organisation for assisting the soldiers. The YMCA secretaries provided yeoman service throughout the division's time in the Pacific. On the Treasury Islands, YMCA secretaries were in the first wave of invaders and earned the admiration of the troops by setting up tea facilities. One of the secretaries was disconcerted when a Japanese mortar bomb destroyed his tea urn. It is difficult to understate their beneficial effect on the troops' morale.

## The enemy

Throughout the struggle for the Solomon Islands, the Japanese, many of whom were battle hardened from the war with China, fought doggedly, brutally and skilfully. The New Zealanders faced Imperial Japanese Army and Navy units, who were formidable and deadly opponents[82] and did not fight according to accepted western norms. The commanders of a Japan that had become increasingly militaristic and nationalistic since the 1930s believed that their country's superior spirit would overcome any material advantages of the effete West. Surrender was forbidden by Imperial Rescript. It entailed complete disgrace and social ostracism for the individual Japanese soldier and his family. The brutality that was part of Japanese discipline meant that Allied prisoners were treated with contempt.[83] As Harry Bioletti recalled: 'The one fear in the jungle was being captured by the Japanese because they would butcher you physically. … You did not want to be captured by them because the Prisoner of War Conventions meant nothing to them. They didn't subscribe to it.'[84]

The soldier companions deployed with civilian coastwatchers became 3NZ Division's first casualties and prisoners of war. When the Japanese struck in December 1941, coastwatchers on Little Makin, Pikate and Avaiang in the Gilberts were captured. As the Japanese thrust into the southern Gilberts in September 1942, they captured still more. Most were sent to grim POW camps[85] or to work camps in Japan as slave labour. Those unfortunate enough to be grouped together with other prisoners on Tarawa were treated brutally and beheaded on 15 October 1942, the first New Zealanders killed by the enemy in the South Pacific in the Second World War.

On Vella Lavella, some New Zealand soldiers were enveloped and almost overrun. A New Zealand private from 35 Battalion, 14 Brigade was captured by the Japanese, strung up to a tree and bayoneted.[86] The body was later recovered. By 1942, word of Japanese atrocities had reached the Allies and it was clear that the war in the Pacific was not going to be a chivalric contest.

Operations on Vella Lavella were focused on mopping up Japanese units which fought doggedly as 14 Brigade pushed them to the north of the island. Few Japanese prisoners were taken and the enemy succeeded in evacuating their forces. On the Treasury Islands the New Zealanders faced composite Imperial Japanese Special Naval Land Forces. Some prisoners were taken, but most of the Japanese defenders were wiped out. A veteran describes an occasion on Mono when his unit took casualties and had to wipe out Japanese defenders entrenched in rifle pits. No prisoners were taken.[87] The Japanese defenders in the Green Islands fought desperately and very few were taken prisoner. Those Japanese taken prisoner were generally isolated from their comrades, were sick and starving or had been rendered unconscious.

New Zealand soldiers were sometimes willing to accept Japanese surrender.[88] However, Japanese attempts to 'play surrenders' and kill their would-be captors made soldiers wary of accepting surrenders. Surprisingly, there seems to have been little of the hatred of the Japanese that American units had. This may have been due to limited exposure to combat and the dehumanising effects it had. On Vella Lavella, some New Zealand soldiers felt sorry for pitiful-looking Japanese prisoners held in barbed wire enclosures and gave them cigarettes.[89]

## James Michener, *Tales of the South Pacific* and Bali Ha'i

The popular but erroneous post-war perception that the Allied troops who had served in the South Pacific had been living in a tropical idyll was cemented by the novelist James Michener. He had been a US Navy lieutenant stationed on Espiritu Santo. After the war he won a Pulitzer Prize for a volume of short stories entitled *Tales of the South Pacific*.[90] This in turn inspired Richard Rodgers and Oscar Hammerstein to write the 1949 smash-hit Broadway musical, *South Pacific*, later made into a classic movie. Set on the fictional island paradise of Bali Ha'i, with lush green foliage and golden sunsets, it featured American Navy nurses, Seabees, exotic (and available) native women and a mysterious French plantation owner. Michener later stated that the inspiration for Bali Ha'i was a tiny, miserable village on Mono Island.[91] *South Pacific* continues to be performed as a musical and the myth of a South Pacific paradise continues to be perpetuated. Little wonder that the soldiers of 3NZ Division in the post-war years had to endure jibes about being 'Pacific playboys', 'Pineapple pickers' and 'Coconut Bombers'.

# Columbia's Apprentice 15

## Fighting with the Americans

Exasperated by coalition warfare in the Second World War, Winston Churchill quipped that 'There is only one thing worse than fighting with allies – and that is fighting without them'.[1] Churchill recognised that allies inevitably brought problems as well as benefits. That thought would have resonated in both Washington and Wellington as they pursued the common objective of ejecting the Japanese from the Solomon Islands. At times the exasperation extended down to the commanders in theatre and even to ordinary servicemen. However, the relationship was generally co-operative and friendly, particularly in comparison with that between the Australians and the Americans nearby.

The twin disasters of the sinking of the two British battleships HMS *Repulse* and *Prince of Wales* by Japanese bombers on 10 December 1941, followed by the rout of British forces in Malaya and the capitulation of Singapore on 15 February 1942, meant that British strength in the Pacific had evaporated. There remained only one power that could contest Japanese supremacy: the United States. New Zealand had to adjust to the reality that its very national existence had passed from familiar British hands to unfamiliar American ones. The war in the Pacific, although it would involve different nationalities, was dominated by American commanders and resources.

Before the Japanese attack on Pearl Harbor, Australasia had not featured in American war plans. The Americans viewed Australia and New Zealand as simply parts of the British Empire and diplomatic and military relations were conducted through London. Indeed, there had been tension between Washington and Wellington over American attempts to acquire various Pacific Islands as air links. New Zealand had sent a warship to cement its claims to some of these islands. In the period before the attack on Pearl Harbor, the Americans were the wild card in the pack. There was never any certainty, given the depth of isolationist feeling among the American public, that America would join the war against Japan if it attacked only the possessions of the European colonial powers,

The relationship changed after Pearl Harbor. The dynamic which initially drove the military relationship between America and New Zealand was the crisis of 1941–42. New Zealand had to operate under the aegis of American protection if it was to survive, and the Americans needed the base facilities of Auckland and the co-operation of the New Zealanders. However welcome the American involvement, New Zealand would have preferred to fight alongside British forces. American and New Zealand soldiers were uneasy, coincidental allies. There was also the question of perspective. For Wellington, the American relationship was of major importance. For the Americans, their relationship with New Zealand was a small, unscripted element in their strategic plans.

For both the Americans and New Zealanders, making their new alliance work involved a learning curve. 3NZ Division found itself in the forefront of that process.

The war in the South Pacific was dominated by the Americans, and 3NZ Division had to work within an American framework. It provided garrisons, combat troops for operations, medical facilities (particularly Malaria Control Units), labour for the essential task of shifting supplies and troops for intelligence operations. The Americans provided transport, food and equipment, naval and aerial support, and assigned the New Zealanders tasks. Overall, on a tactical and operational level, the relationship was comfortable, with the parties respecting each other's abilities. On a political and strategic level, however, the relationship was often marred by miscommunication, obfuscation, misunderstanding and divergent national interests.

The United States – New Zealand relationship did not begin well. It was evident that the Americans would impose their will on their junior partner when they superimposed their own command structures on Australasia and when the brigades on Fiji were returned to New Zealand because it suited them. The disdainful Ghormley was ambivalent about using New Zealand troops in anything but a garrison role. He did not confide in Fraser regarding Operation *Watchtower*, and he tried to avoid engaging with Wellington generally. The American command structure flowed from Washington through Nimitz and Ghormley. Wellington had little influence on American strategic or operational decision making and there was no formal mechanism for co-ordinating New Zealand/American actions. The Pacific War Council was nothing more than window dressing and used by Roosevelt to pay lip service to consultation with his allies.[2] The Americans were determined that they would run the war their way. Unlike in Europe where the battle-hardened British could initially influence strategies, in the South Pacific the sheer weight of the American contribution ensured their domination.

One of Barrowclough's main strengths was that he understood the delicacy of the situation. Barrowclough operated comfortably within the American command structure, meticulously observing the chain of command. He strove hard to avoid friction, often by dealing with matters informally. For example, problems with loading LSTs for *Squarepeg* led him to write to Rear Admiral Wilkinson. However, he added that 'I am not disposed to enter any formal or official complaint as I am sure the difficulties have arisen purely from a misapprehension or from a well-

Amphibious training for 37 Battalion Combat Team, Blue Beach, Ducos Peninsula, Noumea, 10 July 1943, observed by (left to right) Brigadier C. J. Duff, Lt. Col. J. I. Brooke, Major-General Rush B. Lincoln (US Army), Lt Col. H. W. Blake, Major General H. E. Barrowclough, Major G. W. Waddell, Major Guttensohn (G 3 Section 1 Island Command).

*(Alexander Turnbull Library, War History Collection, Ref. PA Coll 5547-035)*

meaning but mistaken zeal.'[3] Similarly, in dealing with claims that 3NZ Division had hoarded supplies, Barrowclough wrote to Major General Breene, denying the allegation in 'an entirely personal and unofficial note.'[4]

Puttick was also conscious of possible American sensitivity. He proposed that Fijian soldiers should make up the division's missing brigade. This made sense considering the close relationship between the FDF and the division, which supplied most of its officers. Halsey rejected the idea twice. Consequently Puttick did not want 'to risk irritating Halsey by raising a third time a matter which he has already given a decision on.' He felt that Halsey 'would suspect some ulterior motive such as my ultimate intention to endeavour to secure the whole brigade or to deprive US command of Solomons battalion.'[5] In seeking American permission to reduce the New Zealand garrison on Tonga in 1943, Puttick thought that the strategic position justified this but conceded it was not his place to come to such conclusions, saying 'I would be glad to have your instructions on the matter'.[6]

Barrowclough asked for and received from Fraser a charter which gave him the ability to appeal to the New Zealand government and to withhold his troops if he considered the proposed operation to be excessively risky. Barrowclough had to walk a fine line between encouraging the Americans to use his troops in combat, but by the same token not putting them into a position where New Zealand soldiers would be slaughtered. Fortunately Barrowclough never had to use his charter.

Barrowclough appears to have got on well with Americans. After assuming command on Vella Lavella, he found his own staff numbers inadequate and temporarily retained American staff.[7] He probably had contact with American officers in 1918 as commander 1st Battalion, Rifle Brigade, when the New Zealand Division 'hosted detachments of Americans to give the latter experience prior to Americans being employed'.[8] American naval commanders appeared to respect Barrowclough, whereas the Australian General Thomas Blamey did not cut the type of dash to impress MacArthur. Barrowclough may well have been able to influence American use of his division. He was able to persuade COMSOPAC to request it be deployed into the Forward Area rather than undertaking garrison duty. Similarly, when the Americans were contemplating using it in the New Georgia campaign, Barrowclough urged Admiral Wilkinson to 'give us a task which would give us an opportunity of undertaking real offensive action. I referred to the fact that General Harmon had congratulated us on the records we had established in amphibious operations.' Wilkinson promised to discuss this with COMSOPAC.[9]

In May 1944 Rear Admiral Robert B. Carney USN, Chief of Staff,

Major General Harold Barrowclough, with General Griswold of the US Forces, Vella Lavella Island, Solomon Islands, 1943.

*(Alexander Turnbull Library, Ref. WH-0226-F)*

COMSOPAC wrote to Barrowclough declaring 'how completely satisfactory our relations have universally been with the New Zealanders in general. Your own handling of the tasks assigned to the 3rd Division have always been in such perfect consonance with the South Pacific credo that they could not help but win the respect and admiration of all our people.'[10] Admiral Nimitz, too, recognised New Zealand co-operation: 'New Zealand has made, is making, and will continue to make a very vital effort to participate in the South Pacific War. Their willingness to participate has won for them a very friendly feeling in Washington with our high military and naval authorities.'[11]

Whereas General Douglas MacArthur and his subordinate, General Robert L. Eichelberger, held a low opinion of the Australian Army in general and the Australian militia in particular, USN commanders such as Halsey[12] and Wilkinson were fulsome in their praise of New Zealand troops. Nevertheless, in earlier arguing for a combat role for 3NZ Division, Barrowclough pointed out that the Americans in their cups were apt to point out that they were defending New Zealand 'with the result that ears were thickened and eyes blackened, and a little blood was apt to run.'[13] Similarly, the New Zealand liaison officer at COMSOPAC, Colonel C.D.F.W. Salmon, found that the Americans had prejudices about the British and New Zealanders and that there was 'a complete unawareness of the part (if any) and what extent New Zealand is playing in the war in the Pacific.' Some Americans thought that New Zealand was putting all its energy into the Middle East and leaving America to fight New Zealand's battle in the Pacific.[14] The Americans also had their frustrations. Halsey complained about 'the more or less "jackass" command set-up we have to go through when dealing with the New Zealand Government.'[15] They perceived a 'lack of co-ordination' by government departments, 'duck shoving' and difficulty in ascertaining responsibility.[16]

Although Barrowclough's relations with the Americans were generally good, he did face marginalisation by American planners, who tended to treat 3NZ Division as a unit to be deployed at their pleasure and even broken up for specific combat operations. In doing so they tended to deal with the operational commanders such as Row rather than Barrowclough. In respect of Vella Lavella, Barrowclough received unofficially a copy of a message instructing General Griswold, the US Army Commander in New Georgia, to arrange for 3NZ Division to take over from three American divisions. Barrowclough feared his forces would be split between Vella Lavella and New Georgia and would face imminent danger from Japanese troops. When visited by Rear Admiral Wilkinson, Admiral Ford and Major General Barrett on 4 September 1943, he did not raise the issue with them, but rather referred obliquely to the dangers of dispersed garrisons and expressed the hope that in view of the division's capabilities it would be employed amphibiously.[17]

> On arrival at my H.Q. I found a series of most conflicting arrangements being made by the various H.Q. of the American forces situated here. They were all planning our move without reference to me … The US set up in this theatre with its multiplicity of headquarters and services is extremely complicated and one had difficulty getting definite instructions on any particular point.[18]

On 10 September Barrowclough was told that the division's brigades would be split, with 8 Brigade probably deployed in a 'largely defensive occupation of an Island Base'.[19] Yet a month later it was committed to an offensive operation – *Goodtime*.

Barrowclough actually became one of the few non-Americans to command American troops when he took control of Allied forces on Vella Lavella, and the land forces in Operations *Goodtime* and *Squarepeg*. In contrast, American Army commanders resisted having their troops commanded by Australians. MacArthur resorted to creating 'Task Forces' to avoid troops being placed under the command of Australian General

Thomas Blamey. Lieutenant-General Robert C. Richardson feared that American troops would be 'placed under a non-professional Australian drunk', meaning Blamey.[20]

Barrowclough appears to have adopted a low-key, informal approach to the Americans under his command. On the Green Islands he dealt with allegations of improper behaviour from several junior officers against Captain Rochester, USN. Barrowclough suggested delaying an official complaint, then told Wilkinson that Rochester 'has probably lost some prestige with his own unit and you may think it advisable to recall him earlier than might otherwise have been the case.' Rochester was recalled and matters were resolved informally.[21]

A fire at the PT boat base on Vella Lavella on 14 December 1943 resulted in two deaths. The incident tested Barrowclough's handling of inter-allied relations because the personnel involved were American. He constituted a court of inquiry, with a legally qualified New Zealand officer as president, assisted by US Navy and US Marine Corps officers. Barrowclough reported to the Commanding General, Forward Area that the base commander could have prevented the accident, but drew back from a finding of negligence, indicating that no further action should be taken.[22]

Where appropriate, Barrowclough could be stern with American troops under his command. On the Green Islands in 1944 he faced the problem of maintaining field hygiene, an absolute necessity in the tropics. An area had been designated for refuse disposal, but rubbish was nonetheless building up and creating a hazard. Barrowclough outlined the problem to a meeting of officers. He then pointed to an American officer and asked what orders he would give to his men. The American replied, 'I guess, General, I will tell them to get it out of sight.' Barrowclough coolly responded that if one of his own officers had said that he would cease to be an officer.[23]

Similarly, Brigadier Row had to make clear to American officers that they were subject to Barrowclough's commands. A group of American officers dissatisfied with their allocation of shipping space for *Goodtime* arrived at Row's HQ to explain that they wanted to take more equipment. Row curtly dismissed them: 'Gentlemen, you have your orders – carry them out.'[24]

Barrowclough's commands involved limited numbers of American troops, mainly Seabees and garrison personnel, and there would have been few American casualties in the event of a blunder. Moreover, he had no control over American aerial and naval operations. He understood that he had limited independence, even referring American fitness reports back to American officers for completion. While on the Green Islands,

Barrowclough was the General Officer Commanding. When an American officer, Captain A.E.R. Wilkinson, asked him to complete his fitness report, Barrowclough felt that it would have been 'presumptuous … to attempt to fill in the Report of Fitness form in the same way as it might be filled in by a United States Army or Marine Officer.'[25] On Vella Lavella he ordered part of an American parachute regiment to occupy defensive positions on the north coast though they were not meant for garrison duty. When General Alexander Vandegrift, the commander of the 1st Marine Amphibious Corps, protested, Barrowclough readily agreed to their being moved with the reservation that in the event of in an invasion he might order them back.[26]

Conversely, COMSOPAC wanted a say in the division's internal administration. This was manifested by Halsey's concerns regarding its under-strength nature, expressed bluntly to Prime Minister Fraser.[27] A second instance occurred when Barrowclough decided to replace Brigadier Row after Operation *Goodtime*. As Salmon told Puttick:

> The Admiral [Halsey] and Admiral Carney would like to be informed of any changes of command personnel before such changes are made. This request has come because of a recent change made by 3 Div. of Brigade Commander [Brigadier Row to Brigadier Goss]. Admiral Carney put it that he had learned this accidentally from one of his officers, and although in no sense questioning the change of appointment or the reasons for it (he looks upon this as NZ's own domestic matter) that he would have liked to have heard of it officially before it was made just in case they had any viewpoints to express; and he would appreciate it if the NZ Chiefs of Staff would advise COMSOPAC in the future.

Salmon considered that this principle would also apply to any command change for forces deployed outside New Zealand, including RNZAF and Royal New Zealand Navy.[28] There was certainly an implication that American commanders should have a say in the promotion or demotion of New Zealand commanders. Fortunately, the issue was not pressed.

The willingness of the soldiers of 3NZ Division to work alongside the Americans is exemplified by the way they embraced American military doctrines and experience. Officers and NCOs were sent to an American Combat Intelligence Course on Guadalcanal.[29] American close air support techniques were studied and a course in air support control was held at Tontouta.[30] Officers were despatched to the United States to learn about amphibious warfare,[31] and courses were held on New Caledonia in the use of American grenades, mines and other weapons.[32] For both

Admiral Halsey (left) shares a drink with Brigadier Row on Guadalcanal while planning for Operation *Goodtime*.

*(From* Bougainville and the Northern Solomons *by John Rentz, p. 94)*

armies there was much to be learned about jungle fighting and there was willingness on both sides to share information and apply lessons learned, for example from the bitter American experience on New Georgia.[33] Likewise, after *Goodtime* a critique was conducted and the lessons learned were disseminated.[34] New Zealand and American units frequently trained alongside one another. For example, in Exercise *Mayflower* in early February 1943, 29 Battalion and 1 Scots Battalion trained alongside an American battalion and with US aircraft.[35]

Command arrangements were generally cordial, but there were exceptions. When Goss took over from Row on the Treasury Islands, he experienced friction with two American officers, who were feuding with each other. The Americans resolved this by removing their truculent officers.[36] General Murray wrote 'a most complimentary report on Goss', and the Americans recommended Goss for an American decoration. Barrowclough had hesitated to recommend Goss for this because of the difficulties with the feuding Americans, but he endorsed the American suggestion.[37]

The New Zealanders also had to work within the American command structure. This raised the issue of the legality of American officers giving commands to New Zealand soldiers. They were subject to New Zealand's Army Act, which defined a superior officer as 'an officer in His Majesty's Forces',[38] indicating a restriction to officers of the British Empire. Barrowclough stepped lightly around an issue which had the potential to derail combat operations. He issued an Administrative Order which stipulated that Allied Officers and NCOs were to be treated as if they held a corresponding rank in the New Zealand Defence Forces. Refusal to obey their proper orders rendered any New Zealander liable for disciplinary action under s 40 of the Army Act.[39] Because New Zealanders generally operated within their own unit structures and American senior officers issued commands through those structures, problems rarely occurred. However, problems did arise on occasion. On New Caledonia a drunken New Zealand driver refused to leave his vehicle when ordered by an American colonel. He struck an American MP who attempted to manhandle him. The soldier was charged with using insubordinate language to his superior officer. The Deputy Judge Advocate General declined to confirm the conviction on the basis that the American was not a superior officer and the particular charge had not been properly laid.[40]

One of the things that smoothed relations between the nationalities was that they were separated into their own units and under their own officers. David Williams found that as a New Zealand officer he only gave orders to his countrymen. Problems were avoided because in dealing with different nationalities you would 'work through the channel of command'.[41] Essentially, goodwill between Americans and New Zealanders made things work, albeit sometimes under strain.

On Vella Lavella (September–October 1943) and the Green Islands (February 1944) New Zealand land units fought without direct assistance from their American counterparts, although United States naval and air support was involved. Operation *Goodtime*, in October 1943, provided a sterner test of the American–New Zealand military relationship, being a complex amphibious operation requiring intense preparation, staff work, logistical support and naval covering fire. Seabees fought alongside the New Zealanders, although their main role was construction. Although the Americans were dominant on the water, the New Zealanders dominated in land operations.

Training and reconnaissance for the landings involved considerable co-operation. The USN had given Barrowclough amphibious warfare manuals,[42] and training in embarking and disembarking on the New Hebrides and Guadalcanal used American ships and personnel. USMC specialists inspected likely invasion beaches, accompanied by Lt. Col. Trench and Solomon Islanders. American and RNZAF aircraft regularly took aerial photos. The first Cowan patrol on the Treasury Islands involved a multinational team of New Zealand, Solomon Islands Defence Force (S.I.D.F.) and USAAF personnel. Overall, the success of the interaction with United States forces can be gauged from the fact that American commanders intended to use the division for further assaults in 1944, and some expressed their regret at its break-up.

Despite the generally good relationship, incidents occurred that led to unnecessary New Zealand casualties. In October 1943, Barrowclough offered a battery of twelve Bofors 40-mm guns to the Americans to supplement their AA defences on Vella Lavella. The offer was accepted, gun sites prepared, and officers delegated to meet each LST and arrange for the speedy off-loading and emplacement of the guns. Yet Barrowclough found the captains reluctant to disembark the guns. Consequently when Japanese bombers struck, some had to fire from the decks of the LSTs. Bombs hit LST 446, destroying a gun and killing the crew.[43] Barrowclough believed that 'If my instructions had been carried out we would have suffered no casualties to that crew and it is just possible that with its better position ashore the gun might have saved the ship.' He stressed to Wilkinson the difficulty 'if arrangements which I make for the protection of these LST's are to be overruled by relatively junior Naval Officers who are quite unfamiliar with our plans.'[44] Wilkinson expressed his condolences but felt sure 'from the very fact that the gun was struck that it was in the best position to defend the ship against the planes coming directly at it.'[45]

Shortly afterwards a potentially serious 'friendly fire' situation arose during Operation *Goodtime*. Each landing craft used by the Allies was equipped with a Browning machine gun operated by the coxwain's mate. As the second wave of landing craft approached Falamai Beach, an American machine gunner sprayed the tree line where New Zealand troops were located. The temptation to return fire was resisted.[46]

The Japanese in the Solomons had become increasingly dependent on motorised barges, which became targets for Allied fighters. Unfortunately problems of identification heightened the risk of 'friendly fire'. On 16 October 1943, a USN barge K51-5 with personnel from 35 Battalion Combat Team was on a supply mission south of Mundi Mundi. A *Corsair* strafed the barge, killing the coxswain and a New Zealand soldier and wounding two others. The New Zealanders were perplexed by the attack as no Japanese barges had been in the area for at least three weeks. A second incident occurred shortly after. On 5 December 1943, 3NZ Division soldiers became stranded on a reef at Suanatalia off Vella Lavella. Their barge was strafed by American aircraft.[47] The barge was a Japanese one salvaged by New Zealand troops at Vella Lavella and, given the shortage of seaborne transport, had been pressed into service. To identify it as being under Allied control, a large American flag was draped across the deck and a large white star painted on the roof of the wheel house. The barge was put to various uses. On this occasion the barge was being used to transport a padre to visit his flock on adjoining islands. The barge had become grounded on a coral reef. Five of the New Zealanders had gone over the side in an attempt to push the barge off the reef. This probably saved lives when the *Corsair* pilots began their strafing run. Two soldiers, Corporal J. J. Jod and Sapper F. L. Knipe, were killed and a third soldier was wounded. The American explanation was that the flight leader had been 'test firing' his guns and his wingman had followed his example. While acknowledging 'a flagrant breach of safety regulations' and gross negligence, Major General Harmon reported that one of the pilots had been killed in combat and the other had received the maximum punishment of forfeiture of half a month's pay and a formal written reprimand. Harmon said of the New Zealand dead that 'we mourn them as brothers-in-arms'.[48]

On the other side of the ledger, during *Goodtime* a Seabee named Ostman panicked and disobeyed orders to stay in his fox-hole during the night.[49] A fellow Seabee recalled:

> He ran off into jungle. Shortly thereafter shots were heard and Ostman was missing in action. A year or so later a bulldozer digging a new road uncovered his body. It was determined that he had been buried next to the New Zealand Aid location. We figured that as he ran toward the New Zealand area in the dark they probably shot him thinking he was a Jap. Nonetheless, there was no ill-feeling towards New Zealanders and we were impressed with their courage and very friendly personalities.[50]

One of the areas where New Zealand made a significant contribution to the Americans, particularly in January 1943, was the provision of personnel for malaria control. The Americans were short of such personnel on Efate and welcomed men from the New Zealand Malaria Control Unit.[51] The New Zealanders gained valuable experience, while the Americans considered that 'the performance of this unit has been outstanding'.[52] Conversely the Americans provided the New Zealanders with Japanese language specialists.[53]

Shipping was critical for 3NZ Division but was in short supply, and communication difficulties between Wellington and the Americans exacerbated this. Barrowclough complained in discussions with General Harmon that the division's shipping requirements 'were not fully communicated to US AFISPA'. Harmon indicated that if the division's needs were furnished, 'shipping will be promptly arranged'.[54] Immediately before the division's shift to Guadalcanal, Barrowclough considered shipment an American responsibility.[55] He maintained that 'they have to fulfil their part of the bargain by supplying the shipping required'.[56] He needed at least 15 refills of ammunition to be delivered to Guadalcanal before he felt comfortable landing his troops, and was not prepared to certify that the division was combat ready when it held only one day's supply of ammunition.[57] Moving a division from New Caledonia to Guadalcanal was beyond the capacity of New Zealand shipping. Indeed, all the division's major movements after July 1942 were accomplished using American ships protected by American air and naval power. Without American shipping support and protection 3NZ Division could have accomplished nothing.

However, New Zealand provided some logistical support in return. New Zealand was often a source of heavy earthmoving equipment for American units. New Zealand also supplied food to American units in New Zealand, which impacted on the need for New Zealand agricultural workers. The men of 3NZ Division were regularly used to providing work parties to load and unload ships, a vital but unsung role.

One area where New Zealand and American units had to mesh was in logistics. All American personnel on Vella Lavella, the Treasury Islands and the Green Islands came under Barrowclough's command. This meant that 3NZ Division Army Service Corps became responsible for the duties of island quartermaster. The ASC units of 3NZ Division had to fit into the American supply system and 'worked in effect, as a U.S. Army organisation'.[58] It therefore had to adopt the same general American systems in the operation of supply, petrol, oil and lubricants dumps. American units were co-operative but it was found desirable to appoint a New Zealand Supply Liaison Officer to the American supply (G4) system.[59]

Indeed, there were growing differences in equipment and weapons between New Zealand and American forces. American equipment changed considerably during the war, but the change did not flow through to New Zealand units because both sides decided that the division should retain its own British-style equipment. This meant it was not logistically efficient in a theatre where material had to be shipped over long distances and supplies at the front were scarce, even in 1943. By then most American weapons were equal or superior to British equivalents. In late 1944, as 3NZ Division was being disbanded, American commanders again raised the possibility of American weapons and equipment being provided if the division were to be reconstituted 'because of obvious logistic difficulties hereto.' Even then Barrowclough demurred, preferring retention of the

British-made 25-pounder artillery. Puttick also doubted the wisdom of such a re-equipment due to the time involved in shipping the weapons to New Zealand and then training New Zealand troops to use them.[60]

The war in the South Pacific brought thousands of Americans and New Zealanders into contact. Some of these contacts resulted in friendships that spanned decades. Others, fuelled by testosterone, alcohol and nationalism, resulted in fights and misunderstandings born of cultural differences. The Kiwis soon found things to appreciate. Among them was the lightweight US jungle outfit. Although Geoffrey Perret considers that the US Army 'never managed to produce a truly satisfactory jungle suit,'[61] those supplied to 14 Brigade were immeasurably more comfortable than the woollen New Zealand outfits painted with brown and green paint used by 8 Brigade. The currency had its attractions too. On arrival in New Caledonia, Kiwi troops were paid in American decimal currency, which Bombardier Gordon J. Thomas found 'a dozen times easier than the British money', with its complex structure of pounds, shillings and pence. Also cigarettes and tobacco were readily available, 'a real change after the shortages at home!'[62]

Nowhere was the cultural difference between New Zealanders and Americans more obvious than in food tastes. New Zealanders had developed a cuisine based on meat, butter and milk. The ethnically diverse Americans had a much wider culinary spectrum. Compounding matters was the fact that food spoiled quickly in the tropics, and dehydrated food had to be used. The soldiers of 3NZ Division had their first exposure to chili con carne, sauerkraut, Vienna sausage and spam. The Americans also used dried beans and dried eggs, which were not popular with the New Zealand soldiers. The greatest wastage was food cooked but not eaten. For their part, the Americans 'grew to detest New Zealand mutton which they strongly suspected of being goat'.[63] Some New Zealanders, however, believed the Yanks were getting better food than they were.[64] In fairness, even for the Americans, the food provided by their army was not popular or palatable.

Although most New Zealand soldiers would undoubtedly have disapproved of stealing from their fellow citizens, in wartime theft became commonplace and almost a sport. In Europe 2NZ Division acquired a reputation for it,[65] and in the South Pacific 3NZ Division got a similar reputation for stealing from the Americans. An American joke was that it would take the 'thieving Kiwis' two days to defeat the Japanese – one day to catch them and one day to steal their equipment.[66] Historian John McLeod notes that division troops pilfered New Zealand Army stores and equipment and also found American stores 'very attractive … and many were unable to restrain themselves from "borrowing" arms, equipment and ammunition. Although HQ… tried to prevent this and have "borrowed" stores handed in, they were simply ignored ...'.[67] The men delighted in their larceny, referring to themselves as 'Barrowclough's Forty Thousand Thieves'.[68] They sang about their prowess too, in a ditty called 'The Jungle Smashers', sung to the tune of the Marine Hymn:

> Oh they call us 'Jungle Smashers'
> and say we fight the Japs
> And we wear the shoulder flashes
> just to show we've been in scraps
> But the booty we've taken there is nothing when it's seen
> By the blooming pile we've captured from the United States Marines.[69]

Not that the New Zealanders were alone in helping themselves to goods from their own side – US Marines on Guadalcanal stole GI supplies.[70] The 93rd NCB became known as 'Harold Lynn [the commander] and his Thousand Thieves'.[71] Theft by American units in MacArthur's South West Pacific Area was endemic. 'Port Battalions and combat troops pressed into unloading duty ruthlessly pilfered holds of their more valuable goods. Even more mundane commodities were not safe.'[72]

The range of items pilfered was extensive and included ammunition cases, the hinges from ammunition boxes and even parts of bombs. This caused Lieutenant-Colonel W.A. Bryden to threaten a court martial for anyone interfering with ammunition dumps.[73] Yet officers sometimes turned a blind eye to their men's larceny. A court of inquiry into the theft of clothing from the wharves of Noumea in 1944 found that one officer was 'aware that his men had been thieving' but took no action. Another 'was conniving at thieving by the men'.[74] Lieutenant-Colonel Bennett criticised some of the division's officers for 'shirking their responsibilities' in seizing unlawfully held 'US arms warlike stores and equipment and ammunition from officers and other ranks.'[75]

In Fiji in 1942, lack of engineering equipment led to misappropriation.[76] The fact that their allies had so much more equipment than the New Zealanders contributed to the problem. On Guadalcanal 3NZ Division engineers engaged in road building marvelled 'at the wealth of material possessions of American troops. There were many gaping mouths as we wandered about the dumps at Lunga Point and several truckloads of useful matter passed back … to decorate the New Zealand engineer camps.'[77]

Similar attitudes prevailed regarding the appropriation of goods for personal consumption. 'The Provost Corps certainly had some trouble in checking up on the correct number of bottles ex the holds of several ships. A whisky case which went overboard was retrieved with grappling irons as well as other things.' And the 'engineers enjoyed some notoriety' in the 'extraction of bottles from the wire netting enclosure at Samambula Camp'.[78] Again, in comparison with American forces, the Kiwis were deprived: the former were provided with ice cream, beer and other luxuries unheard of for New Zealand units.[79]

To the New Zealanders, the American bases codenamed 'Acorns' were veritable Aladdin's caves. The rationale was that since much of this equipment was not being used by the Americans and the New Zealanders had an obvious need, it was all right to take it. As Barrowclough noted, 'There is a tendency with all of us to admire the initiative of a good Quartermaster and to "ask no questions" as to where he acquired this or that article. No one is justified in this complacent attitude.'[80]

Americans often considered that broken equipment should be abandoned and replaced,[81] whereas the New Zealanders, with their more limited resources, repaired equipment where possible. There was a belief that once equipment left the continental United States it was 'written off', and the Americans confirmed this by abandoning prefab buildings, tractors, trucks and equipment on New Caledonia. When the New Zealand engineers on the Green Islands began to pack up their D8 tractors for transport back to New Caledonia in 1944, the Americans told them to leave them and promised that new ones would be provided in New Caledonia. Abandoned American equipment was 'fair game', though it was sometimes debatable whether it was genuinely abandoned. Barrowclough acknowledged this when he said, 'I do not mean to say that a unit is never justified in appropriating any of the thousand and one articles which are commonly found strewn all over the country. For example, it might be quite proper to take an empty and abandoned petrol drum if it was wanted as a field oven or a boiler for hot water for washing mess utensils.'[82] As one soldier recorded in his diary, 'it amazes us though to see the Yank wastage'.[83]

Sometimes it was simply a case of misunderstanding and expediency. On New Caledonia in 1943 New Zealand engineers found themselves undertaking 'service engineering', such as maintaining water distribution points and constructing roads, rather than training to be combat engineers. The expectation had been that the Americans would provide service engineering for the division. Consequently the engineers often had neither the training nor the equipment to carry out such tasks.[84] Construction materials known as 'class IV supplies' were supposed to have been supplied by the Americans, but they were in chronically short supply and 'scrounging' for construction materials ensued.[85]

At the same time, Americans could be generous. Some quartermasters gave New Zealand soldiers food and equipment – 'take what you want'. Ron Tucker recalled that on Nissan his unit was short of tea. They went to the American camp where the cook had a plentiful supply of loose tea. He gave them tea and a pot explaining, 'We don't drink tea – drop the pot back'.[86] On the Green Islands, the American units were much better equipped with tarpaulins than the New Zealand troops and the Kiwis responded to an invitation to help themselves.[87] Trade of goods occurred at an individual level as well, even though both armies frowned on it. A New Zealander in possession of American binoculars he had paid for raised issues of ownership. Barrowclough commented: 'It has been made clear to troops that it is an offence to accept gifts or transfers of US Army stores but there is no general Force order prohibiting our personnel from being in possession of American property.'[88] New Zealand soldiers were given access to PX facilities. They acquired American windbreakers and Gordon Campbell Davie purchased cheap shoes.[89] A thriving trade in Japanese souvenirs, often manufactured, took place with American personnel. In New Caledonia, one New Zealand soldier purchased an American carbine.[90] Another soldier was charged with disobeying a command to hand over US firearms.[91]

Soldiers found crashed American aircraft an irresistible source of raw materials for handicrafts. One exasperated American ground crewman on Vella Lavella complained that 'you Noo Zealanders are worse than a pack of Boston Bums'.[92]

Opportunities for pilfering were understandably greatest in rear areas. A veteran described how members of 29 Battalion were ordered to unload American supply ships in New Caledonia and proceeded to help themselves to clothes and equipment.[93] New Zealand troops were frequently detailed to provide labour, and some resented being 'wharfies for the Yanks'.[94] One veteran summed up his perception of the New Zealand contribution: 'I always thought we were nuisance value to the Yanks but came in handy for rolling many fuel drums to dumps.'[95]

Sometimes there were misunderstandings. In April 1944 Barrowclough received a memo from COMFAIRSOUTH 'alleging neglect in the development of ACORN camps and making certain allegations regarding the non-delivery to the ACORNS of certain equipment.' He noted that 'this was more or less a revival of complaints made by Commander Cotten some time ago. I investigated them and found them without justification and Cotten withdrew his charges. It is to be regretted that COMFAIRSOUTH on a short and cursory visit to the island (Nissan) should have rushed into print with charges he cannot possibly substantiate.'[96] Barrowclough offered to send his provost marshal around the camps on Green Island to arrange delivery of any misappropriated items and take disciplinary action. Later, the Americans acknowledged that 'the material seems to have been abandoned at the Russells by the Acorns' and some of the misplaced equipment was recovered.[97]

A huge amount of American material flowed into the South Pacific and some became genuinely spoiled or damaged. Manual bookkeeping methods meant it was sometimes difficult to ascertain the fate of items. Barrowclough was astonished and appalled that the Americans had not marked their gear for identification. Slipshod accounting and ill-defined areas of responsibility led to gear being abandoned.[98]

Other misunderstandings arose. For example, the Americans complained that on the move of 3NZ Division to another area it 'was found that some $150,000.00 worth of subsistence was held by them in excess of actual requirement. Another large excess of our supplies, including over 2,000 tons subsistence, was held by NZ forces in Tonga. In both instances considerable spoilage had ensued due to building up of such large reserve stocks.'[99] Barrowclough pointed out he had been directed to maintain levels of supply and some of the rations had been inherited from preceding American units. When 3NZ Division had moved northwards it had not been replaced and the extra rations taken over. It was therefore inevitable that the division's rear formation would be holding excess rations.[100]

There was no thriving black market, as there was in Italy. Anything stolen had to be either used or eaten. Similarly, there was little opportunity for spiriting items back to New Zealand. Mail was censored and possession of American equipment was not officially condoned. Fortunes were not made from the theft of American items. More legitimate trade also took place. On the Green Islands, Bob Conner, a Seabee, noted in his diary: 'bought some shell beads for Lib that one of the New Zealanders made'.[101] Japanese souvenirs such as samurai swords, some manufactured, were sold to the Americans, as was illicitly brewed alcohol.

Barrowclough maintained impeccable honesty throughout,[102] and was strongly against theft from the Americans. Orders were issued that American equipment was to be surrendered. Possession of such things was an offence subject to trial by court martial and was to be 'severely punished'.[103] However, there were few, if any, instances of disciplinary proceedings for pilferage. Two soldiers charged with theft of American equipment were court-martialled and acquitted.[104]

George Bernard Shaw quipped that the English and Americans were divided by a common language,[105] and this was true of the New Zealand–American relationship in wartime Pacific. New Zealanders found some of the expressions used by the Americans 'distinctly quaint and odd'.[106] Doubtless the feeling was reciprocated. The problem was broader:

> Even their common language sometimes proved a barrier as much as a bond, by encouraging confusion and misunderstanding. It was not simply a matter of different idioms, or of words used in different senses. American staff officers, articulate, enthusiastic, with an inexhaustible appetite for detail were frankly baffled by the scanty and laconic reports they received from Australian and New Zealand officers in the field. National traits magnified the confusion; Australians would tend to describe a completely satisfactory defensive action, in which an enemy attack had been repelled with heavy casualties, in terms which would imply to Americans that the defenders had been routed. Australian staff officers were being anything but facetious when they suggested that what the ANZACS and the Americans needed most urgently was a corps of interpreters.[107]

The problem might have been eased if the Americans had accepted Barrowclough's request to have an American officer attached to his divisional headquarters. David Williams, a New Zealand officer with 36 Battalion, commented: 'They used phrases which were strange to us, but we got the message.' When travelling on the US troopship *President Coolidge*, Williams was bemused to hear the announcement over the ships tannoy, 'Lay down to the galley for chow.'[108]

Sometimes even something as basic as insignia on uniforms could produce confusion. Harry Bioletti, a New Zealand officer, was part of an advance party that went to New Caledonia in 1943 and stayed at American camps. To his amusement, at breakfast time young American officers would look hard at him wondering whether the two pips on his epaulette meant that he was a two-star general.[109] There were also issues of military etiquette. Should New Zealand officers return the salute of lower-ranking US soldiers, as was the American practice? Although contrary to British practice, orders were issued for the New Zealand officers to return such salutes in order to avoid giving offence.

A commander in the US Shore Patrol at Noumea warned New Zealand officers 'to choose their drinking companions carefully and to keep a guard on their tongues at all times.' He warned that certain types of American officers, whom he variously described as 'mean', 'ornery' and 'just plain crazy', posed a danger. 'There are many New Zealanders who fail to realise that they do not speak quite the same language as Americans and they occasionally use a word or phrase which although harmless to them offers an excuse for offence.'[110] A New Zealand gunner on New Caledonia stole an Army Jeep and was pursued by American MPs. When questioned by an American MP officer he defiantly quipped: 'If you would speak decent English I might be able to understand you.'[111]

The most serious example of miscommunication led to New Zealand suffering its highest-ranking fatal casualty in the war. After being appointed GOC of 3NZ Division, Major General Owen H. Mead arranged to fly from Fiji to Tonga on an RNZAF *Hudson* on 25 July 1942. Because of American security precautions, the aircraft was required to maintain radio silence and the navigator could not check the aircraft's position. A navigational error occurred and was later found to be the primary cause of the aircraft's loss. However, the court of inquiry found that the aircrew 'carried out everything in their power to rectify the previous error in navigation and finally lost the machine while carrying out directions from the ground issued through WT Tonga.'[112] The *Hudson* had arrived near Tonga and radioed that it had only an hour's fuel left. The American naval station Bleacher had the plane on radar, but the officer in charge mistook it for another aircraft and issued directions that led to it flying away from Tonga to its doom.[113] A court of inquiry held in New Zealand was not able to question American personnel. No action was taken against the radar operator and a memo to the Chief of Air Staff advised that 'it would be most unwise to give relatives full details and in both the public and service interests I feel that the passing of details of the accident should be restricted.'[114]

Amphibious operations are complex and it is unsurprising that the movement of 14 Brigade to its landing beaches on Vella Lavella resulted in confusion and casualties. Rear Admiral Wilkinson apologised for this, commenting that 'we had the loading data and you had the beach data; it became again a problem of exchange of information.'[115]

The problem of cultural differences and lack of communication is exemplified by an incident before the invasion of Guadalcanal. The troops of the 1st Marine Division had to unload cargo ships and combat-load them because Wellington watersiders refused to do so. Vandegrift was unimpressed by his 'first introduction to practical socialism'.[116] On the other hand, the Americans had not explained to the watersiders that the ships were being reloaded for battle.

* * *

The New Zealand and American forces were sharply divided in the area of race relations. American forces were strictly segregated along racial lines,[117] and many US soldiers, particularly those from the South, expected segregation to apply to New Zealand units and their facilities. This caused resentment and tension.

Bill Ashton records that when his artillery unit was in Fiji in 1942 his unit fraternised with Fijians. The Americans treated the Fijians as 'niggers'.

> The only 'blacks' the US Army employed were in store and supply and as drivers but never as combat troops. This outlook and atmosphere did not make a good impression and when the Suva Everymans Club which was open to ALL troops of all races was asked by the Yanks to admit 'whites' only and of course they refused, the American hospitality organisation bought the entire building the Club was in, in downtown Suva and converted it to THEIR type of recreational centre, British and Colonial feelings were running pretty high. The bigotry of the 'good ole boys' units from the American South had to be seen to be believed! As they objected to being in the same company as our Maori troops and obviously considered them as 'Nigrahs'! Our Allies!! We were being educated.[118]

The American Army believed that 'blacks wouldn't fight, couldn't fight' and were 'too unskilled, too unhealthy, too undisciplined' to be good service troops. If it had been 'possible to fight and win without them, chances are that no more than a token number of blacks would have worn khaki.'[119] The 93rd Division, composed of black soldiers, was spread around the Pacific as garrison troops, and blacks were used as service troops. Black soldiers also garrisoned the Cook Islands.

On 9 February 1943, 206 New Zealanders from 30 Battalion were working on the docks at Noumea, which brought them into contact with black soldiers. 'The dry phlegmatic ways of the negroes amused our boys. They could sleep anywhere and stacks of bailed hay proved too much of a temptation for many tired coloured boys. During their meal hour, they played complicated card games.' They, like the New Zealanders, took the opportunity of purloining cases of beer.[120]

The presence of black units around Bourail in 1943 caused anxieties to New Zealand and French authorities as these men appeared poorly disciplined.[121] When the governor complained to the New Zealanders, Brigadier Dove replied that if there were specific cases of New Zealand soldiers misbehaving, severe disciplinary action would be taken. However, he had no responsibility for black American troops.[122]

There was conflict in New Zealand after American servicemen arrived there in June 1942, but it is unclear whether race played a part. Allegations were certainly made that Americans had insulted Maori.[123] Although there were no Maori units within 3NZ Division,[124] Halsey welcomed the possibility of having a Maori battalion and assured Wellington that Maori would not be subject to discrimination. Barrowclough had his doubts:

> Whilst senior officers might accept them, I am seriously afraid Maori officers and soldiers would be subjected to indignities which they should not have to endure. Have heard of similar incidents in relation to Negro officers serving here. Americans' relations with their Negro troops might be disturbed as a result of Negroes observing equality of status as between Maori and Pakeha.[125]

It is possible that the division's overwhelmingly European composition may have aided its acceptance with some Americans.

Historian John Dower maintains that the element of race conflict made the Pacific war particularly vicious and that desecration of enemy dead was a common practice, especially the removal of gold fillings from the teeth of enemy dead.[126] Barrowclough on the Green Islands experienced this unsavoury aspect at first hand.

> The success of the operation on the afternoon of the 20th [February 1944] soon became generally known and numbers of American soldiers appeared from everywhere hunting for souvenirs. Most of the legitimate souvenirs had already been taken by our troops, guns, swords, rifles, etc., but this did not deter these American visitors who thoroughly turned over the dead enemy bodies, even extracting the teeth of the dead. We put a stop to this ghoulish business and sent them packing.[127]

Likewise, Barrowclough had to order the burial of Japanese dead in the aftermath of *Goodtime*.[128]

Generally, the American attitude towards the Kiwis was one of bemused tolerance. The Kiwis were somewhat reserved and exotic but nonetheless spoke a similar language and had similar value systems. The contact between the two nationalities produced some interesting cross-fertilisation. On New Caledonia the Kiwis learned to play baseball and the Yanks were introduced to the game of cricket. Tea, the primary drink of the Kiwis, had to give pride of place to 'cawfee' but that was because it was properly percolated and not stewed in an urn for several hours.[129]

The Seabees universally impressed the New Zealanders. Generally composed of older men skilled in heavy construction work, they were able to complete complex engineering feats in very short time. David Williams commented: 'No New Zealand officer would dare presume to give these very competent professionals orders.'[130] The respect was reciprocated, with one Seabee on the Green Islands writing in his diary: 'only a few snipers remain and the New Zealanders – wicked fighters – have them under control ... our boys can say only the best for the New Zealanders.'[131]

The New Zealanders discovered that the Americans were made up of various service branches, each with its own idiosyncrasies. Sometimes this clash of cultures led to literally explosive results. On Vella Lavella in October 1943, two Americans from the 2nd Marine Corps Parachute Battalion drove their truck into a New Zealand-run rubbish dump. The rubbish was to be burned and a bulldozer would then bury the ashes. After they had dumped their waste, the Americans observed that the New Zealand soldier responsible could not get the rubbish lit because it was too wet. One of the Americans helpfully suggested that they obtain some aviation fuel from barrels located in a dump some 100 feet away. The New Zealander said that he would if he could. The Americans then produced a wrench from their truck and one of them unscrewed the cap on one of the barrels. The New Zealander grabbed a five-gallon can that was in the Americans' rubbish, placed it in the fuel barrel and filled it. He then returned to the rubbish dump, where he threw the fuel on the rubbish and lit it. To their horror 'a small line of flame ignited and raced back to the fuel barrels with unbelievable speed'. The resulting explosion destroyed not only the fuel dump but also the truck. The three soldiers were miraculously unhurt because they had all run into the surf. 'What the New Zealander had not known was that the Marines, as a force of habit, when disposing of trash at sea punched a hole in their gas cans so that garbage would sink, to prevent leaving a trail for enemy submarines to follow. Habits die hard, and even on land, the Marines punched holes in the cans. When they filled the five gallon container, Brutind and Carpenter forgot they would be leaving a trail of high octane fuel from the fuel drums to the trash.'[132]

Although New Zealand and American soldiers were segregated into their own national units, proximity and curiosity encouraged contacts. A young Seabee truck driver on Stirling Island was impressed by the friendliness of the New Zealanders manning anti-aircraft emplacements:

> They were always waving and shouting greetings to us as we drove by. One day we decided to stop and chat with these friendly fellows. Of course, there was always a pot of tea brewing and they graciously invited us to have some. From that day on and for many months to follow, tea with that particular gun crew became a matter of routine.

> They would share their baked goods from home with us and we in turn would sometimes provide a tin of pineapple slices or pears that we managed to procure in our travels.

The New Zealanders were acutely conscious that they were not as well dressed or equipped as the Americans and that the Americans were the dominant partner. There was an attitude of 'we will show them' and quite often this manifested itself in the form of friendly rivalry.

The New Zealanders set new records for the loading and unloading of ships. Another example of this involved the Signals Corps. Barrowclough and an American general on Vella Lavella decided to secretly test the efficiency of the American and New Zealand signals systems. A signal given the category 'most immediate, most secret' was given to each signals unit. The New Zealanders, however, had a system whereby a warning preceded the signal so that it ensured that the best operators and cypher experts were on standby and a dispatch rider was on hand to deliver the signal. As a consequence the New Zealand signal was received and acknowledged within 15 minutes. Barrowclough had the satisfaction of visiting the American signals establishment to find out how they were doing only to be told, 'It is almost coded up and ready for transmission, Sir'.[133]

Particularly in frontline areas, there appears to have been an attitude of 'we are all in this together'. Gordon Campbell Davie's artillery unit in the Treasury Islands was frequently visited by soldiers from a neighbouring American AA unit. The shared experience of Japanese air raids no doubt helped them get on well.[134] David Williams, an officer in 8 Brigade, remembers that the New Zealanders and Americans in the Solomons shared the same dangers and discomforts and were comrades in arms.[135] The New Zealanders on New Caledonia sometimes hosted American soldiers in their base area of Bourail. In 1944 this caused concern because it was found that an American deserter had found shelter and food with the New Zealanders. He commented that 'The New Zealand authorities are very lax in checking American personnel who eat at these camps regularly.'[136]

The New Zealanders were not above 'poking the borax' at the Americans. A filmed staged landing of bayonet-bearing US Marines on Green Island brought cheering and catcalls from watching New Zealand soldiers.[137] Occasionally behaviour was reckless. Soldiers from 3NZ Division Tank Squadron on Guadalcanal were perturbed by bullets hitting the New Zealand camp from nearby American troops 'fishing with automatic weapons'. They reciprocated when their tanks deviated slightly from the practice area and fired till their ammunition was expended. 'The following day we heard that our shots had passed over the American camp and we had kept them in their foxholes all day.'[138]

Generally the more unpleasant interactions between Americans and New Zealanders occurred in the rear areas and were alcohol induced. American MPs were usually tolerant of drunken New Zealanders.[139] One MP officer was sworn at by a New Zealand lance corporal whom he arrested, but generously explained that the soldier 'was heavily under the influence of liquor and in my opinion was not responsible for his actions.' However, there was one instance of New Zealand soldiers being clubbed by black MPs.[140] A drunken New Zealand driver visiting a dance at Camp Hadsell, Bourail, cursed an American officer and made insulting remarks about his division and all Americans. The officer told New Zealand MPs that he merely wanted the drunk removed, but the latter and a companion returned half an hour later. This time the officer ordered his MPs to put them off the camp ground and reported the incident to New Zealand HQ.[141] New Zealanders were not the only ones to get drunk. Brigadier Dove complained about drunken American officers causing a disturbance outside HQ, NZEFIP. It turned out that they were delivering a case of whisky to a New Zealand officer.[142]

In assessing the American – New Zealand relationship and the role of the division, a veteran, Warrant Officer C.R. Larsen, wrote that 'there can be no doubt that the tasks on Vella Lavella, Treasury, and Nissan were admirably suited to the capabilities of the New Zealand units involved. The American command showed tact and wisdom, as well as insight into the characteristics of the New Zealanders, in giving them an autonomous role. It was psychologically better to allow the New Zealanders to carry out their tasks according to the way they had been trained.'[143]

The Americans dominated the relationship with New Zealand by virtue of their greater troop numbers and weaponry. However, the relationship was a complex one and not simply that of a dominant nation and a subordinate one. New Zealand pursued its own objectives and protected its own interests and the Americans did likewise. The relationship was at times uncomfortable but generally mutually beneficial.

# 16 Aftermath

An immediate effect of the disbandment of 3NZ Division was the transfer of its personnel to a battle-weary 2NZ Division in Italy. 3NZ Division was effectively cannibalised so 2NZ Division could remain an effective formation. Of the 3675 men in the 14th Reinforcements which arrived on 29 January 1945, 2115 were former 3NZ Division troops. Military historian Christopher Pugsley considers that 'Freyberg was fortunate in the calibre of the ex-3 Division men. They had the experience necessary to replace the officers and N.C.O.s going home.'[1] Another historian, John Crawford, has also paid tribute to the contribution of the Pacific men: 'The well trained and highly motivated 3 Division personnel sent to Italy played a central part in rejuvenating 2 New Zealand Division and in its highly successful offensive across northern Italy in 1945.'[2] Their arrival meant that 2NZ Division could take part in offensive operations and be part of the drive on Trieste. One veteran recalled that soldiers in 2NZ Division welcomed him and other veterans from 3NZ Division because they were so short of men.[3] Other veterans had less cordial welcomes with jibes about 'coconut bombers'.

Barrowclough had ensured that his men were well trained and this undoubtedly helped in their integration. Techniques developed by artillery units in the South Pacific proved useful in Italy.[4] The feared surplus of officers was dealt with by several 3NZ Division officers volunteering to drop a grade in rank to serve in 2NZ Division – for example, Lieutenant-Colonel Brydon had to drop in rank to major in order to serve in an artillery unit in 2NZ Division.[5] This was a poor reward for service in the Pacific and sent a message regarding the relative importance of the two divisions. Those officers who wanted to further their careers in the New Zealand Army recognised that service in Europe was the key to advancement. For Barrowclough there were no command opportunities in 2NZ Division despite his seniority and experience of divisional command. Barrowclough had been a well-respected brigadier in 2NZ Division and had been recommended for divisional command by Freyberg. By 1944 Freyberg and indeed most of his commanders were all played out. Barrowclough had hopes that he would succeed Freyberg but ultimately Freyberg clung on to divisional command. Freyberg was not about to hand command to him and he was eventually sent to Montgomery's 21st Army Headquarters as an observer.[6]

The main reason for 3NZ Division's disbandment had supposedly been the acute manpower crisis New Zealand was facing, particularly in the agricultural and industrial areas. Those soldiers not sent to 2NZ Division in Italy were often demobilised and manpowered into essential industries. For many, this meant that they merged back into the civilian life from which they had come. Some spent time in agricultural work or dairy factories before resuming their careers in the post-war world. And it is likely that the demobilised soldiers of 3NZ Division had no significant impact in the agricultural and industrial sectors. Gillespie notes that 'the response by the farming community was the most disappointing. By 10 May only about 1,000 men of an estimated 7,000 had been asked for by the farmers.'[7] There was certainly wastage of manpower, with farmers being offered more labour than they could use. The estimates of labour required for the farming sector proved too high. Instead of 7000 men being required for dairying, in July 1944 only 4286 were able to be placed.[8] Ironically, while the soldiers of 3NZ Division were being directed into industry, 'industry was repeatedly being combed through to find fit men suitable for armed service who could be taken into the forces without hampering essential production.'[9]

* * *

The role of 3NZ Division in the Pacific had some effect on New Zealand's ensuing relationship with the region. Before 1939, apart from Samoa and the Cook Islands, New Zealand had little direct relationship with the Pacific Islands. The defence of what were British possessions was seen as a problem for Britain and more particularly the Royal Navy. New Zealand found itself taking over extensive, and to a large extent unwanted, British defence responsibilities in the South Pacific because of the area's strategic importance to New Zealand. The need to secure strategic points spanned Norfolk Island, Tonga, Tahiti, Samoa, New Caledonia and the Solomon Islands. Although those defence responsibilities for New Zealand may have been short-term ones, they are significant. At one point it was contemplated that New Zealand take over Norfolk Island from Australia. The inhabitants were considered to be Polynesians having greater kinship with New Zealand.[10] Certainly Wellington in 1944 contemplated a far more vigorous Australasian voice in the South Pacific, and a strong awareness of the strategic importance of the islands to the north has remained.

As the decolonisation of the Pacific took place in the 1960s and 1970s, New Zealand officials found themselves dealing with officials of Pacific Island nations who had a favourable recollection of New Zealand's troop deployment. Even the good relationship between 3NZ Division and the French administration on New Caledonia had potential political resonance. 3NZ Division was one of the first significant deployments of New Zealand forces into the South Pacific.[11] Recently there have again been similar deployments to Guadalcanal, Bougainville and East Timor, and the goodwill created by 3NZ Division has been a tangible asset for their successors.

At Falamai the men from 8 Brigade rebuilt the church,[12] and in the post-war years provided scholarships for the islanders. Veterans from 36 Battalion established the Mono Trust Fund, which provided cash grants to the island's primary school, funds to allow islanders to seek higher education, the provision of water supply for Falamai, sports equipment and books. On a visit to Mono Island in 2003 a New Zealand ministerial delegation was welcomed and the recapture of the island was recalled. When Major Richard Taylor of the New Zealand Army visited Nissan in 2002 he was met by locals with copies of the unofficial histories who proceeded to give him a guided tour showing where the fighting had occurred.[13] New Caledonia, with its cemetery for New Zealand war dead at Bourail, has a special connection. Regular visits have been made by veterans and the New Zealand Army, and ceremonies are held on Anzac Day. New Zealand troops deployed into the Solomons with RAMSI are, whether they are aware of it or not, the heirs of 3NZ Division.

For Fiji the impact of 3NZ Division was profound. The Fijian Defence Force (FDF) is effectively the child of 3NZ Division. Ironically it was the one offspring of 3NZ Division that was not disbanded in 1944.[14] In 1939 the Fiji military forces had consisted of a force headquarters and a territorial battalion. By the end of the war it had grown to an infantry brigade group, a heavy artillery regiment and various supporting units.[15] As the official history notes, 'Emphasis must be placed on New Zealand's contribution to the defence of Fiji, particularly in the earlier stages of the war, and to the provision of materials and technical personnel without whom little would have been accomplished.'[16]

The officers and NCOs of the Fijian military forces during the Second World War were overwhelmingly personnel seconded from 3NZ Division,[17] and a chapter of Gillespie's *The Pacific* is devoted to the Fijians.[18] With the arrival of New Zealand troops on 1 November 1940, Brigadier Cunningham became Commandant FDF. The provisioning of Fijian troops became the responsibility of the NZ Army Service Corps.[19] As the New Zealand forces grew to brigade strength, the FDF came under the operational control of 8 Brigade.[20] The Fijian commandos were trained and led mainly by New Zealanders.[21] Specialist units such as First Field Company, Fiji Corps of Engineers, First Brigade Section, Fiji Corps of Signals, First Field Battery, Fiji Artillery Regiment, and First Bearer Company, Fiji Medical Corps were all dependent on New Zealand personnel. When the Fijian military grew to brigade group size, it became necessary to request assistance from New Zealand. Altogether, 58 additional officers and 214 non-commissioned officers were required. These men were drawn mainly from New Zealanders who had already served in Fiji with the 3NZ Division.[22] Officers from the division, such as Brigadier W.H. Cunningham, Brigadier J.G. Wales and Captain C.W. Tripp, had immense influence in the development of the FDF by virtue of their leadership and administrative talents. In many ways the FDF is a reflection of the New Zealand Army.

The New Zealand connection continued after 1945: 'Some 60 officers and 200 other ranks, nearly all specialists, remained with the Fiji Defence Force, for which New Zealand also provided a Commander, until Fiji became independent in 1970.'[23] Fijian personnel have trained with New Zealanders. The strong links between the New Zealand Army and the Fijian military survive despite several military coups. A portrait of William Cunningham hangs in the Officers Mess in Queen Elizabeth Barracks, Suva.[24]

Despite American dominance in the Pacific War, the importance of Australia to New Zealand defence remained manifest. Attempts at an Anzac defence in 1941 came to nothing, but earlier there had been a division of defence responsibilities in 1939 of Fiji to New Zealand and Papua New Guinea to Australia.[25] The interest in common strategic defence was recognised in the 1944 Canberra Pact. Although there had been considerable Australian resentment at New Zealand's refusal to bring its division back from the Middle East, the Australians supplied New Zealand with much of the British-designed weaponry and munitions which equipped 3NZ Division. The continued existence of 3NZ Division had much to do with the likely Australian reaction to its disbandment. New Zealand contemplated its two-brigade division being deployed for the invasion of Japan alongside Australian forces as part of a Commonwealth Corps.

The defence links between the New Zealand Army and the Australian Army in World War II had been tenuous and amounted to the training of New Zealanders in 'Independent Companies' for commando forces and special operations. Lessons from Australian jungle fighting were disseminated to 3NZ Division, but both armies had to learn independent lessons from the Americans on amphibious operations because of the MacArthur/Nimitz division. Post-war defence links with Australia would be propelled by the demands of 'forward defence'.

3NZ Division's deployment into the South Pacific subtly changed the defence relationship with Britain. The British were willing to learn from Australasian jungle fighting. They had suffered disasters in Burma in 1942-43 and eagerly sought to recruit New Zealand officers to reform the 14th Army.[26] The experience of 3NZ Division in jungle warfare earned British respect that would continue with Commonwealth operations in Malaysia in the post-war world. Furthermore, during the war New Zealand had been obliged to take over defence responsibilities not only for itself but also for British possessions within the New Zealand Naval Station and for islands like Fanning.

For the Americans the deployment of 3NZ Division was a milestone. The division earned recognition from the Americans as being one of the best Allied units in the South Pacific: American personnel were placed under the direct command of a New Zealand major-general. 3NZ Division's successful operations earned kudos from Wilkinson, Halsey and Nimitz. The fact that the New Zealanders were adaptable and willing to get along with American commanders would engender a respect for New Zealand forces' fighting abilities which would continue in Korea, Vietnam and Afghanistan.

The placing of New Zealand forces under American command was precedent setting. For the first time New Zealand land forces came under non-British command, and moreover the operations were successful and casualties small. The movement away from Commonwealth defence to reliance on American protection took decades, but it is arguable that 3NZ Division's deployment was an important milestone.

The legacy of 3NZ Division in the post-war New Zealand Army is not straightforward. By 1950 the Army had largely reverted to its pre-war form, with no regular units but a cadre of officers and NCOs whose role was to form the backbone of a 'Third New Zealand Expeditionary Force', developed from mobilised citizen soldiers.[27] The focus of this Expeditionary Force was to be a deployment to the Middle East. However, the Malayan Emergency required Commonwealth troops and a Fijian battalion was raised, with Fijian veterans of the Pacific War providing the company leadership.[28] New Zealand soldiers and NCOs were sent to 1 Fijian Infantry Regiment, but 'it was a case of learning on the job'.[29] The commander, Major Ron Tinker, was a New Zealander and a veteran of the Long Range Desert Group. The Fijian soldiers were mainly recruits. Similarly, a New Zealand SAS Squadron was created from scratch led by Major Frank Rennie, a veteran of 3NZ Division.[30] That squadron was replaced in 1957 by 1st Battalion, New Zealand Regiment, the first regular unit in the New Zealand Army.[31] Walter. S. MacKinnon, who served with an AA unit in the Pacific, later became a major general and commander of the New Zealand Army. He became the Patron of 3rd NZ Division Association. However, veterans of 2NZ Division such as Major General Stephen Weir predominated in the post-war New Zealand Army.

Experience in Malaya from 1952 to 1960 provided basic expertise in jungle warfare for a new generation of New Zealand soldiers. Training was provided by the British and was based on their experience in Burma in World War II. It was this experience that the Army would build on for later operations in Vietnam. Because 3NZ Division was made up of citizen soldiers who largely returned to their civilian lives at the end of the war, the New Zealand Army lost the expertise that had been so hard won, except for individuals like Frank Rennie who continued as career soldiers. Faced with the jungles of south-east Asia, a new generation of the New Zealand Army had to relearn its skills.

In the same way, the experience that 3NZ Division gained on amphibious assaults also faded.[32] Interest in amphibious operations has only recently been revived with the purchase of HMNZS *Charles Upham*, a roll-on/roll-off vessel, and HMNZS *Canterbury*. The state of the art in amphibious operations has changed hugely since 1944 with the advent of helicopters and specialised amphibious vehicles,[33] but amphibious capability remains a valuable military asset for an island nation.

The New Zealand Army Service Corps produced a 'Report on N.Z.A.S.C. Operations with 3NZ Division in South Pacific', which set out lessons learned and made recommendations. The report ranged widely, from the size of war establishments through to field bakeries and liaison with American units, but it was very specific to the South Pacific.[34] A similar type of report was produced by Brigadier Dove.[35] Barrowclough also produced a report detailing the operations of 3NZ Division, which went to Peter Fraser in late 1944. This document was explanatory rather than analytical.[36] The war was still raging and there was not the luxury of retrospection and analysis of what went wrong and what went right in the South Pacific.

While the experiences of 3NZ Division did not crystallise into doctrine, and the lessons learned, like those on desert and mountain warfare by 2NZ Division, tended to fade away, nonetheless those experiences became part of the fabric of the Army's history. A 'Vella Lavella Barracks' was opened by Major General McKinnon at Waiouru on 30 October 1990. A Valentine Mk V, of 3NZ Division Tank Squadron, stood guard at the Queen Elizabeth II Army Museum for a number of years but is no longer on display. A small display in the museum commemorates 3NZ Division. It is arguable that for the modern soldier the events of the Pacific War are as obscure as battles on the Gallipoli Peninsula.

Working alongside non-British military personnel was hard for the Army but it adjusted. This experience would stand it in good stead in subsequent deployments with American and UN Peacekeeping Missions. In a carry-over from both Freyberg's and Barrowclough's Charters, every senior New Zealand military commander in the post-war period who has had troops under his command deployed operationally overseas has possessed a 'Command Directive'. For example, the Directive to Commander New Zealand Army Force Far East regarding New Zealand Forces in South Vietnam, 1967, paragraph 22, provides a Right of Appeal in the event that his force was given a task which 'adversely affects the national interest of New Zealand', or which 'adversely affects the well being of New Zealand services personnel'. The Right of Appeal ultimately was to NZ Army HQ.[37]

Perhaps because of the dominance of 2NZ Division and the fact that some personnel from 3NZ Division served in Italy, there was no ruction in the post-war New Zealand Army between those who served in the Mediterranean and those who served in the Pacific. In contrast, there were clashes in the post-war RNZAF between those who had served in the European air war and those who had served in the Pacific. The RNZAF contribution in the Pacific had been numerically greater, the challenges had been very different and there was a sense that the Pacific was the harder theatre.

Back in New Zealand, many 3NZ Division soldiers who did not go on to join 2NZ Division in Italy faced widespread public ignorance about what they had accomplished and the perception that they had lived in comfort in the Pacific islands while 2NZ Division had fought the real war in Africa and Europe. The experience of individual soldiers varied, but for most it was not an enjoyable war. In the Solomons they faced a tropical environment that one historian has referred to as 'nature's killing machine'[38] and a number had their health broken. They had to face an implacable foe known to torture and execute prisoners. For many, lack of basic facilities and boredom were major problems.

Yet their service in the Pacific seemed to be unappreciated, not only by the New Zealand public but by other veterans too. A 3NZ Division man who saw combat on the Treasury Islands described how he found Anzac Days particularly hard because of the disdain shown by 2NZ Division veterans to the 'Coconut Bombers' of 3NZ Division. On one occasion a 2NZ Division veteran had flicked his Pacific Star with his finger and disdainfully inquired, 'What did you do to earn this?'[39] On another occasion a veteran of 2NZ Division acidly commented about 3NZ Division: 'You guys just hid away in the Pacific.'[40]

One soldier from 3NZ Division posted to Italy recalled with bitterness the opinion of 2NZ Division troops: 'They thought we spent our time lying under coconut trees talking to black sheilas.' The bitterness endured into the post-war world. For some veterans their service in the Pacific was a source of shame. Another veteran of 3NZ Division who had been a 'Base Wallah' on New Caledonia, and later Guadalcanal, felt that he could not wear his medals on Anzac Days or even stand alongside his friends because he had not earned his medals and the conditions of those in the Mediterranean had been far worse. Ironically, he had been downgraded on his return to New Zealand because of a tropical ear infection which would remain with him for the rest of his life and had missed out on deployment to Italy.[41] Some saw significance and an intentional slight in the fact that 2NZ Division veterans led the parade in Wellington to celebrate the 60th anniversary of VJ Day. A number of veterans made the point to me that a soldier goes where he is sent and they had no choice where they were deployed.

Despite the anxiety caused by the threat of Japanese invasion in 1941–42, the New Zealand public regarded the Pacific as an American theatre and interest evaporated once the immediate danger had passed. As a veteran of the fighting in the Solomons has commented:

> Not unnaturally an attitude developed that the war in the Pacific was a kind of secondary war; if you had been serving in the Pacific you had 'only been to the Pacific'. Was there really any proper fighting going on there? Did not New Zealanders in the Pacific just sit under palm

> trees, eat bananas and drink beer … The first reaction of most people sent to the Pacific was usually disgust. You knew what the man in the street – and the woman – felt and said about forces sent to the Pacific, the 'banana pickers', the 'coconut bombers'.[42]

Returning veterans had to endure jibes about 'Coconut Bombers', a term some perceived as an insult and others as light-hearted humour. Quite often the troops referred to themselves as 'Coconut Bombers'. The origins of the term are obscure and none of the veterans I interviewed were able to explain what it meant. It possibly had its origins in the trench raids of the First World War where parties of men carrying haversacks of grenades lobbed them into enemy trenches. They were called 'trench bombers'. In Fiji in 1940, with no grenades available, troops were provided with wooden imitations and may have ironically described themselves as 'coconut bombers'. The expressions 'pineapple pickers' and 'banana fusiliers' plainly convey an impression of indolence, as though they had spent their war in a luxuriant idyll. In the same way that prisoners of the Japanese were unable to convey the awfulness of their experience and had to submit to ill-informed aspersions about sitting out the war in safety, 3NZ Division veterans have had difficulty conveying their experiences. At least one veteran applying to join his local RSA turned on his heel and left never to return after being called a 'coconut bomber'.[43]

The disdainful attitude to the soldiers of 3NZ Division can be partially attributed to the garrison roles that the division played in Fiji, Norfolk Island, Tonga and New Caledonia. An attraction of war for some is adventure and the chance to prove themselves. Initially, the South Pacific offered only monotonous garrison duty. To the young men who enlisted to fight the Axis in North Africa, this was often a huge blow. Although vital, garrison duty is unglamorous and because these places were not invaded, the public would have assumed an absence of danger or discomfort. The troops themselves struggled with the sense of inactivity and purposelessness. One veteran recalls being on a 3NZ Division troop train when a woman onlooker called out, 'Look, there are soldiers', only to have one of the soldiers exclaim, 'No, we are not soldiers, we are Coconut Bombers'.[44]

The small number of combat operations carried out by 3NZ Division was dwarfed by those of 2NZ Division. The war in North Africa and Europe was on a larger scale and progress toward victory was measurable. The commanders in Europe were colourful characters and household names in New Zealand. There was a feeling that the war would be decided in Europe, a view evidenced by the unwillingness of Maori to provide a battalion for service in the Pacific. Europe had clear strategic goals in terms of enemy capitals, whereas the South Pacific lacked readily identifiable battlegrounds. Few had ever heard of Vella Lavella, the Treasury Islands or the Green Islands.

Furthermore, 2NZ Division had a superb publicity machine attached to it. Newsreels, photos and news stories about it were plentiful. Churchill made favourable references to the division in the British Parliament. Awards for gallantry, including Victoria Crosses, were made to its soldiers.

3NZ Division had a publicity unit but very little news made it into New Zealand newspapers. A New Zealand photographer was present at Operation *Goodtime* but his camera malfunctioned and the only photographs available came from American sources. The New Zealand public's ignorance about 3NZ Division arose partly from 'the constant conflict between the military need for secrecy and the media demand for information' and the Americans were intent on preserving operational security. Compounding matters was the friction between MacArthur's South West Pacific Headquarters and that of Halsey's South Pacific Headquarters. There was some discomfiture when MacArthur's publicists broke the news of Operation *Goodtime*.[45] General Harmon was intent on keeping the presence of New Zealand troops on Vella Lavella secret 'in order to keep the Japanese guessing about the Allied order of battle.'[46]

Barrowclough complained about the low quality of the journalists attached to the division and their lack of success in getting items into the New Zealand media: 'I have seen more newspaper publicity given to the rounding up of some bushman who has gone berserk than was given to the operations of two Battalions in difficult country and under circumstances where we had a pretty heavy list of casualties'.[47] Those complaints were echoed by the rank and file.[48] The journalists did, however, face difficulties. The Public Relations Office was formed relatively late and only arrived in New Caledonia in April 1943. It consisted of war correspondents, artists, photographers, a mobile recording unit and an archives section. Initially, there was only one war correspondent who sent his reports to the Director of Publicity in Wellington. He was instructed to 'not "over-colour" such experiences as mud, mosquitoes and monotony'.[49] Once the division moved into the forward zone, the correspondent had to submit material to the Americans for censorship and competed with Australian and American journalists. American war correspondents complained that they had 'the greatest possible difficulty in getting censorship approval of any articles containing any reference to New Zealand troops and any such reference invariably delayed the despatch.'[50] Some stories were 'killed because verification was unavailable'.[51] The difficulties of providing coverage were exacerbated when the division operated in brigades on different islands, and it was not until Operation *Squarepeg* that a second journalist was appointed, allowing one to be with the soldiers while the other at Guadalcanal handled the despatch of news.[52]

There was little incentive for journalists to travel to the tropics to observe 3NZ Division. It was generally in garrison mode and lacked sensational stories. It is no coincidence that the most famous piece of archival film footage about 3NZ Division involves soldiers producing a home-made washing machine.[53] Two official war artists, Russell Clark and Allan B. Barns-Graham, produced artworks showing not only the lassitude of garrison life but also the immediacy of combat. Sadly, their works were not exhibited to any extent and were completely overshadowed by the war artist of 2NZ Division, Peter McIntyre. Worse, Barns-Graham's works were denigrated in the post-war period as being inferior. The scope of their efforts was limited: 'The jungle does not lend itself to any dramatic or spectacular incidents and in spite of the grim nature of such fighting, much of the work portrays seemingly peaceful scenes. The artists' struggle was rather with humidity, heat and rain.'[54]

The division's official photographers faced myriad problems, from having to supply their own cameras through to totally inadequate facilities for processing film. The Americans eventually assisted with the supply 'of

Kiwi sappers of 20 Field Company with an improvised washing machine made from a 44-gallon drum and a packing case.

*(Archives NZ, WAII, 7, 3 official photographer)*

cameras, paper and all the material necessary for a photographic service'.[55] Although 3200 negatives were exposed, few images found their way into the New Zealand media. The publicity the division received amounted to some New Zealand Film Unit footage of garrison life, some photographs and recorded messages from the soldiers. Any news items were rarely front-page material.

The need for operational security often created anxieties for the families of the men. Kathleen Bee, the wife of a newly married soldier in 34 Battalion, only knew that her husband had been shipped overseas suddenly from his camp in Papakura. She did not become aware that he was in Fiji until much later.[56] A sergeant who wrote to his wife telling her where he was and where his unit was moving to was sentenced to 90 days detention in 1944.[57]

* * *

There were practical reasons for 3NZ Division's piecemeal return to New Zealand. Barrowclough was concerned that too large a contingent of troops would place strain on the ferries and rail system, and shipping space was limited. There was also a need for operational security. For these reasons there were no parades, no brass bands and no welcoming crowds. Units were simply broken up and the soldiers demobilised or sent as reinforcements to the Mediterranean. By the time Japan surrendered in August 1945, 3NZ Division was a distant memory. The New Zealand representative at the signing of the Japanese surrender on USS *Missouri* was not a veteran of 3NZ Division, but rather Air Vice-Marshal Isitt.

The men of 2NZ Division, by contrast, returned to New Zealand on troopships to a well-publicised and public welcome. Some of its members took part in the victory celebrations in London. They had a sense of solidarity, accomplishment and pride in what they had achieved. The men of 3NZ Division were robbed of this and their experiences began their slide into obscurity. The lack of recognition of what 3NZ Division had achieved was to persist in the post-war years. No attempt was made to thank them for their contribution to victory in the Pacific, let alone explain to them what they had achieved. Although the soldiers of 3NZ Division were not in combat for the same length of time as their contemporaries in 2NZ Division, they faced comparable challenges, privations and discomforts.

Despite what it achieved, the legacies of 3NZ Division proved to be ephemeral and localised. Partly this was because the division was largely composed of citizen soldiers who rapidly merged back into civilian society.

8 Brigade troops training on the Treasury Islands. Left to right: Lt William Tricklebank, Lt A. Siddall, Major John Ross Marshall (later a prime minister of New Zealand), Captain H. McKechnie.

*(Alexander Turnbull Library, War History Collection, Ref. WH-0558, photographer unknown)*

Barrowclough is the prime example, rapidly moving from being a major general back to being a lawyer. The division itself ceased to be on the order of battle of the New Zealand Army and its soldiers were scattered by demobilisation or absorbed into 2NZ Division. Demobilisation at the end of the war resulted in a huge loss of corporate knowledge. A similar phenomenon occurred with 2NZ Division – and for that matter with most of the military units of the western democracies.

Perhaps sensing that his division's history would be overlooked and swept into the dustbin of history, Barrowclough attempted to memorialise what his men had accomplished in a series of volumes of unofficial histories prepared by the men themselves and distributed to each veteran. The Army Board in 1944–45 also published two volumes on the New Zealand contribution in the Pacific. The veterans would, however, have to wait for Oliver Gillespie's *The Pacific* for the 'Official History'. Even then, Gillespie's volume dealt with garrison units, Fijian commandos and the air and naval aspects, rather than focusing on 3NZ Division. There are few published personal accounts of New Zealanders in 3NZ Division.

There were sad and bitter emotional and physical legacies from 3NZ Division's Pacific service. Many veterans continued to suffer broken health from tropical diseases. Although New Zealand's battle casualties in the South Pacific were mercifully small – some 97 killed as a result of combat and 189 wounded – there were 34 fatal non-combat casualties caused by road accidents, drowning and explosion of lamps and 16 from tropical illnesses, which added to the toll. The loss of each of the soldiers killed in the South Pacific had a huge impact on their families and friends, spanning the generations. The impact of ill-health on the lives of the veterans due to their service in the tropics is incalculable.

There were positives too, however. For the approximately 20,000 New Zealand men and women of 3NZ Division their deployment overseas had, in many instances, presented them with opportunities and helped them develop skills they may never otherwise have encountered or acquired. The veterans of 3NZ Division often figured prominently in post-war New Zealand. The discipline and skills they learned served many of them well in their civilian lives. Harold Barrowclough became Chief Justice from 1953 to 1965. He was instrumental in setting up the Court of Appeal, and presided during a period momentous in the development of the judicial system. In the political sphere, John ('Jack') Marshall, a company commander in 36 Battalion, was to become Prime Minister of New Zealand in 1972. His nemesis and subsequent Prime Minister Robert Muldoon was with 37 Battalion and became part of the New Caledonia Garrison Headquarters Intelligence Unit. Guy Powles, New Zealand's first Ombudsman, had served with 144th Independent Battery as Lieutenant Colonel.

For years, however, despite the fact that many wartime New Zealand families had members serving 'in the islands', there has been little public interest in, or even awareness of, what 3NZ Division achieved in the South Pacific. And as the generation who fought in the Second World War passes, the veil of obscurity descends ever more tightly. However, the achievements of 3NZ Division were significant and the sacrifices its soldiers made were substantial. They deserve to be rescued from that obscurity.

# 17 The Achievements of 3NZ Division

The creation and deployment of 3NZ Division into the South Pacific represented a significant investment in terms of manpower, money and scarce military resources by New Zealand. The questions that need to be asked are firstly, 'What did 3NZ Division achieve?' and secondly, 'Was the cost worth it?'

In answering the first question, it is important to appreciate that the mission of the division changed over time, and as it did so the division itself changed as well. In the early part of the war the men of the embryo division were entrusted with the mission of securing Fiji against seizure by Axis forces. They were sent to Fiji lacking equipment, barely trained and with officers of mainly World War I vintage. Fiji served largely as a training ground for men intended to be sent to 2NZ Division in the Mediterranean. The role of securing Fiji against Axis attack was initially secondary, but as the likelihood of war with Japan grew, so too did the importance of the garrison role. When Japan entered the war, Fiji was held by a comparatively weak brigade. Fiji became of frontline importance and troops and resources flowed into the country. It was the American decision to garrison Fiji with their own forces that led to the ejection of the New Zealand forces and their return to New Zealand. The New Zealand garrison had fulfilled its mission of holding the line until more powerful American units arrived. If Fiji had not been garrisoned, albeit with a relatively weak force unsupported by significant air and naval forces, then Japan would have been tempted to seize it. Had Japan been able to seize

Fiji, it would have proved a useful base from which to launch air and sea raids and cut the Australasian link to the United States. Arguably, the Fijian garrison was New Zealand's first line of defence.

When the Fijian garrison returned to New Zealand, the New Zealand government recognised the importance of being seen to be contributing to its own defence. How could we ask the Americans for their men to fight in the South Pacific if we were not prepared to commit our own? It was also important that British Commonwealth forces be seen to be fighting in the South Pacific. British forces and prestige had received a severe blow with the fall of Singapore. To maintain credibility the Union Jack had to be seen in the South Pacific. The men of 3NZ Division were the standard bearers for the Commonwealth in the South Pacific. Another factor that preyed on Prime Minister Fraser's mind was that if Allied focus shifted to Europe then the sneaky Japanese would be likely to erupt from their bases once more and threaten New Zealand. The further back the frontline could be pushed, the better. For these reasons 3NZ Division was committed to offensive operations, albeit with a lingering fear of casualties.

In performing its mission as an offensive force, the division was hamstrung by its understrength structure. Nonetheless, the division transformed itself into an effective fighting force capable of undertaking complex amphibious operations with its American ally and conducting demanding jungle warfare. The division accomplished successfully every mission its American taskmasters gave it and in a very cost-effective way.

In order to complete its offensive mission the men of the division had to display considerable flexibility and work alongside American forces. This was not easy, but the soldiers accomplished it to the extent that they were valued by their American counterparts.

A major contribution that 3NZ Division made was the garrisoning of New Caledonia. Because it did so, the Americans were able to move the Americal Division from New Caledonia to Guadalcanal. The Americal Division relieved the battered Marines on 'The Canal' and cemented Allied victory in that see-saw battle.

The next contribution the division made was in the deployment of 14 Brigade to Vella Lavella and the brigade's elimination of the Japanese defenders there. At that time, three American divisions had been involved in the gruelling New Georgia campaign and their combat power had become burned out. They needed to rest and recuperate. By taking on the combat role on Vella Lavella, the New Zealanders afforded the badly stretched Americans a much needed respite. By securing Vella Lavella, 14 Brigade triggered the withdrawal of Japanese forces from by-passed Kolombangara and completed the struggle for the New Georgia Islands.

The Division's 8 Brigade made the next contribution during Operation *Goodtime*. The Allies were chronically short of troops in the South Pacific, particularly those with amphibious capabilities. The seizure of the Treasury Islands was a complex and dangerous affair but was carried out with alacrity by 8 Brigade. The pay-off was the establishment of radar installations, an airfield and a naval base, all of which assisted the invasion of Empress Augusta Bay, Bougainville.

The next contribution was made by 14 Brigade supported by divisional assets including tanks. Operation *Squarepeg*, the seizure of the Green Islands, was another complex and dangerous amphibious assault exposed to Japanese air attack. The seizure of the Green Islands permitted the momentum of the South Pacific campaign to be maintained and enabled air and naval facilities to be set up. These air and naval facilities were then used to complete the isolation of the main Japanese base at Rabaul.

The final achievement of 3NZ Division arose, ironically enough, from its demise. The soldiers were well trained and proved to be the leavening with which the burnt-out 2NZ Division was able to regain its vigour and continue its final operations in the Italian campaign. New Zealand could not afford to maintain two divisions in different theatres. The strategic decision to disband 3NZ Division was a painful and difficult one and did not in any way reflect on the fighting qualities of its personnel.

In carrying out its battlefield missions 3NZ Division was remarkably successful for a formation that had not experienced combat before 1943. Vella Lavella was cleared of Japanese. *Goodtime* was uniformly successful; the Treasury Islands were rapidly secured and radar, aerial and naval facilities were swiftly established. Likewise, the Green Islands were quickly cleared of Japanese. Another measure of military effectiveness is the success of logistics. Even in an area as remote as Vella Lavella, the front-line units received their supplies of rations and ammunition. The supply line stretched back to New Zealand, and although most shipping was American, the divisional logistical units attended to processing and distribution. Similarly, the health of the troops was maintained by superb medical and logistical support infrastructures.

A notable feature of the division's operations was its soldiers' proclivity for unconventional operations, generally of an intelligence-gathering nature. Soldiers like Sgt Bert Cowan were able to use their skills to good effect. The division's combat operations were of an almost autonomous nature, albeit with the support of the US Navy and Allied air power. The New Zealanders had their own weapons (which were generally incompatible with American weapons), and their own distinct command structures and training. It is arguable that if the division had been deployed alongside American units on, for example, Bougainville, its distinct needs would have severely strained the American logistical system.

So was it all worthwhile? Did the soldiers of 3NZ Division 'earn their salt' and contribute meaningfully to Allied victory in the Pacific? The answer, I believe, has to be yes! However important air and sea power were in the battle for the South Pacific, it required boots on the ground to secure the islands. Ground forces were required to hold vital ports, airfields and strategic sites. They were also required to wrest territory from a Japanese enemy determined to retain it. Particularly in the early part of the war when the Allies lacked trained soldiers in the South Pacific, the men of 3NZ Division were of considerable value to the Allied cause.

American historian John Prados argues that the real turning point of the Great Pacific War was not the Battle of Midway but rather Guadalcanal and the attritional battles that occurred in the Solomon Islands.[1] At Midway the Japanese carrier fleet was dealt a grievous blow, but overall the Japanese still had significant striking power and they remained on the offensive. It was the Japanese capture of Guadalcanal and their efforts to set up an airfield there that triggered the American counter-invasion. Japanese air, land and sea forces were ground down in the South Pacific campaign, and 3NZ Division took a proud role in that.

Combat is the ultimate test of any military unit's training, motivation, weaponry and leadership. 3NZ Division passed that test. It had trained intensively in amphibious and jungle warfare, and was well equipped and led. If it had survived into 1945 it is likely that it would have been a key element in New Zealand's contribution to the Commonwealth Corps for the invasion of Japan.

# Notes

## Preface

1 For a full account of *Operation Goodtime*, see Reg Newell, *Operation Goodtime and the Battle of the Treasury Islands, 1943*. Jefferson, North Carolina: McFarland & Co, 2012.

## Chapter 2: Defence Dilemmas and Strategic Nightmares

1 W. David McIntyre, *The Rise and Fall of the Singapore Naval Base 1919–1942*. London: Macmillan, 1979.
2 Andrew Field, *Royal Navy Strategy and Tactics in the Far East, 1919–1939*. London: Frank Cass, 2003.
3 Archives NZ EA1, 156/2/1 Imperial Conference 1937 – Paper No. 3 – Navy, pp. 2–3.
4 Christopher Thorne, *Allies of a Kind: The United States, Britain and the War against Japan 1941–1945*. London: Hamish Hamilton, 1978, p. 35.
5 Archives NZ, N1, 16/3/1 Part 1, Combined Operations Staff Exercise for Senior Officers of the New Zealand Permanent Force.
6 Archives NZ, EA1 156/2/1 Imperial Conference 1937 paper No. 3, p. 6, 12 March 1937.
7 Archives NZ, AD MO 7/3 Part 1, 16th Meeting of Chiefs of Staff, December 1938.
8 Archives NZ, EQA 86/27/10 Pacific Defence Conference 1939.
9 Pacific Defence Conference.
10 Chatfield to Ismay, 23 April 1939 TNA, Public Record Office, CAB 21/497/22.

## Chapter 3: New Zealand's Achilles Heel: The vulnerable northern approaches

1 John Buckley, *Airpower in the Age of Total War*. London: UCL Press, 1999.
2 Archives NZ, Air 101, I COS 6 ONS Report considered by Cabinet, 6 May 1938 and approved.
3 W. David McIntyre, *New Zealand Prepares for War*. Christchurch: University of Canterbury Press, 1988, p. 18.
4 Gordon L. Rottman, *World War II Pacific Island Guide: A Geo-Military Study*. London: Greenwood Press, 2002, p. 96.
5 McIntyre, *New Zealand Prepares for War*, pp. 172–73.
6 Archives NZ, AD Series 12, 528/3 Vol. 1 – Chiefs of Staff Report, 30 July 1940.
7 Statutory Regulations 1941/9.
8 Order in Council, 29 January 1941.

## Chapter 4: Into the Pacific: Fijian genesis

1 Archives NZ, EA1/86/15/2 Pt 4 NZ Defence Forces, COS 40, 5 June 1940.
2 Archives NZ, WAII, 1, DAZ 121/9/B/3/1.
3 The Third Division Histories Committee, *Pacific Kiwis*, Wellington: AH & AW Reed, 1947, pp. 10–11.
4 Harry Bioletti, narrative 25 February 2007, author's collection.
5 Eric Bergerud, *Fire in the Sky: The Air War in the South Pacific*. Oxford: Westview Press, 2000, p. 99.
6 Bioletti narrative.
7 Archives NZ, WAII, DAZ 174/1/1-14.
8 *Pacific Kiwis*, p. 10.
9 Basil Renshaw narrative, author's collection.
10 Conversation with Brian Cunningham, October 2006.
11 Archives NZ, EA 86/1/1 Defence of the Pacific Section, Letter from a Major, General Staff Security Intelligence, 1 July 1941.
12 Archives NZ, WAII, 1, DAZ 121/9/B/3/1 Conference 9.
13 *Pacific Kiwis*, p. 23.

14 Third Division Histories Committee, *Headquarters*. Dunedin: AH & AW Reed, 1945, p. 95.
15 Archives NZ, WAII, DAZ 121/1/7-9 Appendix II.
16 R.A. Howlett, *The History of the Fiji Defence Forces 1939–45*. Suva: Fiji Government Printer, 1948, p. 103.
17 Archives NZ, AD Series 12 32/35 Memo for War Cabinet, 4 August 1941.
18 Archives NZ, EA 81/4/3-3 COS Paper 98, 15 August 1941.
19 Archives NZ, WAII, DAZ 121/9/83/1.
20 Martin Caiden, *Flying Forts*. New York: Ballantine Books, 1968.
21 Archives NZ, WAII, DAZ 121/1/17.
22 Archives NZ, NI030/38/17, Report on Visit of Prime Minister to Fiji and Tonga, 31 December 1941.

### Chapter 5: Japan Enters the War

1 The International Date Line meant that 7 December at Pearl Harbor was 8 December in Fiji.
2 Archives NZ, AD Series 12, S28/3, Vol. 2.
3 Archives NZ, EA 81/4/3-3 COS Paper No. 108, 8 December 1941.
4 Ibid.
5 Archives NZ, EA 81/4/3-3 COS Paper No. 109, Defence of Fiji, 20 December 1941.
6 Archives NZ, WAII, DAZ 158/1/1-3.
7 Archives NZ, AD Series 12, 528/3 Meeting of COS 20 December 1941, COS Paper No. 109.
8 Ibid.
9 Archives NZ, AD Series 12, 528/3 Cable PM NZ to PM UK, 24 December 1941.
10 Archives NZ, EA 86/1 PM NZ to Freyberg, 26 December 1941.
11 Third Division Histories Committee, *The Gunners*. Wellington: AH & AW Reed, 1948, p. 14.
12 Order in Council, 25 February 1942.
13 Archives NZ, WAII, 1, DAZ 121/9/B/3/5.
14 Archives NZ, WAII, 1, DAZ 121/9/B/10/5.
15 Howlett, *The History of the Fiji Defence Forces 1939–45*.
16 Martin Caiden, *The Rugged, Ragged Warriors*. New York: Bantam Books, 1979, pp. 306–7.
17 Archives NZ, WAII, 1, DAZ 121/9/B/10/1.
18 Archives NZ, EA 528/3/Vol.4.
19 Ibid.
20 Ibid.
21 *Documents Relating to New Zealand's Participation in the Second World War 1939–45* Volume III, Wellington Historical Publications Branch, pp. 327–28.
22 Archives NZ, Air 118, 81f Defence of Pacific, Narrative, p. 97.
23 Jack Cantwell interview, 2013, author's collection.
24 *Pacific Kiwis*, p. 29.

### Chapter 6: Confusion and Obfuscation: Forming a division

1 Archives NZ, AD Series 12, Box 21, Secret Cables, E. Puttick to Park, 16 July 1942.
2 Puttick to NZ Minister of Defence, 31 July 1942.
3 Archives NZ, AD Series 12, 28/15/1 Operation Kiwi, Puttick to Jones, 31 July 1942.
4 Archives NZ, AD Series 12, 28/15/1 Operation Kiwi, Puttick to Jones, 3 August 1942.
5 War Cabinet Minute, 11 August 1942.
6 Archives NZ, AD Series 12, 28/15/1 Operation Kiwi, Notes by DCGS as a result of visit to Rear COMSOPAC, 10 August 1942.
7 Archives NZ, AD Series 12, 38/15 Cable DCGS to COMSOPAC, 10 August 1942.
8 Archives NZ, AD Series 12, 28/15 Cable COMSOPAC to DCGS 11 August 1942.
9 Archives NZ, AD12, Box 21 Secret Cables E Puttick, Nash to Fraser, 3 November 1942.
10 Ghormley to Nimitz, 7 September 1942, Personal Papers of Fleet Admiral Nimitz, Series XIII Folder 14, US Navy Historical Centre.
11 Oliver A. Gillespie, *The Pacific*, Wellington: War Histories Branch, Department of Internal Affairs, 1952, p. 74.
12 Archives NZ, AD Series 12, 28/15/1, Operation Kiwi DCGS to COMSOPAC ADM, 18 August 1942.
13 Archives NZ, AD Series 12, 28/15/1, Lt Col A.D. Mead to Brigadier K.S. Stewart, 20 August 1942.
14 Puttick to Jones, 3 September 1942, *Documents* Vol. III, p. 360.
15 Archives NZ, AD Series 12, 28/15/2, Barrowclough to Army HQ, 1 September 1942.

16 Archives NZ, AD Series 12, 28/15/2, DCGS to Barrowclough, 4 September 1942.
17 Archives NZ, EA Series 1, 84/3/1 Intelligence General PM NZ to NZ Minister, Washington, 24 September 1942.

### Chapter 7: Growing Pains

1 Gillespie, *The Pacific*, p. 84.
2 Lindsay Adams narrative, author's collection.
3 Archives NZ, WAII, AD Series 12, 28/15/1 Supply Mission to Nash, 17 September 1942.
4 Archives NZ, EA1, 86/20/2 Norfolk Island Assumption of Defence.
5 Archives NZ, EA 86/20/1, Captain P. Olding to Puttick, 13 October 1942.
6 Archives NZ, AD Series 12, 28/15/1, Puttick to COMSOPAC, 21 October 1942.
7 Archives NZ, AD Series 12, 28/15 Vol. 1 Cable COMSOPAC to COMSOPAC ADM, 16 October 1942.
8 Archives NZ, AD Series 12, 28/15/1, Puttick to Jones, 2 November 1942.
9 Nimitz Command Summary, Book Three, p. 1348.
10 Coates to PMNZ, 24 February 1943, *Documents*, Vol. III, p. 385.
11 COMSOPAC to Barrowclough, 11 June 1943.
12 Archives NZ, AD Series 12, 28/15, Halsey to Fraser, 21 August 1942.

### Chapter 8: New Caledonia: The land of the Niaouli trees

1 Gillespie, *The Pacific*, pp. 94–95.
2 Archives NZ, DAZ 138/1/7.
3 Third Division Histories Committee, *Pacific Service*. Wellington: AH & AW Reed, 1948, p. 54.
4 Ibid, p. 57.
5 *Pacific Kiwis,* p. 52.
6 Gillespie, *The Pacific*, p. 101.
7 War Diary GOC 3NZ Division, 2 June 1942.
8 Jeffrey Plowman, *Rampant Dragons: New Zealanders in Armour in World War II*. Christchurch: Kiwi Armour, 2002, pp. 42–43.
9 Archives NZ, AD Series 12, 28/15 Vol. 2, Barrowclough to Army HQ, 2 February 1943.
10 Archives NZ, AD Series 12, 28/15, Notes on Tour of Inspection, DCGs.
11 COMSOPAC to Barrowclough, 11 June 1943.
12 John Crawford (ed.), *Kia Kaha: New Zealand in the Second World War*. Auckland: OUP 2000, p. 148.
13 War Diary, GOC 3NZ Division, 30 May 1943.
14 Archives NZ, AD Series 12, 28/15, War Cabinet to Minister of Defence, 27 June 1943.
15 Archives NZ, EA 28, 28/15/4, Barrowclough to Army HQ, 25 June 1943.
16 Archives NZ, AD Series 12, 28/15, Barrowclough to Army HQ, 7 July 1943.
17 War Diary GOC, 3NZ Division, 30 May 1943.
18 Archives NZ, WAII, 1, AD Series 12, 28/15/1, Barrowclough to Army HQ, 4 February 1943.
19 Gillespie, *The Pacific*, p. 111.
20 Archives NZ, AD Series 12, 29/15, Halsey to Fraser, 21 August 1943.
21 Archives NZ, AD Series 12, 28/15 Vol. III, Army HQ to HQ NZEFIF, 14 July 1943.

### Chapter 9: To the Solomons: Into the forward area

1 *Pacific Service*, p. 60.
2 *Pacific Kiwis,* p. 64.
3 Bombadier Gordon Thomas diary, entry 9 September 1943.
4 Peter Stone, *Hostages to Fortune: The Fall of Rabaul*. Yarram, Australia: Oceans Enterprises, 1994, p. 221.
5 Stanley L. Falk, 'Douglas MacArthur and the War against Japan' in William M. Leary (ed.), *We Shall Return: MacArthur's Commanders*. Kentucky: University of Kentucky Press, 2004, pp. 11–12.
6 Gordon L. Rottman, *Saipan and Tinian 1944*. Oxford: Osprey Publishing, 2004, p. 34.

### Chapter 10: Fighting on Vella Lavella: Initiation to battle

1 John Miller, *Cartwheel: The Reduction of Rabaul*. Washington D.C.: Center of Military History, US Army, 1990, pp. 172–73.
2 Archives NZ, EA 28, 28/15/4, Report on Ops 3NZ Division, Barrowclough to Fraser, 31 December 1943.
3 Archives NZ, WAII, 1, DAZ 155/1/20, Narrative 1 Commando Fiji Guerrillas.
4 Archives NZ, WAII, 1, DAZ 159/1/22, copy of diary kept by Sgt H.B. Brereton while temporarily at 1 Fijian Commandos.
5 Gillespie, *The Pacific*, p. 127.

6 Archives NZ, WAII, DAZ 151/1/21, Appendix V.
7 Archives NZ, WAII, DAZ 503/1/VIII–IX. In contemporary accounts the words 'landing barge' and 'landing craft' are used interchangeably.
8 Archives NZ, WAII, DAZ 158/1/21, Report No. 1 Combat Team 15 October 1943.
9 Archives NZ, EA 28, 28/15/4, Barrowclough to Fraser, 31 December 1943.
10 Third Division Histories Committee, *Pacific Saga*. Wellington: AH & AW Reed, 1948, pp. 69–70.
11 Third Division Histories Committee, *The 35th Battalion: A record of service of the 35th Battalion with the Third Division in the Pacific*. Wellington: AH & AW Reed, 1947, p. 45.
12 Archives NZ, WAII 1, DAZ 126/1/13.
13 Archives NZ, WAII, 1, DAZ 121/1/1/8, Daily Intelligence Summary No. 11, 30 September 1943.
14 *The 35th Battalion,* p. 86.
15 Archives NZ, WAII, 1, DAZ 157/1/22.
16 Ibid.
17 3NZ Division Association Newsletter No. 28, 1993. *A Soldier Remembers,* p. 29.
18 Archives NZ, DAZ 158/1/21 War Diary, 27 Battalion, 5 October 1943.
19 Archives NZ, WAII, 1, DAZ 155/1/21, Appendix.
20 Archives NZ, WAII, 1, DAZ 447.33/4, Eyewitness Reports 'Clash at Warambari Bay, Vella Lavella', undated.
21 Archives NZ, WAII, 1, 28/15, Vol. 1 Pacific Operations – 14 Brigade Group – 3 (NZ) Division Report on Combat Operations – Vella Lavella. Ref: NGOF AG 370.2-W, 29 Oct 1943.
22 Archives NZ, WAII, DAZ 126/1/14, Appendix 4A.
23 Alan Henderson, David Green and Peter Cooke, *The Gunners: A History of New Zealand Artillery*. Auckland: Penguin Books, 2008, p. 74.
24 Archives NZ, AD Series 12, 28/15, Vol. 1 Pacific Operations Report on Combat Operations.
25 Archives NZ, EA 28, 28/15/4, Barrowclough to Fraser, 31 December 1943.
26 *Pacific Saga*, p. 78.
27 Ibid.
28 Ibid, p. 79.
29 John N. Rentz, *Marines in the Central Solomons*. Washington DC: USMC, 1952, pp. 135–36.
30 Army Board, *Guadalcanal to Nissan*. Wellington: The Army Board 1945, pp. 27–28.
31 Third Division Histories Committee, *Stepping Stones to the Solomons*. Wellington: AH & AW Reed, 1946, pp. 51–55.

### Chapter 11: The Treasury Islands: Operation Goodtime – A diversionary operation

1 Henry I. Shaw and Douglas T. Kane, *Isolation of Rabaul: History of US Marine Corps Operations in World War II,* Volume II. Washington: US Government Printing Office, 1963, p. 88.
2 Archives NZ, Puttick Papers, Barrowclough to Puttick, 11 October 1943.
3 Archives NZ, WAII, 1, DAZ 151/1/23, Report on Operations Treasury Island, 23 November 1943 (hereinafter 'Row Report').
4 Ibid.
5 Archives NZ, WAII, 1, DAZ 151/1/23, Appendix B to 8 NZ Brigade GPCO No. 1, Order of Battle.
6 Row Report, p. 4.
7 Archives NZ, WAII, Series 9 Brooke-White to Barrowclough, 18 October 1943.
8 Archives NZ, WAII, 9, S14 Operations, Row to Barrowclough, 20 October 1943.
9 Ibid, Barrowclough to Row, 22 October 1943.
10 Row Report.
11 Ibid.
12 John Rentz, *Bougainville and the Northern Solomons*. Nashville: Battery Press, 2001, p. 93.
13 Minesweeping units were deployed to sweep for mines. Archives NZ, WAII, 1, DAZ 151/1/23, Annex Dog Minesweeping Plan, 18 October 1943.
14 Samuel Eliot Morison, *History of the United States Navy in World War II, Volume III, Breaking the Bismarck's Barrier: 22 July 1942 to 1 May 1944*. Edison, N.J.: Castle Books, 2001, p. 295.
15 Rentz, *Bougainville and the Northern Solomons*, p. 92.
16 Ibid, p. 94.
17 Archives NZ, WAII, 1, DAZ 151/1/22 Part 1.
18 Row Report.

19 Archives NZ, WAII, 1, DAZ 151/1/23, Recce to Mono Island, (No. 2).
20 Cowan interview, 2003.
21 Ibid.
22 *Headquarters and Communications*, p. 55.
23 Row Report.
24 Ibid.
25 Row Report.
26 Archives NZ, WAII, 1, DAZ 438.3/3, Japanese View Monograph 34.
27 Rentz, *Bougainville and the Northern Solomons*, pp. 96–97.
28 Archives NZ, WAII, 1, DAZ 151/9/1/20, Prisoner of War Interrogation Report No.1, 31 October 1943.
29 Rentz, *Bougainville and the Northern Solomons*, p. 97.
30 J.D. Ladd, *Assault from the Sea 1939–45: The Craft, the Landings, the Men*. New York: Hippocrene Books, 1976, pp. 190–91.
31 Rentz, *Bougainville and the Northern Solomons*, p. 97.
32 Row Report.
33 Army Board, *From Guadalcanal to Nissan*, p. 31.
34 'Thirty-Six Battalion, Third New Zealand Division', Robert Gordon Dunlop in Bruce M. Petty, *New Zealand in the Pacific War*. London: McFarland and Company, 2008, p. 26.
35 Archives NZ, WAII, DAZ 154/1/24, Appendix 3, p. 1.
36 Tassone was awarded the Silver Star.
37 Frank Cooze, *Kiwis in the Pacific*. Wellington: self-published, 1945, p. 37.
38 Les Taylor diary.
39 George Hodgson interview.
40 Row Report.
41 Dunlop, p. 26.
42 Row Report.
43 Newell, *Operation Goodtime*, pp. 144–49.
44 Archives NZ, WAII, DAZ, 152/1/38, Appendix 2, p. 3.
45 Row Report.

### Chapter 12: The Green Islands: Operation *Squarepeg*

1 Archives NZ, Series 9, S14 Operations, Halsey to Nimitz/King, 29 April 1944.
2 National Archives US, FE 25/A16-3 Commander Third Amphibious Force to Commander in Chief US Pacific Fleet, Seizure and Occupation Of Green Islands (hereinafter 'Wilkinson Report').
3 Wilkinson Report.
4 War Diary GOC 3NZ Division, 31 December 1943, p. 38.
5 Archives NZ, Puttick 5, W1427/5.
6 *Pacific Kiwis*, p. 89.
7 Wilkinson Report, p. 4.
8 Frank Rennie, *Regular Soldier: A Life in the New Zealand Army*. Auckland: Endeavour Press, 1986, p. 50.
9 Ibid.
10 Archives NZ, DA 428/3/2, 'Past a Joke' Official War Correspondent NZEF, 6 February 1944.
11 *Pacific Kiwis*, p. 95.
12 Rennie, *Regular Soldier*, p. 95.
13 Archives NZ, WAII, DAZ 156/1/40, Appendix, 30 Battalion Commando Raid.
14 Archives NZ, WAII, 1, 158/1/26, p. 13.
15 Gillespie, *The Pacific*, p. 256.
16 Wilkinson Report, p. 3.
17 Archives NZ, WAII, 1, DA 438.3/3, The Japanese View.
18 Morison, *History of the United States Navy in World War II*, p. 414.
19 Archives NZ, WAII, 1, DAZ 158/1/26, War Diary 37 Battalion.
20 J.M.S. Ross, *Royal New Zealand Air Force*. Wellington: Government Printer, War History Branch, 1955, p. 243.
21 Ibid, p. 244.
22 Ron Tucker, correspondence with author.
23 Archives NZ, WAII, DAZ 121/1/1/15, Appendix 1.
24 Wilkinson Report, p. 9.
25 War Diary GOC 3NZ Division, 16 February to 19 February 1944.
26 Third Division Histories Committee, *The Tanks*. Wellington: AH & AW Reed, 1947, p. 47. *Tanks, MMG and Ordnance*, p. 47.
27 Gillespie, pp. 186–87.
28 *Tanks, MMG and Ordnance*, pp. 48–49.
29 Robert W. Conner, 93rd NCB, diary entry.

### Chapter 13: Death of a Division

1 Archives NZ, AD Series 12, NZSOPAC to Defender, 23 July 1943.
2 Archives NZ, AD Series 12, Box 21, Secret Cables Puttick to Freyberg, 16 August 1942.

3 *Documents* Vol. II, No. 176, pp. 142–44, PMNZ to PMUK, 19 November 1942.
4 Archives NZ, AD Series 12, Box 21, Secret Cables Nash to Fraser, 5 December 1942.
5 Michael Bassett and Michael King, *Tomorrow Comes the Song: The Life of Peter Fraser.* Auckland: Penguin Books, 2000.
6 J.V.T. Baker, *War Economy.* Wellington: Government Printer, 1965, p. 81.
7 NZPD Vol. 262, p. 496, 19 March 1943.
8 Ibid, p. 502.
9 *Documents* Vol. II, No. 216, pp. 185–86, PMNZ to PMUK, 19 April 1943.
10 Ibid, PM to Freyberg, 7 May 1943.
11 Ibid, No. 222, pp. 189–90.
12 Ibid, No. 23, p. 191, PMUK to PMNZ, 3 May 1943.
13 McIntosh Papers, McIntosh to Stevens, 14 May 1943.
14 Brian Hewson, 'Goliath's Apprentice' (unpublished manuscript), p. 61, author's collection.
15 Archives NZ, AD Series 12, Box 21, Puttick to NZLO, 11 June 1943.
16 Thorne, *Allies of a Kind.* See CAB, 14 March 1945.
17 NARA Despatch No. 618, 22 June 1943. Relations between New Zealand Government and South Pacific Command, Food Requirements 1943–44.
18 Archives NZ, Puttick Papers, Manpower Situation, 6 June 1943.
19 Baker, p. 490.
20 *Documents* Vol. III, No. 414, p. 430, Nash to Halsey, 4 December 1943.
21 J.T. Henderson, Berendsen interview 1970 (unpublished), p. 17.
22 Archives NZ, Puttick Papers, Observations on Current Army Problems, 24 February 1943.
23 Archives NZ, Puttick Papers, Puttick to Barker, 30 December 1943.
24 Archives NZ, AD Series 12, 28/15/1, Part 4, Operation Kiwi, Salmon to Halsey, 20 August 1943.
25 *Documents* Vol. III, No. 1 389, pp. 404–5, PMNZ to Halsey, 30 August 1943.
26 *Documents* Vol. II, No. 358, p. 328.
27 Archives NZ, Air 118/81f The Defence of the Pacific 1942, pp. 194–202.
28 J.T. Henderson, Issit interview, p. 8.
29 Archives NZ, WAII, 9, SI Barrowclough to Puttick, 12 February 1944.
30 Archives NZ, Puttick Papers, Puttick to PMNZ, 19 February 1944.
31 Ibid. Withdrawal of Overseas Forces, Puttick to PMNZ, 29 February 1944.
32 Baker, pp. 491–92.
33 War Cabinet Minute cited in Lissington, p. 65.
34 Gillespie, *The Pacific*, p. 197.
35 Archives NZ, AD Series 12, 28/2 Freyberg to Minister of External Affairs, 10 June 1944.
36 *Documents* Vol. II, No. 385, p. 353.
37 War Diary GOC 3NZ Division, 7 June to 25 June 1944.
38 Ibid.
39 Archives NZ, WAII, 87/21/1, Barrowclough to Army HQ, 26 June 1944.
40 Archives NZ, AD Series 12, 28/15/1, Operation Kiwi, Barrowclough to Army HQ, 26 June 1944.
41 Archives NZ, WAII, 1, AD 491/8, Appreciation of the Situation Regarding the Strength of NZ Military Forces Overseas by Lt. Gen. Puttick, 4–21 August 1944.
42 Gillespie, *The Pacific*, p. 203.
43 Harry Bioletti, correspondence with author, 23 March 2007.
44 Archives NZ, EA1, 81/1/6 War Cabinet – Land Force in the War against Japan, 1 August 1945.
45 *Documents* Vol. III, 458, pp. 488–89, Churchill to Fraser, 5 July 1945.

### Chapter 14: 'Mud, Mosquitos and Monotony': The hard slog

1 Bergerud, *Fire in the Sky*, p. 97.
2 Jack London, *South Seas Tales.* Honolulu: Mutual Publishing, 1998, p. 199.
3 Army Board, *From Guadalcanal to Nissan: With the Third Division Through the Solomons.* Wellington: Army Board, 1945, p. 15.
4 Archives NZ, AD Series 12, 28/15/1, Part 4 Operation Kiwi, Barrowclough to Army HQ NZ, 20 September 1943.
5 Robert Dunlop, correspondence with author, 14 November 2009.
6 Allan Rogers interview, 20 September 2006.
7 Archives NZ, WAII, 1, DA 428/3/2, Lt. D.W. Bain, Message No. 41, 5 November 1943.
8 Barbara Bolt, 'Mail Call – New Zealanders

at War in the Pacific', *The New Zealand Genealogist*, March/April 2005, p. 94.
9 Stout, *Medical Services in New Zealand and the Pacific*, p. 74.
10 Ibid, p. 75.
11 Ibid, p. 74.
12 Harry Bioletti, correspondence with author, 2007.
13 Historical Record of 37th Battalion, entry 12–14 March 1944.
14 Third Division Histories Committee, *Pacific Pioneers*. Wellington: AH & AW Reed, 1945, pp. 67–68.
15 Ibid, p. 68.
16 Routine Orders No. 195, 20 January 1944, author's collection.
17 Bill Ashton narrative, author's collection, pp. 30–31.
18 Archives NZ, WAII, 1, daz 121/9/2, Barrowclough, 19 October 1943.
19 Archives NZ, WAII, 1, DAZ 121/9/A8 1, Detention Barracks.
20 Gordon Campbell Davie interview, 2006.
21 Archives NZ, WAII, DAZ 121/9/2 Box 460, Court Martials.
22 *The 36th Battalion*, pp. 68–69.
23 Archives NZ, WAII, DAZ 30/1/16 Vol. II.
24 *Pacific Pioneers*, p. 39.
25 Albert S. Cowdrey, *Fighting for Life: American Military Medicine in World War II.* New York: The Free Press, 1994, p. 63.
26 Ibid.
27 David Williams interview, 16 September 2006.
28 Archives NZ, WAII, 1, DAZ 182/6/1-6.
29 Ibid, Report NCO I/C Detachment 35 BN CT Area to OC (NZMCU).
30 Report Lt. R.D. Dick to DC (NZ) MCU, 15 November 1943.
31 Stout, *War Surgery and Medicine*, p. 536.
32 Ibid, p. 531.
33 Ibid, p. 537.
34 Ibid, p. 483.
35 Army Base Records Personnel File, William Cunningham.
36 Stout, *War Surgery and Medicine*, p. 698.
37 Cowdrey, p. 64.
38 Archives NZ, WAII, 1, DAZ 139/1/42.
39 Archives NZ, WAII, 1, DAZ 140/1/28.
40 Nancy Taylor, *The Home Front*, Vol. 1. Wellington: Historical Publications Branch, 1986, pp. 716–17.
41 David Williams interview, 2007.
42 *Pacific Saga*, p. 93.
43 Archives NZ, WAII, DAZ 155/1/13 14, Brigade Routine Orders 4.
44 Archives NZ, WAII, 1, DAZ 121/4/26.
45 John McLeod, *Myth and Reality: The New Zealand Soldier in World War II.* Auckland: Reed Methuen, 1986, p. 137.
46 *Base Wallahs,* p. 157.
47 *Pacific Service*, p. 55.
48 Gordon Campbell Davie interview, 2000.
49 *Pacific Kiwis,* p. 47.
50 Archives NZ, AD Series 28/15/1 Barrowclough to Army HQ, 1 May 1943.
51 *Headquarters*, p. 186.
52 Ibid.
53 Archives NZ, WAII, 1, DAZ 121/9/6/3/1 Conference 10, 24 January 1941.
54 Archives NZ, WAII, 1, DAZ 121/9/B3/5.
55 Harry Bioletti interview, 5 September 2000.
56 Bert Cowan interview, 29 August 2001.
57 Archives NZ, WAII, 1, DAZ 121/9/A8/2, Sgt Spencer to DAAG, 27 November 1943.
58 *Base Wallahs,* pp. 142–51.
59 Archives NZ, WAII, 1, DAZ 117/15/1, Unit History Kiwi Company.
60 *Base Wallahs*, p. 144.
61 Ibid, p. 148.
62 Ibid.
63 Ibid, p. 150.
64 McLeod, *Myth and Reality*, p. 136.
65 Archives NZ, AD Series 12, 87/12/1, Barrowclough to Army HQ, 1 May 1943.
66 David Williams interview, 2006.
67 *Base Wallahs,* p. 148.
68 *Pacific Pioneers*, p. 112.
69 Archives NZ, WAII, 1, DAZ 151/9/3, Proceedings of Court of Inquiry, 24 April 1944.
70 Archives NZ, WAII, 1, DAZ 121/9/A8-2, 25 October 1943.
71 Archives NZ, WAII, 1, DAZ 121/9/a82, Discipline.
72 The Third Division Histories Committee, *Pacific Kiwis*, Wellington: AH & AW Reed, 1947, p. 23.
73 Ibid, p. 124.
74 Cooze, *Kiwis in the Pacific*, p. 13.

75 Archives NZ, AD 28/15/1, Barrowclough to Army HQ, 1 May 1943.
76 Archives NZ, AD Series 12, 87/21/1, Barrowclough to Army HQ, 1 May 1943.
77 Gordon Campbell Davie interview, 2006.
78 Bombardier G.J. Thomas, Diary No. 1, 23 August 1943.
79 Letter Major B.H. Pringle, 27 November 1943, author's collection.
80 Robert Dunlop interview, 29 October 2009.
81 *Headquarters*, p. 234.
82 Gordon L. Rottman, *Japanese Army in World War II, Conquest of the Pacific 1941–42*. Oxford: Osprey Publishing, 2005.
83 Meiron and Susan Harries, *Soldiers of the Sun*. New York: Random House, 1991, pp. 475–84.
84 Megan Hutching (ed.), *Against the Rising Sun: New Zealanders Remember the Pacific War*. Auckland: HarperCollins, 2006, p. 97.
85 W. Wynne Mason, *Prisoners of War*. Wellington: Department of Internal Affairs, 1954, pp. 160–61.
86 Archives NZ, WAII,1, DAZ 121/9/18/1/4A, NZ Prisoner of Japanese, 10 October 1943.
87 Allan Rogers interview, 20 September 2006.
88 Bert Cowan interview, 29 August 2001.
89 *Pacific Saga*.
90 James Michener, *Tales of the South Pacific*. New York: Fawcett Books, 1993.
91 James Michener, *The World is my Home: A Memoir*. New York: Random House, 1992, p. 91.

### Chapter 15: Columbia's Apprentice: Fighting with the Americans

1 Peter G. Tsouras (ed.), *The Greenhill Dictionary of Military Quotations*. London: Greenhill Books, 2000, p. 34.
2 Keith Sinclair, *Walter Nash*. Auckland: Auckland University Press, 1976, p. 219.
3 Archives NZ, WAII, 9, S9 Barrowclough to Wilkinson, 21 February 1943.
4 Ibid, Barrowclough to Breene, 2 January 1944.
5 Archives NZ, AD Series 12, Box 21 Secret Cables – E. Puttick Army HQ to NZLO, London, 6 July 1943.
6 Archives NZ, AD Series 12, Unnumbered Files, Box 21, Puttick to COMSOPAC, 23 October 1943.
7 Archives NZ, AD Series 12, 28/15/1 Pt 4, Barrowclough to Army HQ, 20 September 1943.
8 Steve Taylor, 'Major General, The Right Honourable Sir Harold Eric Barrowclough, *New Zealand Armed Forces Law Review*, Wellington, 2004, p. 20.
9 War Diary, GDC 3NZ Division, 4 September 1943.
10 Archives NZ, WAII, 9, S9, Carney to Barrowclough, 29 May 1944.
11 Library of Congress, Manuscript Division, MS16, Halsey Box 6, Nimitz to Halsey, 3 April 1943.
12 Archives NZ, WAII, 1, S14 Operations. Halsey described Barrowclough's role in *Squarepeg* in glowing terms. Halsey to CINC US Fleet, 29 April 1944.
13 Ian McGibbon (ed.), *Undiplomatic Dialogue: Letters between Carl Berendsen and Alister McIntosh 1943–1952*. Auckland: Auckland University Press, 1993.
14 Archives NZ, Air 1, 130/8/7 COS Papers, 22 September 1943.
15 Halsey was referring to air matters but no doubt the sentiment was broader. Library of Congress Manuscript Division, Halsey to Nimitz, 11 June 1943.
16 Archives NZ, Air 1, 130/817 Chiefs of Staff papers, Memo, 22 September 1943.
17 War Diary, GOC 3NZ Division, 4 September 1943.
18 Ibid, 9 September 1943.
19 Ibid, 10 September 1943.
20 D.M. Horner, *High Command: Australia and Allied Strategy 1939–1945*. Sydney: Allen & Unwin, 1982, p. 208.
21 Archives NZ, WAII, 9 S9 Barrowclough to Wilkinson, 24 February 1944.
22 Archives NZ, WAII, 9, S9 Barrowclough to Commanding General, Forward Area, 27 December 1943.
23 David Williams interview, 7 July 2006.
24 Ibid.
25 Archives NZ, WAII, 9, S9 Barrowclough to COMSOPAC, 4 May 1944.
26 Archives NZ, WAII, 9, S9 Barrowclough to C.O. IMAC Corps Troops, Vella Lavella, 25 October 1943.
27 Archives NZ, AD Series 12, 28/15 Halsey to Fraser, 21 August 1943.

28 Archives NZ, AD Series 12, 28/15 Salmon to Puttick, 2 December 1943.
29 Archives NZ, WAII, 1, DAZ 121/1/1/2, Appendix 17.
30 Ibid, Appendix 2.
31 Archives NZ, WAII, 1, DAZ 121/1/1/5.
32 Ibid, Appendix 16.
33 Archives NZ, WAII, 1, DAZ 121/1/1/8 H.Q. 37th Infantry Division, 20 August 1943, Jungle Tactics and Operations.
34 Archives NZ, WAII, 1, DAZ 151/1/23, Combined Operations – Notes on Planning, HQ 9 (NZ) Bde Gp, 30 November 1943.
35 Archives NZ, WAII 1, DAZ 121/1/31.
36 Archives NZ, WAII, 9, S1 Personal Papers, Conway to Barrowclough, 19 June 1944.
37 Ibid, Barrowclough to Conway, 27 June 1944.
38 Section 190 (4) Army Act.
39 Administrative Order No. 1, 15 November 1942.
40 Archives NZ, WAII, 1, DAZ 113/915 Courts Martial, DJAG 68, A/DJAG NZEFIP to Officer 1/C Administration, 22 March 1944.
41 David Williams interview, 7 July 2006.
42 Archives NZ, WAII, 1, S14 Operations.
43 For a graphic account, see James F. Christ, *Mission Raise Hell: The US Marines on Choiseul, October – November 1943*. Annapolis: Naval Institute Press, 2006, pp. 1–5.
44 Archives NZ, WAII, 9, S9 Barrowclough to Wilkinson, 3 October 1943.
45 Archives NZ, WAII, 9, S9 Wilkinson to Barrowclough, undated.
46 George Hodgson interview, 2003.
47 *Pacific Saga*, p. 81.
48 Archives NZ, WAII, 9, S9 Major General H.R. Harmon to Barrowclough, 23 February 1944.
49 'The rule was that no one moved at night. If you moved you were shot.' Recollection of Tom Sen, interview, 25 June 2000.
50 Letter from R.P. Townsend, 27 May 2001, author's collection.
51 Archives NZ, WAII, DAZ 182/6/1-6, Report of NZ Malaria Control Unit Detached Party – Lt. L.J. Dumbleton, 12 August 1943.
52 Ibid, Commander James J. Saperio USN to Barrowclough.
53 Third New Zealand Division Histories Committee, *Headquarters and Communications*. Dunedin: AH & AW Reed, 1947 pp. 30–31, 48.
54 Archives NZ, AD Series 12, Box 12, Secret Cables – E. Puttick HQ 3NZ Division to Army HQ, 24 June 1943.
55 Archives NZ, WAII, 9, S9 Barrowclough to Lt. Col. W.G. Bassett, 1 August 1943.
56 Ibid.
57 Ibid.
58 Archives NZ, AD1, 375/1/80, Report on NZASC Operations with 3 Division in South Pacific, Lt. Col. C.A. Blazey, May 1945, p. 16.
59 Ibid.
60 Archives NZ, AD Series 12, 28/5, Puttick to Park, 28 March 1944.
61 Geoffrey Perret, *There's a War to be Won: The United States Army in World War II*. New York: Random House, 1991, p. 301.
62 Bdr G.J. Thomas, diary entry, 23 August 1943.
63 Glen Barclay, *A History of the Pacific*. London: Sedgwick & Jackson, 1978, p. 202.
64 Gordon Campbell Davie interview, 20 June 2006.
65 John McLeod, *Myth and Reality*, pp. 132–35.
66 Bdr G.J. Thomas, 49 Battery 38 Field Regiment, NZ Artillery No. 1 diary, 24 August 1943.
67 McLeod, pp. 136–37.
68 *Pacific Pioneers*, p. 29.
69 Author unknown, Archives NZ, WAII, DAZ 426/33/5.
70 Carl K. Hixon, *Guadalcanal*. Annapolis: Naval Institute Press, 1999, p. 142.
71 Robert W. Conner, 93rd NCB diary entry, 2 January 1944.
72 Stephen R. Taafe, *MacArthur's Jungle War: The 1944 New Guinea Campaign*. Lawrence, USA: University of Kansas Press, 1988, p. 46.
73 38 FD Regt, Routine Order 195, 20 January 1944.
74 Archives NZ, WAII, DAZ 113/9/6, Courts of Inquiry Brig. Dove September 1944.
75 Archives NZ, WAII, DAZ 121/9/A8-2, Lt. Col. Bennett, AA & QMG to 3 Div units, 21 March 1944.
76 *Pacific Pioneers*, p. 29.
77 Ibid, p. 31.
78 Ibid, p. 68.
79 Ron Tucker interview, 9 March 2000.

80 Archives NZ, AD1, 375/1/2, Misappropriation of Property, Barrowclough, 20 December 1942.
81 David Williams interview, 7 July 2006.
82 Barrowclough memo, 20 December 1942.
83 Thomas diary, 24 August 1943.
84 Archives NZ, WAII, DAZ 209/1/25, Assist Dir F L W to QMG, 29 June 1943.
85 Ibid, Appendix III.
86 Ron Tucker interview, 9 March 2000.
87 David Williams interview, 7 July 2006.
88 Archives NZ, WAII, DAZ 121/9/A8/2, Barrowclough to Army HQ, 15 July 1944.
89 Gordon Campbell Davie interview, June 2006.
90 Archives NZ, DAZ 121/9/A8-2 Discipline, Conduct of Troops, Captain DAAG, 1 November 1943.
91 Ibid, 9 May 1944.
92 *Headquarters*, p. 223.
93 George Hodgson interview, 2003.
94 The need to load and unload ships required fit men, who were in short supply. Gordon Campbell Davie interview, June 2006.
95 Andy Lysaght, correspondence with author, 15 January 2007.
96 War Diary GOC, 3NZ Division, 3–5 April, 1944, p. 58.
97 Archives NZ, WAII, 9, 59 Rear Admiral E.L. Gunther to Barrowclough, 9 April 1944.
98 Archives NZ, WAII 9, S9 Barrowclough to Gunther.
99 Archives NZ, WAII, 9, S9 Lt. Col. Henry Bertz memo, 7 January 1944.
100 Ibid, Barrowclough to Breene, 28 January 1944.
101 http://www.seabees.93.net, Robert W. Conner diary, 93rd NCB.
102 On the return of the division to New Zealand, Barrowclough purchased items from his mess at auction. Recollection of Joan Clouston.
103 Barrowclough memo, 20 December 1942.
104 Archives NZ, DAZ 121/9/A8 Discipline, Base Provost Section, 13 June 1943.
105 Susan Ratcliffe (ed.), *The Oxford Dictionary of Thematic Quotations.* Oxford: Oxford University Press, 2000, p. 215.
106 Third Division Histories Committee, *Headquarters and Communications.* Dunedin: AH & AW Reed, 1947, p. 29.
107 Glen St John Barclay, *A History of the Pacific from the Stone Age to the Present Day.* London: Sidgwick & Jackson, 1978, p. 203.
108 David Williams interview, 7 July 2006.
109 Harry Bioletti correspondence, 27 November 2006.
110 Archives NZ, WAII, DAZ 121/9/A8 Discipline – Conduct of Troops, J.A. Tarleton, Noumea Transit Camp, 12 November 1943.
111 Archives NZ, WAII, DAZ 121/9/A8 Discipline.
112 Archives NZ, Air, Series 25, 25/2/634.
113 Ibid, R.W. Goddard to Minister of Defence, 23 October 1942.
114 Ibid, Group Captain to CAS, 13 October 1942.
115 Archives NZ, WAII, 9, S9 Rear Admiral T.S. Wilkinson to Major General Barrowclough. Undated, probably October 1943.
116 Robert B. Asprey, *Once a Marine: The Memoirs of General A.A. Vandegrift.* New York: W.W. Norton & Co, 1964, pp. 102–3.
117 Ulysses Lee, *The US Army in World War II: The Employment of Negro Troops*, Washington: United States Government Printing, 1966. By 1945 some 70,000 black Americans were serving in the US Army – about 10 per cent of the overall total.
118 Bill Ashton, 'An Enjoyable War', unpublished manuscript, 23 December 1997, pp. 14–15.
119 Perret, *War to be Won*, p. 453.
120 *Pacific Kiwis*, p. 46.
121 Archives NZ WAII, DAZ 121/9/8A Discipline, Col. Dove to Island Command, 3 May 1943.
122 Archives NZ, WAII, 1, DAZ 121/9/A8/2, Brigadier Dove to Governor General of New Caledonia, 10 November 1943.
123 Harry Bioletti, *The Yanks are Coming.* Auckland: Century Hutchinson, 1989, pp. 151, 157–58.
124 However, there were soldiers of Maori descent who served in 3NZ Division.
125 Archives NZ, AD12, 28/15/1, Barrowclough to NZ Army HQ, 4 February 1943.
126 John Dower, *War Without Mercy.* New York: Pantheon Books, 1986.

127 War Diary, GOC 3NZ Division, 21 to 25 February, 1944, p. 50.
128 Bert Cowan interview, 29 August 2001.
129 *Pacific Kiwis*, p. 42.
130 David Williams interview, 7 July 2006.
131 Robert W. Conner, 93rd NCB diary entry, 25 February 1944, Vol. 2, November 1943 – December 1944, http://www.seabees.93.net.
132 Christ, *Mission: Raise Hell*, pp. 82–83.
133 Laurie Barber and Cliff Lord, *Swift and Sure: A History of the Royal New Zealand Corps of Signals and Army Signalling in New Zealand.* Auckland: NZ Signals Incorporated, 1996, p. 119.
134 Gordon Campbell Davie interview, 2006, author's collection.
135 David Williams interview, 7 July 2006.
136 Archives NZ, WAII, DAZ 121/9/9/8A Discipline, Office of the Provost General, 23 July 1944.
137 David Williams interview, 7 July 2006.
138 Plowman, *Rampant Dragons*, p. 43.
139 Archives NZ, WAII, 1, DAZ 121/9/A8/2, Lt. A.J. Gadbois to Office of the Provost Marshal, 1 Island Command, 2 July 1944.
140 Ibid.
141 Archives NZ, WAII, DAZ 121/9/A8/2, Lt. E.L. Ayers to OC Base Provost, 15 September 1944.
142 Archives NZ, WAII, 1, DAZ 121/9/A8 2, HQ Base Provost Section, 3 August 1944.
143 Archives NZ, WAII, 1, DA 401.3/1, Vol. 2 Narrative 2NZEFIP.

### Chapter 16: Aftermath

1 Christopher Pugsley, 'The Second New Zealand Division of 1945' in Crawford (ed.), *Kia Kaha*, pp. 97–98.
2 Crawford (ed.), *Kia Kaha*, p. 157.
3 Gordon Campbell Davie interview, 2006.
4 Henderson, Green and Cooke, *The Gunners*, p. 343.
5 Archives NZ, AD Series 12, 28/2, Officers Ex-3NZ Division – Report by H.E. Barrowclough.
6 Archives NZ, AD Series 12, 28/2, Report by H.E. Barrowclough on his visit to Honolulu, 2NZ Division and 21 Army Group, October 1944–April 1945.
7 Gillespie, *The Pacific*, p. 203.
8 Baker, *War Economy*, p. 493.
9 Ibid, p. 497.
10 Archives NZ, EA1 86/20/2, Norfolk Island Assumption of Defence.
11 Samoa 1914 and Fiji 1921 were precedents.
12 Third Division Histories Committee, *Stepping Stones to the Solomons*, 1947. Chapter 8, 'Church of Remembrance', pp. 70–71.
13 Conversation with Richard Taylor, 27 January 2006.
14 See John Tonkin-Covell, 'The Very Long Way Back: The Republic of Fiji Military Forces and the Neutrality Convention' in *New Zealand Journal of Defence Studies*, Vol. 1, March 2007, p. 11.
15 Howlett, *The History of the Fiji Military Forces 1939–1945*, p. 13.
16 Ibid.
17 Ibid, pp. 166–73.
18 Gillespie, pp. 261–72.
19 Howlett, pp. 17–18.
20 Ibid, p. 18.
21 Colin Larsen, *Pacific Commandos: New Zealanders and Fijians in Action.* Wellington: AH & AW Reed, 1946, p. 9.
22 Ibid, p. 177.
23 Rennie, *Regular Soldier*, p. 263.
24 Col. Jonisario Maru, FDF, email 7 July 2007, author's collection.
25 Pacific Defence Conference 1939.
26 Archives NZ, EA 87/3/10 Part 1, NZ Officers for Indian Army.
27 Christopher Pugsley, *From Emergency to Confrontation.* Oxford: Oxford University Press, 2003, p. 22.
28 Ibid, p. 24.
29 Ibid, p. 25.
30 Ibid, p. 92.
31 Ibid, p. 124.
32 Combined operations exercises were carried out by the New Zealand Military in the 1950s but then lapsed. Archives NZ, N2 16/3/1 Part 3.
33 Colonel M.H.H. Evans, *Amphibious Operations: The Projection of Sea Power Ashore.* London: Brassey's, 1990.
34 Lt. Col. C.A. Blazey, CRASC. 3NZ Division, May 1945, unpublished, author's collection.
35 Archives NZ, AD Series 12, 28/15/2.
36 Archives NZ, EA28, 28/15/4, Report on Ops 3 Division, Barrowclough to Fraser.
37 Ministry of Defence File FD 24/3/8.

38 Eric Bergerud, *Touched with Fire: The Land War in the South Pacific*. New York: Viking Penguin, 1996, p. 97.
39 Allan Rogers interview, 20 September 2000.
40 A veteran of 3NZ Division interviewed by the author.
41 Les Bee interview, 28 December 2006.
42 T.E. Dorman, *The Green War*. Christchurch: Caxton Press, 1997, p. 5.
43 Conversation with John Tonkin-Covell, 7 July 2007, regarding his father's experience.
44 Campbell Davie interview, 2006.
45 Archives NZ, Puttick Papers, Puttick to Barrowclough, 4 November 1943.
46 Ibid.
47 Archives NZ, Puttick Papers, W1427/5 Barrowclough to Puttick, 23 October 1943.
48 The Third Division Histories Committee, *Base Wallahs*, Wellington: AH & AW Reed, 1946, p. 140.
49 Ibid, p. 138.
50 Archives NZ, Puttick 5, W1427/5 Barrowclough to Puttick, 23 October 1944.
51 *Base Wallahs*, p. 139.
52 Ibid, p. 140.
53 National Film Unit, 'Wash Day in the Pacific' (Weekly Review), *War Years*. Auckland: Stage Door Video NZ.
54 *Base Wallahs*, p. 140.
55 Ibid.
56 Interview with Kathleen Bee, 28 December 2006.
57 Archives NZ, WAII, DAZ 113/9/5, 19 July 1944.

### Chapter 17: The Achievements of 3NZ Division

1 John Prados, *Islands of Destiny: The Solomons Campaign and the Eclipse of the Rising Sun*. New York: New American Library, 2012.

# Appendix

## The organisation of 3NZ Division at its height, early 1943, New Caledonia

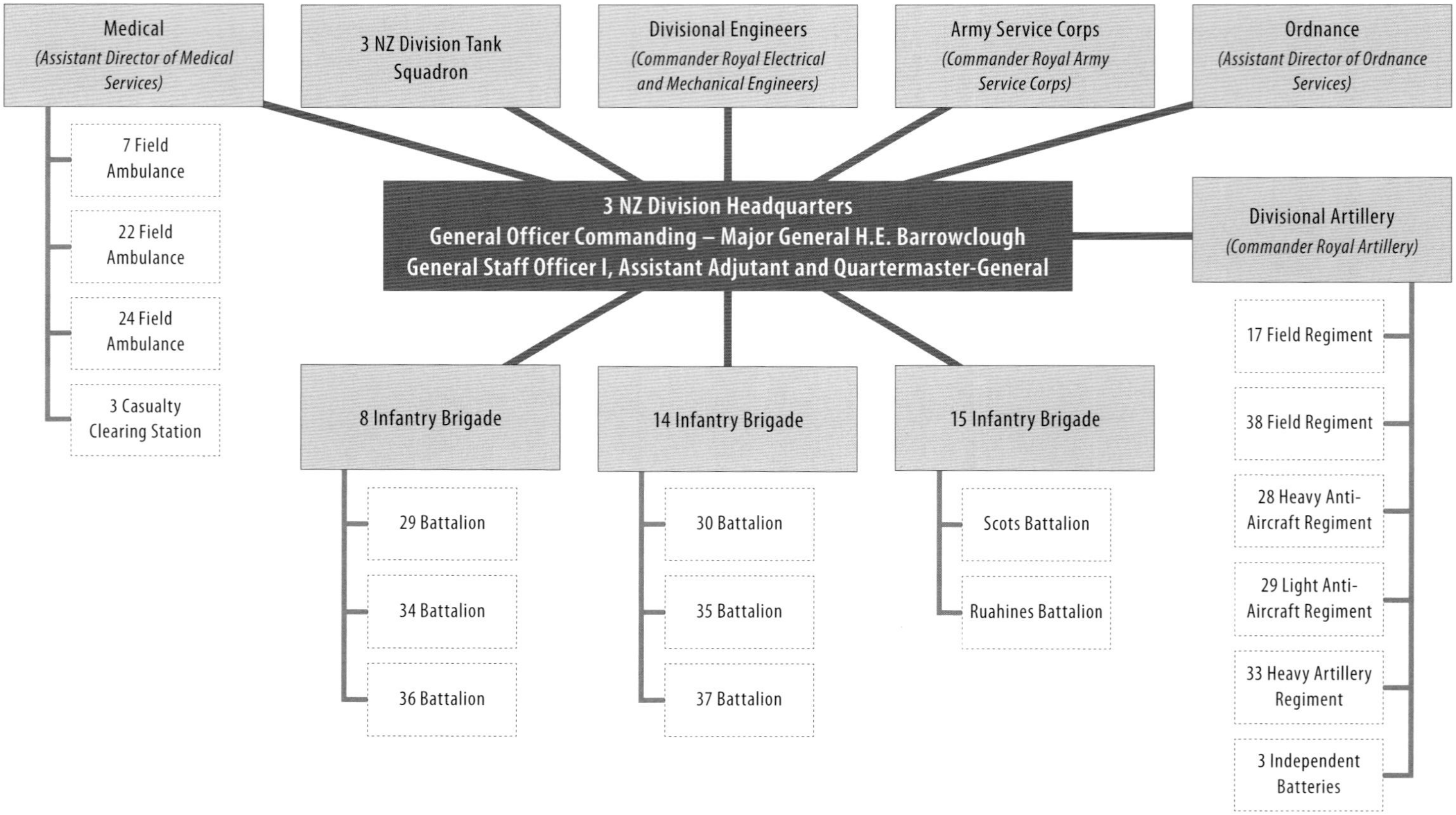

# Glossary

**AA** Anti-Aircraft.

**AA & QMG (also A & Q)** Assistant Adjutant and Quartermaster General, i.e. Senior Administrative Military Officer.

**Acorn** United States Navy code name for a CB unit tasked with constructing, operating and maintaining advanced plane and sea plane bases.

**ADC** Aide de Camp, a military assistant to an officer of high rank.

**Adm** Admiral.

**ADMS** Assistant Director Medical Services.

**ADOS** Assistant Director of Ordnance Services (*see* Ordnance; RNZASC).

**ADS** Advanced Dressing Station (i.e. a medical facility located further back from Regimental Aid Posts).

**AHQ** Army Headquarters (Wellington, NZ).

**AIF** Australian Imperial Force – Australian Army troops who had volunteered to serve outside the borders of Australia and who were deployed overseas. They were considered to be the best trained and equipped of Australian's troops and were initially deployed in the Middle East. In contrast, Australian Militia troops could not be committed for use outside the borders of Australia (which included New Guinea).

**Amb** Ambulance.

**AMCU** Anti-Malarial Control Unit.

**Americal Division** US Army Division formed on New Caledonia in January 1942. It was composed out of two National Guard Regiments and a regiment.

**ANZAC** Acronym for 'Australia and New Zealand Army Corps' from WWI, but also used in WWII to refer to the Australia–New Zealand defence area. Despite both being part of the British Empire, Australia and New Zealand did not have a unified command organisation during the war.

**APA** Auxiliary Ship Cargo Attack (US Navy acronym). These were large US transports used to transport troops, including troops of 3NZ Division (*see also* Unholy Four).

**APC** Coastal transport ship (US Navy acronym).

**APD** Army Personnel Destroyer (US Navy acronym). This was a 'four-stacker' obsolete American destroyer modified by the removal of funnels to provide accommodation area for troops. It had originally been designed to provide fast transport for USMC raiding parties in line with the raiding philosophy developed by the USMC in the interwar years. APDs were used in WWII for the transport of elements of NZ 8 Brigade and NZ 14 Brigade to Japanese-held areas in the Solomons.

**AR** All Ranks, i.e. officers and other ranks.

**ARCH NZ** Archives New Zealand.

**Argus** US codeword for radar units primarily involved in fighter control, e.g. Argus Unit Seven deployed on Green Island in 1944. This involved New Zealand radar sets and operators as well as specialist US personnel. The USN purpose for Argus units was 'to provide during the development stage of a United States Naval Base a comprehensive air warning, surface warning and fighter direction organisation which will co-ordinate all radar operations under the area commander.' Typically, an Argus unit was made up of 20 officers and 178 men.

**Arisaka** Japanese .25 calibre rifle.

**ASC** Army Service Corps.

**A/T** Anti-Tank.

**B-Force** The designation given to New Zealand soldiers deployed to Fiji in 1940. This unit was later designated 8 Brigade Group and became the core of what would become 3NZ Division.

**B-17 Flying Fortress** USAAF strategic heavy bomber produced by Boeing and a state-of-the-art weapon in the period before America's entry into World War II. Proponents of air power saw it as a means of coastal defence for the United States and a means of defending the Philippines from Japanese attack. Although tough, the bulk of B17s in the Philippines and Hawaii were destroyed in the initial Japanese aerial onslaught in December 1941 and its early promise of air power remained unfulfilled.

**Barrowclough's Charter** The instructions given by the NZ Government to Major General H.E. Barrowclough in relation to the committal of New Zealand forces to combat. Barrowclough, like Freyberg, had the power to decline to commit New Zealand forces to high-risk military operations. A certificate was required from Barrowclough to the New Zealand Government confirming that the risks were reasonable before 3NZ Division was to be committed to combat.

**Bde** Brigade. A unit of roughly 7000–8000 troops of various types, usually made up of three Infantry Battalions or three Tank Battalions.

**Beachhead** A designated area on a hostile shore which is the objective of an amphibious operation. When seized it allows the attacker to land troops and equipment with the aim of further operations inland.

**Beachmaster** An officer (generally naval) tasked with controlling the beaching of landing craft and amphibious vehicles on a beach.

**Beach Red** A particular area of the beachhead. It was common for the beach areas to be given a colour designation for planning purposes, e.g. Beach Red, Beach Green, Beach Yellow, etc.

**Betty** Allied code name for Mitsubishi G4M Medium Bomber.

**BGS** Brigadier, General Staff (Chief Staff Officer at Corps or Army level).

**Binary Division** A division with two brigades (usually there were three brigades).

**Bn/Btn/Batt** Battalion, a unit of approximately 700–900 troops, predominantly infantry, commanded by a lieutenant colonel. It contains three or four rifle companies and a company of supporting weapons, or three squadrons of tanks plus HQ.

**Bofors** A 40 mm, single-barrelled light AA gun of Swedish design.

**Bogey** Unidentified aircraft.

**BRA** Brigadier Royal Artillery.

**Bren Gun** A light machine gun used by Commonwealth forces.

**Bren Gun Carrier** A light, open-topped tracked vehicle designed to carry a Bren gun but also used for reconnaissance and general transport and haulage work (*see also* Universal Carrier).

**Bty** Battery – a tactical and administrative unit of artillery, roughly corresponding to a company in other branches of the army.

**Canberra Pact** Defence treaty signed between New Zealand and Australia in 1944 recognising common defence interests.

**CAP** Combat Air Patrol, a protective aerial umbrella usually provided over a specified area for vessels by fighter aircraft.

**Capt** Captain.

**Carrier** Bren gun carrier.

**Cartwheel** The Allied code name for the two-pronged drive up the coast of New Guinea (by MacArthur's forces) and the Solomon Islands (by Nimitz's forces) designed to isolate and neutralise the main Japanese base in the South Pacific at Rabaul. Operations began on 31 June 1943 and were completed by 1 March 1944, leaving the garrison of 98,000 men bypassed and ineffective.

**CAS** Close Air Support, a term used to describe air power dedicated to the needs of army units.

**Casualty Clearing Station** First Aid post.

**CB** Construction Battalion. Also 'Seabee', a USN term for Naval Construction units which performed prodigious feats of engineering, particularly airfield and base construction. These units were integrated into 3NZ Division operations.

**CCS** Casualty Clearing Station, a medical unit sited between a Medical Dressing Station and a Field Hospital.

**Cdo** Commando, a word which implies that a soldier has specialist skills in raiding warfare.

**Cdr** Commander.

**CFG** Commandos, Fijian Guerrillas. The term

referred to Fijian Army Units established initially for resistance to the Japanese invasion of Fiji and later for operations behind Japanese lines in the Solomons.

**CGS** Chief of the General Staff.

**CID** Committee of Imperial Defence (British).

**CIGS** Chief of the Imperial General Staff. A United Kingdom designation signifying a position of powerful influence within the British defence establishment. General Alanbrooke filled this role for most of the war.

**CinC** Commander in Chief.

**CINCPAC** US Commander in Chief US Pacific Fleet (Admiral Nimitz).

**CO** Commanding Officer.

**Coastwatchers** Allied personnel deployed on various Pacific Islands with the purpose of covertly observing and reporting on Japanese aerial and naval movement. The Japanese also deployed Coastwatchers.

**Colonel's Revolt** A term used to describe a scandal within the New Zealand Army which became public in 1938 when various high-ranking New Zealand officers breached accepted conventions by publicly criticising the NZ Government of Michael Joseph Savage for the depletion in the levels of NZ militia. Four officers were sacked but the inadequacy of NZ defence numbers had been highlighted. H.E. Barrowclough was part of the NZ Defence League, a pressure group set up with the aim of strengthening the NZ military, and which gave support to the concern about the depletion of NZ military strength. He was considered by some to be 'the 5th Colonel'. He had resigned his commission some time before the revolt.

**Combat Loading** The loading of transport and cargo ships in such a way that items needed for combat could be easily accessed and unloaded first. Not as efficient as 'commercial loading' but essential for the success of an amphibious operation.

**COMFAIRSOUTH** Commander Fighters Air South Pacific.

**COMSOPAC** Commander South Pacific Area, initially Ghormley and then Halsey.

**Condition Red** Air raid warning status: air raid imminent.

**COS** Chiefs of Staff. Term used to describe either British or NZ heads of service of the Army, Air Force and Navy.

**Coy/Co** Company: three platoons of infantry.

**Cpl** Corporal.

**CRA** Commander Royal Artillery (NZ) (of Division).

**CRE** Commander Royal Engineers (NZ) (of Division).

**CREME** Commander Royal Electrical & Mechanical Engineers.

**CTF31** Combined Task Force 31. A USN naval force active in the Solomon Islands, commanded by Admiral Theodore Wilkinson. This force provided transport and naval gunfire support to 3NZ Division.

**D-Day** Designated Day on which an operation is to commence. When a plus symbol is used it signifies days after D-Day; when a minus symbol is used it signifies days before D-Day, e.g. D+5 refers to 5 days after the invasion, D-5 refers to 5 days before the invasion.

**DADME** Deputy Assistant Director Mechanical Engineers.

**DADOS** Deputy Assistant Director Ordnance Services.

**DCGS** Deputy Chief of General Staff (NZ).

**DCM** Distinguished Conduct Medal.

**DD** Destroyer (USN acronym).

**DDMS** Deputy Director Medical Services.

**Defence Medal** NZ Medal awarded to NZ troops in areas considered 'non-operational', including the garrison areas of Fiji, Tonga, New Hebrides, Guadalcanal and New Caledonia.

**DEME** Director of Electrical & Mechanical Engineering.

**Div** Division, a unit of approximately 12,000–14,000 soldiers.

**Div A & QMG** Divisional Adjutant and Quarter Master General.

**Div Arty** Divisional Artillery.

**Div G** Divisional General Staff Branch.

**Div HQ** Divisional Headquarters.

**Div Tps** Divisional Troops.

**Div Workshops** Ordnance Unit responsible for the maintenance of weapons and equipment.

**DSO** Distinguished Service Order.

**Ech** Echelon – a movement of troops in a group, implying that a portion of a unit is separated from a parent unit (*see also* Flight). In terms of the reinforcements to 2NZ Division, 1st, 2nd and 3rd Echelons refer to the main contingents despatched from NZ.

**Exercises Styx, Scylla & Tonta** Training exercises in river crossing, beach landings and mountain warfare carried out on New Caledonia in early to mid-1943.

**Exercise Cyclops** Code name for amphibious landing practice by 8 Bde and parts of Div HQ in Necal in 1943.

**Exercise Efate** Code name for amphibious training practice by 8 Bde at Efate, New Hebrides in 1943.

**Fd Am** Field Ambulance.

**Fd Arty** Field Artillery.

**Fd Coy** Field Company of Engineers.

**FDF** Fijian Defence Force.

**Fd Regt** Field Regiment of Artillery.

**Fd Wksps** Field Workshops.

**Fiji Expeditionary Force** A NZ Army contingent despatched by the Government of William Massey which left Wellington on 5 February 1920 commanded by Major Edward Puttick (later GOC NZ Army) with the aim of crushing a strike by Indian sugar workers. A request had been made for military support by the Governor of Fiji because the strike was perceived as being anti-British. An unopposed landing was made and after one Indian casualty the strike failed. Noteworthy for being the first peacetime deployment of NZ soldiers.

**Flight** An army expression meaning a movement of troops from one area to another, usually by sea.

**FMAC** First Marine Amphibious Corps (also IMAC).

**FMC** Field Maintenance Centre (NZ).

**FO** Forward observer, an artillery spotter usually deployed close to the front to observe the fall of artillery shells and report suitable targets for artillery.

**Forearm** Allied code name for the invasion of Kavieng.

**Free French** The French who after the fall of France in 1940 opted to align themselves with General de Gaulle rather than with the collaborationist French Government based at Vichy. The French Government in New Caledonia aligned itself with the Free French.

**G Branch** Staff of division involved with operational matters.

**Gen** General.

**GHQ** General Headquarters.

**GI** US Army soldier ('Government Issue').

**GOC** General Officer Commanding.

**GSO** General Staff Officer (made up of various grades, GSO1, GII, etc).

**HE** High Explosive.

**Higgins Boat** Landing craft for infantry and light vehicles (LCVP).

**HMG** Heavy Machine Gun.

**HMNZS** His Majesty's New Zealand Ship.

**HMS** His Majesty's Ship.

**HQ** Headquarters.

**Hudson/Ventura** US twin-engine plane made by Lockheed. Frequently used for patrol reconnaissance and anti-submarine work by both the US and RNZAF. The Ventura was a development model of the Hudson.

**I/C** In Command.

**IFF** Identification, Friend or Foe.

**IGHQ** Imperial General Headquarters (Japanese).

**IJA** Imperial Japanese Army (Kogun).

**IJAAF** Imperial Japanese Army Air Force.

**IJN** Imperial Japanese Navy (Tikoku Kaigun).

**IJNAF** Imperial Japanese Naval Air Force (Koku Butai).

**Ind Bty** Independent Battery.

**Inf** Infantry.

**Jay Force** New Zealand Army Unit involved in the post-war occupation of Japan.

**Kaigun** Imperial Japanese Navy.

**KIA** Killed in Action.

**Kiwi A, B, C, D** New Zealand Army designation for the optional force ratios for the proposed 3NZ Division. These ranged from purely garrison troops through to defensive options. Ultimately Kiwi C was chosen.

**Kiwi Company** Unit of WAAC with 3NZ Division.

**Kogun** Imperial Japanese Army.

**Koku Butai** Imperial Japanese Naval Air Force.

**LAA** Light Anti-Aircraft.

**LAD** Light Aid Detachment. An engineering unit attached to a battalion to assist in repair and maintenance of vehicles and equipment.

**LCI** Landing Craft, Infantry – a large landing craft capable of holding 200 men. Of shallow draught but with seagoing ability, it was the workhorse of the Pacific War.

**LCM** Landing Craft, Mechanised.

**Lethbridge Mission** A military mission (No. 220) despatched by the British Government in 1943 to the 'Pacific and Indian Theatres to investigate measures for the prosecution of the war against Japan.' It sent small parties into the forward area to gather information and also sought the despatch of New Zealand officers to India/Burma.

**Lewis Gun** A light machine gun used by Allied forces.

**LMG** Light Machine Gun.

**Logan Force** A unit which landed on the northern area of Mono Island with a view to establishing a radar station consisting of 34 Bn, 87 NCB and Argus 6. The unit encountered brisk combat with Japanese units intent on escaping Mono.

**LST** Landing Ship, Tank – a large seagoing landing craft capable of carrying tanks and large numbers of men and supplies. An essential part of amphibious operations in the Pacific.

**LtA/A** Light Anti-Aircraft.

**Lt Col** Lieutenant Colonel.

**Lt Gen** Lieutenant General.

**Lt/Lieut** Lieutenant.

**1 MAC** 1st Marine Amphibious Corps.

**Maj** Major.

**Maj Gen** Major General.

**Mandated Islands** Former German possessions in the Pacific seized by the Japanese in WWI and entrusted to them by the League of Nations.

**MC** Military Cross.

**MG** Machine Gun.

**MIA** Missing in Action.

**mm** millimeter.

**MM** Military Medal.

**MMG** Medium Machine Gun.

**Mort** Mortar.

**MP** Military Police.

**MT** Motor Transport.

**MT Fd Wkshp** Motor Transport Field Workshop.

**Nambu** Japanese 7.7 mm light machine gun.

**NARA** National Archives & Records Administration (US).

**NCB** Naval Construction Battalion, i.e. Seabees.

**NCO** Non-commissioned Officer.

**N Force** New Zealand troops despatched to Norfolk Island: 36 Infantry Battalion, 215 Composite AA Battery, the 152nd Heavy Battery and 9 Mobile Field Troop (1488 men).

**NZEF** New Zealand Expeditionary Force.

**NZEFIP** New Zealand Expeditionary Force in the Pacific.

**NZLO** New Zealand Liaison Officer.

**NZOC** New Zealand Ordnance Corps.

**NZPD** New Zealand Parliamentary Debates.

**One Mac** 1 MAC, First Marine Amphibious Corps.

**ONS** Organisation for National Security.

**OP** Observation Post.

**Operation Kiwi** New Zealand code name for deployment of 3NZ Division to New Caledonia and the Solomon Islands.

**Orange** Colour used in US planning to designate Japanese forces.

**Ordnance** A military term referring to artillery, but also in a wider sense encompassing military stores such as ammunition, rations, etc.

**ORs** Other Ranks (i.e. not officers).

**Pacific Star or Clasp** New Zealand medal awarded to military personnel who served in an operational area of the Pacific Theatre. Operational areas were defined to include Guadalcanal, New Georgia, Treasury Islands, Green Island and the Gilbert and Ellis Islands, but not the garrison areas of Fiji, Tonga, New Caledonia, the New Hebrides, Norfolk Island and Fanning Island.

**Pdr** Pounder.

**PM** Prime Minister.

**POW** Prisoner of War (also PW).

**PT Boat** Patrol Torpedo Boat (US Navy).

**Pte** Private.

**PX** Post Exchange.

**RAdm** Rear Admiral.

**RAF** Royal Air Force (British).

**RAMC** Royal Army Medical Corps.

**RAMSI** Regional Assistance Mission to the Solomon Islands.

**RAP** Regimental Aid Post.

**Recce** Reconnaissance (also recn).

**Regt** Regiment.

**Rikusentai** Japanese Naval Infantry.

**RN** Royal Navy (British).

**RNZA** Royal New Zealand Artillery.

**RNZAF** Royal New Zealand Air Force.

**RNZASC** Royal New Zealand Army Service Corps, the organisation responsible for the supply of stores to the New Zealand Army under the Director of Ordnance Stores (DOS). There are also Deputy Directors of Ordnance Stores (DDOS), Assistant Directors of Ordnance Stores (ADOS) and at Divisional level the Deputy Assistant Director of Ordnance Stores (DADOS).

**RNZN** Royal New Zealand Navy.

**rpm** rounds per minute (i.e. rate of fire of weapons).

**RSM** Regimental Sergeant Major.

**SCAT** South Pacific Air Combat Transport Command.

**Sec** Section. In aviation terms, a unit of between 2 and 4 planes; in artillery terms, 2–3 guns; in infantry terms, a third of an infantry platoon.

**Sgt** Sergeant.

**Sigs** Signals.

**SMLE** Short Magazine Lee Enfield Rifle, the standard rifle of Commonwealth forces in World War II.

**SNLF** Special Naval Landing Force (Japanese).

**SOPAC** South Pacific Area of Operations, a US command that encompassed the Solomon Islands. From October 1942 to late 1944 Admiral Halsey commanded this area. He was in turn responsible to the Commander, Pacific Fleet, Admiral Nimitz.

**Sqdn** Squadron, in aviation terms, a unit of 18–36 planes, or armoured vehicles or recce troops.

**Squarepeg** The Allied code name for the invasion of Green Island, February 1944.

**SWPA** South West Pacific Area.

**Territorial** A military unit made up of part-time voluntary soldiers (Commonwealth).

**TF** Task Force, generally a grouping of naval craft with supporting air and other units for the fulfilment of a particular purpose.

**T Force** New Zealand troops despatched to defend Tonga.

**Towpath** A US Army plan for the assault on Rabaul which envisaged the use of 2 US Marine Division and 3NZ Division. Cancelled in November 1943.

**Ultra** Intelligence gained from the interception and decoding of Axis radio communications.

**Unholy Four** The nickname given to four US Navy troop transport ships active in the South Pacific in World War II: USS *President Adams* (APA-19), USS *President Monroe*, USS *President Jackson* and USS *President Hayes*. The nickname apparently derived from the fact that when crossing the international dateline the ships 'lost' a day, so Sunday and Sunday services were missed. The troop ships were active in transporting troops of 3NZ Division (*see also* APA).

**Universal Carrier** A tracked vehicle used by British and Commonwealth forces. Also known as a 'Bren Gun Carrier', due to the ability to mount a Bren machine gun in the forward seat next to the driver. Because they were open-topped they afforded the crew very limited protection (*see also* Bren Gun Carrier).

**USAAF** United States Army Air Force.

**USMC** US Marine Corps.

**USN** United States Navy.

**USNR** United States Naval Reserve.

**USS** United States Ship.

**VAdm** Vice Admiral.

**Val** Allied code name for the Aichi D3A dive bomber.

**VE Day** Victory in Europe Day, 8 May 1945.

**Vickers Machine Gun** Medium machine gun used by Commonwealth forces.

**VJ Day** Victory over Japan Day, 2 September 1945.

**VMF** (US acronym) 'V' signifies fixed wing aircraft, 'M' signifies US Marine Corps and 'F' signifies a fighter unit.

**WAAC** Women's Auxiliary Army Corps.

**War Plan Orange** US plan for the defeat of

Japan prepared by the US War Plans Division. It envisaged holding part of the Philippines and advanced bases in the Pacific while US ships fought their way to the relief of US garrisons. This would culminate in a Trafalgar-like battle with Japanese forces, and following victory Japan would be blockaded into surrender.

**Watchtower** US code name for the Guadalcanal-Tulagi landings, 7 August 1942. Wryly nicknamed Operation Shoestring by participants because of the lack of resources allocated.

**WIA** Wounded in Action.

**Williams Report, The** The report of British General Sir Guy Williams to the New Z Government on 1 October 1941 on the state of NZ defence. Recommendations included strengthening NZ harbour defences, establishing Coast Watchers and strengthening the defences of Fiji and the northern approaches to New Zealand. Many of his recommendations were acted upon.

**W/T** Wireless Telegraphy.

**Zeke/Zero** Allied code name for Mitsubishi A6M fighter (IJNAF).

# Bibliography


Alanbrooke, Field Marshall Lord, *War Diaries 1939–45*. Los Angeles: University of California Press, 2001.

Army Board, *From Guadalcanal to Nissan*. Wellington: The Army Board, 1945.

___ *Pacific Story*. Wellington: The Army Board, 1945.

Asprey, Robert, *Once a Marine: The Memoirs of General A.A. Vandegrift*. New York: WW Norton & Co., 1964.

Baker, J.V.T., *War Economy*. Wellington: Government Printer, 1965.

Barber, Laurie and Lord, Cliff, *Swift and Sure: A History of the Royal New Zealand Corps of Signals and Army Signalling in New Zealand*. Auckland: NZ Signals Incorporated, 1996.

Bartlett, Merrill (ed.), *Assault from the Sea: Essays on the History of Amphibious Warfare*. Annapolis: Naval Institute Press, 1983.

Bassett, Michael and King, Michael, *Tomorrow Comes the Song: A Life of Peter Fraser*. Auckland: Penguin Books, 2000.

Behrens, C.B.A., *Merchant Shipping and the Demands of War*. London: Her Majesty's Stationery Office, 1955.

Bell, Christopher M., *The Royal Navy, Sea Power and Strategy Between the Wars*, Stanford, California: Stanford University Press, 2000.

Bell, Roger, *Unequal Allies: Australian/American Relations and the Pacific War*. Carlton: Melbourne University Press, 1977.

Bergerud, Eric, *Fire in the Sky: The Air War in the South Pacific*. Boulder, USA: Westview Press, 2000.

___ *Touched by Fire: The Land War in the South Pacific*. New York: Viking Penguin, 1996.

Bioletti, Harry, *The Yanks are Coming: The American Invasion of New Zealand 1942–1944*. Auckland: Century Hutchinson, 1989.

Bolton, J.S., *A History of the Royal New Zealand Army Ordnance Corps*. Wellington: Royal New Zealand Army Ordnance Corps, 1992.

Buckley, John, *Air Power in the Age of Total War*. London: UCL Press, 1999.

Buell, Thomas B., *Master of Sea Power: A Biography of Fleet Admiral Ernest J. King*. Annapolis: Naval Institute Press, 1995.

Caiden, Martin, *Flying Forts*. New York: Ballantine Books, 1968.

___ *The Ragged Rugged Warriors*. New York: Bantam Books, 1979.

Callahan, Raymond, *Churchill and his Generals*. Lawrence: University Press of Kansas, 2007.

Christ, James, *Mission: Raise Hell*. Annapolis: Naval Institute Press, 2006.

Churchill, Winston Spencer, *The Second World War* (6 volumes). London: The Reprint Society, 1953.

Clark, Margaret (ed.), *Peter Fraser: Master Politician*. Palmerston North: Dunmore Press, 1998.

Collins, John M., *Military Geography*. Washington: Brassey's, 1998.

Colonial Office, *Among Those Present: The Official Story of the Pacific Islands At War*. London: Her Majesty's Stationery Office, 1946.

Cooke, Peter, *Defending New Zealand: Ramparts on the Sea* (3 volumes). Wellington: Defence of New Zealand Study Group, 2000.

Cooze, Frank, *Kiwis in the Pacific*. Wellington: self-published, 1945.

Cowdrey, Albert E., *Fighting For Life: American Military Medicine in World War II*. New York: The Free Press, 1994.

Crawford, John (ed.), *Kia Kaha: New Zealand in the Second World War*. Auckland: Oxford University Press, 2000.

___ *New Zealand's Pacific Front Line: Guadalcanal – Solomon Islands Campaign, 1942–45*. Wellington: New Zealand Defence Force 1992.

Cross, Robin, *The Bombers.* London: Transworld Publishers, 1987.

Daws, Gavan, *Prisoners of the Japanese.* New York: William Morrow & Co., 1994.

*Documents Relating to New Zealand's Participation in the Second World War 1939–45.* Volume I, Wellington: Historical Publications Branch, 1949.

*Documents Relating to New Zealand's Participation in the Second World War 1939–45.* Volume II, Wellington: Historical Publications Branch, 1951.

*Documents Relating to New Zealand's Participation in the Second World War 1939–45.* Volume III, Wellington: Historical Publications Branch, 1963.

Dod, Karl C., *The Corps of Engineers: War Against Japan.* Washington DC: United States Army, 1966.

Dorman, T.E., *The Green War.* Christchurch: Caxton Press, 1977.

Dower, John, *War Without Mercy.* New York: Pantheon Books, 1986.

Dyer, George Carroll, *The Amphibians Came to Conquer: The Story of Admiral Richmond Kelly Turner* (2 volumes), Washington, DC: US Government Printing Office, 1972.

Evans, M.H.H. (Col.), *Amphibious Operations: The Projection of Sea Power Ashore.* London: Brassey's, 1990.

Farrell, Brian P., *The Defence and Fall of Singapore 1940–1942.* Stroud: Tempus Publishing, 2005.

Fay, Peter Ward, *The Forgotten Army: India's Armed Struggle for Independence 1942–45.* Michigan: University of Michigan, 1995.

Feldt, Eric, *The Coast Watchers.* Hawthorn, Australia: Lloyd O'Neill Pty, 1975.

Field, Andrew, *Royal Navy Strategy and Tactics in the Far East 1919–1939.* London: Frank Cass, 2003.

Freyberg, Paul, *Bernard Freyberg, VC: A Soldier of Two Nations.* London: Hodder & Stoughton, 1991.

Gailey, Harry A., *Bougainville: The Forgotten Campaign 1943–45.* Kentucky City: The University Press of Kentucky, 1991.

Gillespie, Oliver A, *The Pacific.* Wellington: War Histories Branch, Department of Internal Affairs, 1952.

Grey, Jeffrey, *The Australian Army.* Melbourne: Oxford University Press, 2001.

Hamill, I., *The Strategic Illusion: The Singapore Strategy and the Defence of Australia and New Zealand 1919–1942.* Singapore: Singapore University Press, 1981.

Hancock, Kenneth, *New Zealand at War.* Wellington: AH & AW Reed, 1946.

Harries, Meiron and Susie, *Soldiers of the Sun.* New York: Random House, 1991.

Hastings, Max, *Nemesis: The Battle For Japan 1944–45.* London: Harper Collins, 2007.

Haworth, Jennifer, *The Art of War: New Zealand War Artists in the Field.* Christchurch: Hazard Press, 2007.

Hayashi, Saburo and Coox, Alvin, *Kogun: The Japanese Army in the Pacific War.* Quantico: Marine Corps Association, 1959.

Hayes, Grace Person, *The History of the Joint Chiefs of Staff: The War Against Japan.* Annapolis: Naval Institute Press, 1982.

Henderson, Alan, Green, David and Cooke, Peter, *The Gunners: A History of New Zealand Artillery.* Auckland: Penguin Books, 2008.

Horn, Alex, *Wings over the Pacific: The RNZAF in the Pacific Air War.* Auckland: Random Century, 1992.

Horner, D.M., *Blamey: The Commander in Chief.* St Leonards, NSW: Allen & Unwin, 1998.

—— *Crisis of Command: Australian Generalship and the Japanese Threat 1941–43.* Canberra: Australian National University Press, 1978.

—— (ed.), *The Commanders: Australian Military Leadership in the 20th Century.* Sydney: Allen & Unwin, 1984.

—— *High Command: Australia and Allied Strategy 1939–45.* Canberra: George Allen & Unwin, 1982.

Horton, D.C., *New Georgia: Pattern for Victory.* London: Ballantine Books, 1971.

—— *Between the Thunder and the Sun.* London: The Book Guild, 1998.

Howlett, R.A., *The History of the Fiji Defence Forces 1939–45.* Suva: Fiji Government Printer, 1948.

Hoyt, Edwin P., *How They Won the War in the Pacific: Nimitz and his Admirals.* Guildford: Lyons Press, 2003.

Huie, William Bradford, *Can Do! The Story of the Seabees.* Annapolis: Naval Institute Press, 1997.

Hutching, Megan (ed.), *Against the Rising Sun: New Zealanders Remember the Pacific War.* Auckland: Harper Collins, 2006.

Isely, Jeter, A. and Crowl, Philip A., *The US Marines and Amphibious War: Its Theory and Practice in the Pacific.* Princeton: Princeton University Press, 1951.
Larsen, Colin, *Pacific Commandos: New Zealanders and Fijians in Action.* Wellington: AH & AW Reed, 1946.
Leary, William M. (ed.), *We Shall Return: MacArthur's Commanders and the Defeat of Japan.* Lexington: University of Kentucky Press, 2004.
Lee, Ulysses, *The US Army in World War II: The Employment of Negro Troops.* Washington: United States Government Printing, 1966.
Lewis, Jonathan and Steele, Ben, *Hell in the Pacific.* London: Channel 4 Books, 2001.
Lissington, M.P., *New Zealand and the United States 1840–1944.* Wellington: Government Printer, 1972.
Long, Gavin, *The Final Campaigns.* Canberra: Australian War Memorial, 1963.
Lorelli, John A., *To Foreign Shores: US Amphibious Operations in World War II.* Annapolis: Naval Institute Press, 1995.
Loxton, Bruce and Coulthard-Clark, Chris, *The Shame of Savo.* St Leonards, NSW: Allen & Unwin, 1997.
McCarthy, Dudley, *South West Pacific: First Year,* Canberra: Australian War Memorial, 1956.
McGee, William L., *The Amphibians are Coming.* Santa Barbara: BMC Publications, 2000.
___ *The Solomons Campaign 1942–43 from Guadalcanal to Bougainville.* Santa Barbara: BMC Publications, 2002.
McGibbon, Ian C., *Blue Water Rationale: The Naval Defence of New Zealand 1914–42.* Wellington: Reed Publishers, 1981.
___ *Kiwi Sappers – The Corps of Royal New Zealand Engineers: Century of Service.* Auckland: Reed, 2002.
___ (ed.), *Oxford Companion to New Zealand Military History.* Auckland: Oxford University Press, 2000.
___ (ed.), *Undiplomatic Dialogue: Letters between Carl Berendsen and Alister McIntosh 1943–1952.* Auckland: Auckland University Press, 1993.
McIntyre, W. David, *Background to the ANZUS Pact.* Christchurch: Canterbury University Press, 1995.
___ *New Zealand Prepares for War.* Christchurch: University of Canterbury Press, 1988.
___ *The Rise and Fall of the Singapore Naval Base 1919–42.* London: Macmillan, 1979.
McLeod, John, *Myth and Reality: The New Zealand Soldier in World War II.* Auckland: Reed Methuen, 1986.
Marston, Daniel P., *Phoenix from the Ashes: The Indian Army in the Burma Campaign.* Westport, USA: Praeger Publishers, 2003.
Mason, Wynne W., *Prisoners of War.* Wellington: War History Branch, Department of Internal Affairs, 1954.
Matloff, Maurice, *Strategic Planning for Coalition Warfare 1943–44.* Washington: Office of the Chief of Military History, 1959.
Matloff, Maurice and Snell, Edwin M., *Strategic Planning for Coalition Warfare 1941–42.* Washington: Office of the Chief of Military History, Department of the Army, 1953.
Meyers, Bruce F., *Swift, Silent and Deadly: Marine Amphibious Reconnaissance in the Pacific 1942–45.* Annapolis: Naval Institute Press, 2004.
Michener, James, *Tales of the South Pacific.* New York: Fawcett Books, 1993.
Millen, Julia, *Salute to Service: A History of Royal New Zealand Corps of Transport and its Predecessors 1860–1996.* Wellington: Victoria University Press, 1996.
Miller, Edward S., *War Plan Orange: The US Strategy to Defeat Japan 1897–1945.* Annapolis: Naval Institute Press, 1991.
Miller, John, *Cartwheel: The Reduction of Rabaul.* Washington D.C.: Center of Military History, US Army, 1990.
Morison, Samuel Eliot, *History of the United States Navy in World War II, Volume III: Breaking the Bismarck's Barrier, 22 July 1942 to 1 May 1944.* Edison, USA: Castle Books, 2001.
Parr, Alison, *Silent Casualties: New Zealand's Unspoken Legacy of the Second World War.* Auckland: Tandem Press, 1995.
Perret, Geoffrey, *A Country Made by War.* New York: Random House, 1989.
___ *There's a War to be Won: The United States Army in World War II.* New York: Random House, 1991.
Pitt, Barry (ed.), *Purnell's History of the Second World War* (7 volumes). London: Purnell & Sons, 1964.
Plowman, Jeffrey, *Armoured Fighting Vehicles of New Zealand 1939–59.* Christchurch: self-published, 2003.

___ *Rampant Dragons: New Zealanders in Armour in World War II.* Christchurch: Kiwi Armour, 2002.

___ *The Operational History of the 3rd NZ Division Tank Squadron.* http:kiwisinarmour.hobbyvista.com

Plowman, Jeffrey and Thomas, Malcolm, *New Zealand Armour in the Pacific 1939–45.* Christchurch: self-published, 2000.

Potter, E.B., *Bull Halsey.* Annapolis: Naval Institute Press, 1986.

___ *Nimitz*, Annapolis: Naval Institute Press, 1976.

___ (ed.), *Sea Power: A Naval History.* Annapolis: Naval Institute Press, 1981.

Prados, John, *Combined Fleet Decoded: The Secret History of American Intelligence and the Japanese Navy in World War II.* New York: Random House, 1995.

Rees, Nigel, *Horror in the East.* London: BBC Worldwide, 2001.

Rennie, Frank, *Regular Soldier: A Life in the New Zealand Army.* Auckland: Endeavour Press, 1986.

Rentz, John, *Bougainville and the Northern Solomons.* Nashville: Battery Press, 2001.

___ *Marines in the Central Solomons.* Washington DC: USMC, 1952.

Republic Entertainment Inc., *The Fighting Seabees* (film). Hollywood, 1944.

Ross, J.M.S., *Royal New Zealand Air Force.* Wellington: Government Printer, War History Branch, 1955.

Rottman, Gordon L., *Landing Ship, Tank (LST) 1942–2002.* Oxford: Osprey Publishing, 2005.

___ *Japanese Army in World War II: Conquest of the Pacific 1941–42.* Oxford: Osprey Publishing, 2005.

___ *Saipan and Tinnian 1944: Piercing the Japanese Empire.* Oxford: Osprey Publishing, 2004.

___ *US Marine Corps World War II Order of Battle: Ground and Air Units in the Pacific War 1939–45.* London: Greenwood Press, 2002.

___ *US Marine Corps Pacific Theatre of Operations 1943–44.* Oxford: Osprey Publishing, 2004.

___ *US World War II Amphibious Tactics: Army & Marine Corps, Pacific Theatre.* Oxford: Osprey Publishing, 2004.

___ *World War II Pacific Island Guide: A Geo-military Study.* London: Greenwood Press, 2002.

Ruble, Carl W. (ed.), *The Earthmover: A Chronicle of the 87th Seabee Battalion in World War II.* Baton Rouge, USA: Army and Navy Publishing Company, 1946.

Sakai, Saburo, *Samurai.* New York: New English Library, 1969.

Shaw, Henry I. and Kane, Douglas T., *Isolation of Rabaul: History of US Marine Corps Operations in World War II, Volume II.* Washington: US Government Printing Office, 1963.

Sinclair, Keith, *Walter Nash.* Auckland: Auckland University Press, 1976.

Spector, Ronald H., *Eagle Against the Sun: The American War with Japan.* New York: Viking Penguin, 1984.

St John Barclay, Glen, *A History of the Pacific from the Stone Age to the Present Day.* London: Sidgwick & Jackson, 1978.

Stoler, Mark A., *Allies and Adversaries: The Joint Chiefs of Staff, the Grand Alliance and US Strategy in World War II.* London: University of North Carolina Press, 2000.

Stone, Peter, *Hostages to Fortune: The Fall of Rabaul.* Yarram, Australia: Oceans Enterprises, 1994.

Stout, T. Duncan M., *War Surgery and Medicine.* Wellington: War History Branch, Department of Internal Affairs, 1954.

*Medical Services in New Zealand and the Pacific.* Wellington: War History Branch, Department of Internal Affairs, 1958.

Stuart, Ian, *In the Line of Fire: New Zealanders tell their Wartime Stories.* Auckland: Reed Publishing, 2001.

Taafe, Stephen R., *MacArthur's Jungle War: The 1944 New Guinea Campaign.* Lawrence, USA: University of Kansas Press, 1988.

Taylor, Nancy Margaret, *The Home Front* (2 volumes). Wellington: Historical Publications Branch, 1986.

Thorne, Christopher, *Allies of a Kind: The United States, Britain and the War against Japan.* London: Hamish Hamilton, 1978.

Underhill, M.L., *New Zealand Chaplains in the Second World War.* Wellington: War History Branch, Department of Internal Affairs, 1951.

Wahlert, Glenn, *Australian Army Amphibious Operations in the South West Pacific: 1942–45* (edited papers of the Australian Army History Conference held at the Australian War Memorial 15 November 1994). Army Doctrine Centre, Sydney: Southward Press, 1995.

Waters, S.D., *The Royal New Zealand Navy.* Wellington: Historical Publications Branch, 1956.
Watt, Lawrence, *Mates and Mayhem: World War II Front Line Kiwis Remember.* Auckland: Harper Collins, 1996.
Wigmore, Lionel, *The Japanese Thrust.* Canberra: Australian War Memorial, 1957.
Willmott, H.P., *Empires in the Balance: Japanese and Allied Pacific Strategies to April 1942.* Annapolis: Naval Institute Press, 1982.
___ *Grave of a Dozen Schemes: British Naval Planning and the War against Japan 1943–45.* Annapolis: Naval Institute Press, 1995.
___ *June 1944.* Poole, UK: Blandford Press, 1984.
___ *The Barrier and the Javelin: Japanese and Allied Pacific Strategies February to June 1942.* Annapolis: Naval Institute Press, 1989.
Wood, F.L.W., *The New Zealand People at War: Political and External Affairs.* Wellington: Department of Internal Affairs, 1971.

## Articles

Bolt, Barbara, 'Mail Call – New Zealanders at War in the Pacific', *The New Zealand Genealogist*, March/April, 2005.
Crawford, John, 'Major General Harold Barrowclough – Leadership and Command in Two World Wars' in Glyn Harper and Joel Hayward (eds), *Born to Lead? Portraits of New Zealand Commanders*, Auckland: Exisle Publishing, 2003, pp. 144–63.
Gustafson, Barry, 'Savage, Michael Joseph, 1972–1940', in Dictionary of New Zealand Biography, www.dnzb.govt.nz.
Hall, D.O.W., 'Coastwatchers' in *Episodes and Studies Volume 2.* Wellington: War History Branch, Department of Internal Affairs, 1951.
Martin, John E, 'Total War? The National Service Department and New Zealand's Manpower Crisis of 1942', in Crawford, John (ed.), *Kia Kaha: New Zealand in the Second World War.* Auckland: Oxford University Press, 2000, pp. 221–35.
Pugsley, Christopher, 'The Second New Zealand Division of 1945' in Crawford, John (ed.), *Kia Kaha: New Zealand in the Second World War.* Auckland: Oxford University Press, 2000, pp. 94–106.
Ross, J.M.H., 'The Second New Zealand Division of 1945' in Crawford, John (ed.), *Kia Kaha: New Zealand in the Second World War.* Auckland: Oxford University Press, 2000, pp. 94–106.
Smith, Arthur and Hooper, Craig, 'The Mosquito can be more dangerous than a Mortar Round – The Obligations of Command', *Naval War College Review*, Winter 2005, Vol. 58, No.1, pp. 77–87.
Taylor, Steve, 'Major General the Right Honourable Harold Eric Barrowclough, KCMG, CB, DSO, MC, ED' in *New Zealand Armed Forces Law Review*, 2004, pp. 20–31.
Tonkin-Covell, John, 'The Very Long Way Back: The Republic of Fiji Military Forces and the Neutrality Convention', *New Zealand Journal of Defence Studies*, Vol. 1, March 2007.

## Unpublished material

Blazly, C.A., 'Report on NZ ASC Operations with 3NZ Division in South Pacific', May 1945, author's collection.
Ghormley, Robert Lee, Jnr, 'Vice Admiral Robert Lee Ghormley, US Navy', unpublished manuscript, author's collection.
Gubb, Matthew, 'The Military Role of Australia and New Zealand in the South Pacific', MA subthesis in Strategic Studies, Strategic and Defence Studies Centre, Research School of Pacific Studies, Australian National University, 1990.
Hewson, Brian, 'Goliath's Apprentice', unpublished manuscript, author's collection.
Lysaght, Andrew, 'Going Back', unpublished manuscript, September 1996, author's collection.

## Third Division Histories Committee

1 *Stepping Stones to the Solomons: The Unofficial History of the 29th Battalion with the Second New Zealand Expeditionary Force in the Pacific.* Wellington: AH & AW Reed, 1947.
2 *Pacific Kiwis: Being the story of the service in the Pacific of the 30th Battalion, Third Division, Second New Zealand Expeditionary Force.* Wellington: AH & AW Reed, 1947.
3 *Pacific Pioneers: The Story of the Engineers of the New Zealand Expeditionary Force in the Pacific.* Wellington: AH & AW Reed, 1945.
4 *The 36th Battalion: A Record of the service of the 36th Battalion with the Third Division in the Pacific.* Wellington: AH & AW Reed, 1948.

5 *Pacific Saga: The Personal Chronicle of the 34th Battalion and its part in the Third Division's Campaigns.* Wellington: AH & AW Reed, 1948.
6 *The Gunners: An Intimate Record of Units of the 3rd New Zealand Divisional Artillery in the Pacific from 1940 until 1945.* Wellington: AH & AW Reed, 1948.
7 *Pacific Service: The Story of the NZ Army Service Units with the Third Division in the Pacific.* Wellington, AH & AW Reed, 1948.
8 *Shovel, Sword and Scalpel: A record of the service of medical units of the Second New Zealand Expeditionary Force in the Pacific.* Wellington: AH & AW Reed, 1945.
9 *Tanks: An Unofficial History of the Activities of the Third New Zealand Division Tank Squadron in the Pacific* [incorporates MMG and Ordnance]. Wellington: AH & AW Reed, 1947.
10 *Headquarters: A Brief Outline of the Activities of the Headquarters of the Third Division and the 8th and 14th Brigades During their Service in the Pacific* [incorporates Communications]. Wellington: AH & AW Reed, 1947.
11 *Base Wallahs: The Story of the Units of the Base Organisation, NZEF IP.* Wellington: AH & AW Reed, 1946.
12 *Story of the 34th: The Unofficial History of a New Zealand Infantry Battalion in the Pacific.* Wellington: AH & AW Reed, 1947.
13 *The 35th Battalion: A Record of Service of the 35th Battalion with the Third Division in the Pacific.* Wellington: AH & AW Reed, 1947.

# Index

airpower: development of bomber and threat to NZ 21–2; government preference for 21
alcohol 151–2; adulterated liquor 152; beer ration 151; illicit stills 151
*Aloma of the South Seas* (film) 133
American command areas 37, 158
American–New Zealand relations: communication difficulties 174–6; culinary differences 170; 'friendly fire' incidents 167–8; logistics 169; NZ soldiers pilfering US supplies 170–4; pre-war relationship 157–8; race relations 70, 176–8
American weaponry and equipment: development during war 169; incompatibility with NZ 169
amphibious warfare 159, 176, 187; NZ interwar exercises 19; landing craft 101–5; US development of expertise 98
Ashton, Bill 141, 177
Atabrine 144–5
Australia: and deployment of NZ troops in Pacific 185; provision of weaponry to NZ 186

B-17 *Flying Fortress* 33, 214
B Force 26
Barahun (Green Islands) 110, 112, 115
Barakoma, Vella Lavella 81
Barnes-Graham, Allan (war artist) 192
Barrowclough, Major General Harold Eric 8, 46, 47, 49, 51–3, 56–9, 61–4, 66-70, 78-80, 90, 94, 96-8, 100–1, 110, 116, 118, 123, 128–31, 135, 139, 141, 151–3, 159-81, 182-95, 196-9; and disbandment of 3NZ Division 128, 129, 130; early military career 46-7; post-war career 195; relationship with Americans 159, 160–4, 166-9, 174–5, 180
Barrowclough Cup 152
Barrowclough's charter 160, 214
battalion combat teams 77, 79
beachmasters 101
Beaumont, Lt Joseph 81–3, 89
Bee, Kathleen 193, 211
Berendsen, Carl 127
Bioletti, Lt Harry 28, 152, 155, 175
Blamey, General Thomas 160, 163
Blanche Harbour (Treasury Islands) 94
Boys anti-tank rifle 89
Bren gun 28, 33, 89
Brewster, Lance Corporal 143
British food requirements 127, 129
British Trans-Pacific Cable 22
Brooke-White, Col John 97
Brydon, Lt Col W. A. 182
Bullen, Major Arthur 119

Canberra Pact 128, 185, 214
*Canterbury*, HMNZS 187
Cantwell, Jack 42
Carney, Rear Admiral Robert 160, 164
*Cartwheel*, Operation 74, 75, 214
Cassino, Battle of 128
*Charles Upham*, HMNZS 187
*Cherryblossom*, Operation 93, 96
Choiseul 92, 94, 99
Churchill, Winston Spencer 35, 125, 128, 131, 157, 191
Clark, Russell (war artist) 2, 192
coastwatchers 33, 34, 37, 215
Coates, Gordon 32, 56
'coconut bombers' 28, 182, 190
Committee of Imperial Defence 19
COMSOPAC 55, 110, 160–1, 164, 215
*Confident*, HMS 91, 144
Conner, Bob (Seabee) 122, 174
Cooze, Frank 104, 152
Coral Sea, Battle of 14, 40
Cowan, Sgt William Albert (Bert) 92, 100–1, 103, 110, 167, 198
Crawford, John 182
Crete, Battle of 44, 48
Cunningham, Brigadier William Henry 25–9,

32, 36–7, 46, 141, 185; appointment to command Fiji Garrison 25; problems of command and resources 25, 27, 29; health 37
*Cyclops*, Operation 64, 216

Davie, Gordon Campbell 141, 173, 180
Dean, Lt 116
Dove, Brigadier 177, 181, 188
Doveli, Vella Lavella 84
Duff, Brigadier Charles 52, 159
Dunlop, Robert 104, 105–6
Dutch East Indies 13, 36, 74
Dyer, Ralph 148–9

*Efate*, Operation 72, 216
Eichelberger, General Robert L. 161
El Alamein, Battle of 124
Emirau 109
Empress Augusta Bay, Bougainville 94, 96, 97, 108, 109

Falamai, Mono Island 96, 97, 100–5, 167, 184
Fanning Island 19, 20, 23, 34
Fiji 8, 19–25, 27–31, 33–43, 45–6, 48, 50–2, 56–7, 61–2, 69, 78, 127, 141, 144–6, 148–50, 158, 171, 176–7, 184–5, 190, 193, 196, 197; airfields 22, 33, 34; climate and disease 31; Fijian-Indian attitude to war 22–3; hurricane 30–1; inadequate garrison 22, 40; strategic importance to NZ 20, 21, 23
Fijian camps: Namaka 26, 30; Samambula 26, 31, 172
Fijian commandos, guerrillas, South Pacific scouts 38, 185
Fijian Defence Force (FDF) 19, 27, 34, 37, 38, 160, 185; creation of 37, 184–5; post-war links with NZ Army 184–5
First Island Command 58
Fort, Admiral George 95, 96
Fraser, Peter 29, 33, 35, 40–1, 43–4, 47–8, 50, 54–5, 57, 70, 124–6, 128, 131, 158, 160, 164, 188, 197; attitude to casualties 57; and strength of Fiji garrison 40, 41; reasons for NZ participation 43; and creation of 3NZ Division 43–4, 48, 50; and disbandment of 3NZ Division 126, 128, 131
Freyberg, Major General Bernard 35–6, 49, 51, 70, 124–5, 130, 182, 183
furlough scheme for 2NZ Division 69, 126

Gallipoli 8, 9, 98, 188
Ghormley, Vice Admiral Robert Lee 39, 41, 44–5, 46–50, 53–5, 158–9; appointment as COMSOPAC 39; attitude to NZ troops in combat role 45, 47, 158; and garrison for Norfolk Island and Tonga 54; replacement as COMSOPAC 55
Gilfillan, Corporal W. 101
Gillespie, Oliver 183, 185, 194
*Goodtime*, Operation 9, 93–6, 98, 108, 162–8, 178, 191, 198; garrison role of NZ troops 108; invasion of Treasury Islands 93–108; planning of invasion 96–100; reconnaissance patrols 100–1
Goss, Brigadier L. G. 36–7, 164, 165
Graham, Lt D. G. 79
Green Islands 9, 72, 90, 109–11, 113, 116–17, 119, 121–2, 130, 139–40, 145–6, 150, 152, 156, 163, 166, 169, 172–4, 178–9, 191, 198; commando raid 110–16; invasion of 116–20; use of *Valentine* Tanks 118–21
Griswold, General 161
Guadalcanal 15–16, 38, 44–5, 47–8, 49, 54–8, 66, 70–4, 78, 96, 98–101, 117, 137, 139, 145–6, 150, 164–6, 169, 171, 176, 180, 184, 189, 192, 197, 199; advance base for 3NZ Division 73; Battle of 15, 199; deployment of Americal Division to 57; plans to use NZ soldiers 47

Halsey, Admiral William 55–7, 67–8, 70, 74–5, 109, 127–9, 160–2, 164–5, 178, 186, 191; appointment as COMSOPAC 55; attitude to use of NZ soldiers 56, 186; response to offer of depleted 3NZ Division 56
Hannifin, Staff Sgt D. O. 106
Harmon, General Millard 57, 191
Harnett, Marcel 151
Hudson Bomber 39, 73; creation of 'Huddy club' 73; disappearance of 176

Ilalla, Sgt David 100, 101
India 131
Irvine, Sgt G. 147
Isitt, Air Vice Marshall 193

Japanese forces: airpower 14, 16, 21; atrocities 21, 155; attitude to Allied prisoners of war 155; attitude towards surrender 155–6; Imperial Japanese Army 40, 79, 155; Imperial Japanese Navy 15, 16, 41; Special Naval Land Force 156
Japanese barges 90–1, 167

Japanese strategy 13, 15
Java Sea, Battle of 14
Jod, Corporal J. J. 168
Jones, Fred 32, 45, 49, 55
Josselyn, Sub Lt Henry 84, 85
jungle warfare 134–8

Kaimais, Battle of the 52–3
Kavieng 109, 216
King, Admiral Ernest J. 40, 41; attitude to NZ after Canberra Pact 128–9; provision of US aircraft to RNZAF 126
Kirk, Captain Les 106
Kiwi A, B, C, D 45, 48–9, 55, 216
Kiwi Company 150–1
Kiwi Concert Party (Pacific) 148, 149
Knipe, Sapper F. L. 168
Kokoda Track, Battle of 14

Lamour, Dorothy 133, 148
League of Nations 19, 23
*Leander*, HMS 22
Lee-Enfield rifle 89, 142
Lempiere, Private P. 101
Lethbridge Mission 217
Lewis gun 28
Leyte Gulf, Battle of 28
Lincoln, Lt General Rush B. 58, 159
Logan, Major Gordon 106
Loganforce 106
logistics 169; critical importance of 147; NZ troops load and unload shipping 139–41
London, Jack 133
Luke, Sir Harry 25, 32

MacArthur, General Douglas 16, 33, 35, 37, 44, 74, 160–2, 171, 186, 191
McClure, General Robert B. 91
McKinnon, Major General 187–8
mail 153–4
Malaria Control Units 60, 158
malaria, effects of 144–5
manpower shortages by NZ 124, 125
Maori 56, 69, 70, 152, 177, 178, 190; possible service of Maori Battalion in Pacific 69–70; rejection of deployment to Pacific 70, 190
Marquana Bay, Vella Lavella 80, 82, 143
Marshall, General George C. 125
Marshall, Major John 194–5
*Mayflower*, Exercise 165
Mead, Major General Owen H. 8, 37–9, 41–2, 46–7
Michener, James: *Tales of the South Pacific* 156; and origins of Bali Ha'i 156
Midway, Battle of 15, 41, 199
Milne Bay, Battle of 15
Muldoon, Robert 104–5, 135, 195

**NZ Forces**
*2NZ Division* 2, 9, 24, 32, 34–5, 40, 43, 45, 51, 56, 69, 70, 123–5, 128–31, 146, 153, 170, 182–3, 187, 188–9, 190–4, 196, 198; need for reinforcements 182; victory parades and publicity 189
*3NZ Division*: Divisional HQ 36, 51, 64, 175
  Divisional Engineers 60; 18 Troops Coy 26, 27; 20 Field Coy 27, 65, 192; 26 Field Coy 70
  Divisional Infantry:
    8 Brigade 26, 28, 32–3, 36–7, 39, 52, 64, 73, 78, 92–8, 100–1, 105, 108, 118, 142, 145, 154, 162, 170, 180, 184–5, 194, 198; 29 Battalion 27, 60, 92, 101, 107, 165, 173; 34 Battalion 27, 36, 54, 105, 193; 36 Battalion 36, 54, 103–5, 135, 144, 153, 175, 184, 195
    14 Brigade 35–6, 49, 52, 65, 73–4, 78–80, 90, 94, 109–11, 117–18, 152, 155–6, 170, 176, 197–8; 30 Battalion 27, 30, 53, 97, 110, 113, 115, 117–19, 149, 152, 177; 35 Battalion 36, 51, 65, 79, 80, 155, 167; 37 Battalion 35, 36, 79, 80, 117, 121, 147, 159, 195
    15 Brigade 56, 66, 69, 70; Scots Battalion 165
  Divisional Artillery: Field Artillery – 144 Independent Battery 110
  Divisional Signals 39, 51, 63–4, 69, 86, 112, 136, 180, 185
  NZ Army Service Corps 51–2, 61, 63, 169, 185, 187
  3NZ Tank Squadron 118
  4NZ General Hospital 59
  lack of publicity 191; military discipline 141–2; unconventional operations 92, 100–1, 198; weapons and equipment 142–3, 198
  RNZAF 44, 52, 69, 70, 115–17, 124, 126, 128, 131, 149, 164, 166, 176, 188; cost of US supplied aircraft 126, 128; rapid expansion in Pacific 126
  RNZ Navy 127
Nash, Corporal Benjamin Franklin 100
Nash, Walter 40–1, 44, 50, 127–9
National Patriotic Fund 154–5; parcels to troops in Pacific 154

Nauru Island 131
New Caledonia 41, 46, 48, 54–5, 57–65, 67, 69, 71, 78, 99, 129, 136, 139, 141–2, 144–7, 149, 151–3, 164, 166, 169–70, 172–3, 175–6, 178, 180, 184, 189–91, 195, 197; arrival of NZ troops 58; Bourail 145, 177; Bourail cemetery 184; climate and conditions 60–2; garrison 197; Niaouli tree 58, 59; Noumea 71; prospect of Japanese invasion 58, 62; training by NZ troops 63–7
New Georgia 165, 197
New Hebrides 20, 64, 72, 144, 166
New Zealand Chiefs of Staff 19, 21, 23, 34–5, 129
Nimitz, Admiral Chester 15, 16, 37, 40, 54–5, 109, 130–1, 159, 161, 186
Nissan Atoll, Green Islands 111–12, 117, 119, 121
Norfolk Island 22, 54, 184, 190
Northern Independent Commando 38

O'Dowd, Lt Patrick 114

P–38 *Lightning* 73
P–39 *Aircobra* 39
Pacific Defence Conference 20
Pacific Star (medal) 8, 138, 189, 217
Pacific War Council 159
Papua New Guinea 20
Paraso Bay, Vella Lavella 80, 84
Pearl Harbor 13–14, 21, 34, 157–8
Peck, General De Witt 67
Philippines 14, 16, 33, 35–6, 40, 74
Pinipel Island, Green Islands 121
Pokonian Plantation, Green Islands 115, 117
Potter, Brigadier Leslie 36, 38, 78–80, 82–3, 85, 92
Pouembout River, New Caledonia 65
Powles, Guy 195
PT Boats 100, 109, 112, 116, 122, 163
Pugsley, Christopher 182
Puttick, Lt General Edward 32, 44–7, 49, 54–6, 68, 124, 126–9, 131, 160, 161, 170; military career before 1942 44; preference for airpower 126; role in creation of 3NZ Division 44–6, 49; role in disbandment of 3NZ Division 126, 129, 131

Queen Elizabeth Barracks, Fiji 185

Rabaul 14, 24, 74–5, 110, 115–16, 122, 130, 198; Japanese base 14; planned attack on 75; *see also Cartwheel*, Operation
*Rangatira*, SS 26, 35
rations 30
recreation 152–3
Rennie, Lt Frank 17, 112, 114, 187
Richardson, Lt General Robert C. 163
RNZAF *see* NZ Forces
RNZ Navy *see* NZ Forces
Roosevelt, Franklin D. 14, 35, 125, 128, 159
Row, Brigadier Robert Amos 39, 95, 96–7, 98, 103, 163, 165
Royal Navy 17, 18, 183; protector of Australasia 18
Rusden, Private C. M. 101
Rutherford, Major 119

Salmon, C. D. F 161, 164
Sau, Green Islands 121
Saveke, Treasury Islands 101
*Scylla*, Exercise 64, 216
Seabees *see* US Forces: Naval Construction Battalions
Seaward, Colonel C. F. 80
sex 148–50
Shaw, George Bernard 174
Sherson, C. H. 107
shipping shortages 40, 131, 168; and not returning 2NZ Division to Pacific 125, 129
Singapore: major British base 18; fall of Singapore 36; strategy to protect British interests 18, 20, 35
Sirot, Green Islands 110, 118
Smith, Private Joe 106
Soanatalu, Mono Island 100, 107
Solomon Islands 14, 15–16, 20, 40, 53, 70, 74–6, 84, 97, 100, 112, 130, 133–4, 155, 157, 161, 167, 184, 199; strategic importance to Australasia 20, 22
Solomon Islands Defence Force 100, 167
South Pacific Area 37, 218
South West Pacific Area 37, 171, 191
Stewart, Brigadier K. L. 37, 47–8
Stirling Island, Treasury Islands 94, 103, 137, 145–6, 179
Stokes, Lt R. A. 91
Stronach, Captain 118
*Styx*, Exercise 64, 65, 216
Sugden, Lt Col A. H. L. 116
Suva, Fiji 19, 22–3, 25–7, 29–34, 36–7, 39, 42, 177, 185

*Taniwha*, Exercise 64

Tassone, Aurelio 104
Taylor, Les 105
Taylor, Major Richard 184
Thomas, Bombardier Gordon 71, 73, 170
Thompson sub-machine gun 89
Thwaites, Matron Gladys 31
Tinker, Ron 187
Tonga 19, 20, 22–3, 34, 37, 42, 54, 78, 127, 131, 160, 174, 176, 184, 190; T Force 54
*Tonta*, Exercise 64, 67, 216
Torokina, Bougainville 109, 115
*Towpath*, Operation 218
Treasury Islands 72, 78, 92–3, 95–6, 99–102, 106, 108, 110, 112, 130, 137, 139–40, 143, 145, 151, 155–6, 165, 167, 169, 180, 189, 191, 194, 198; *see also Goodtime*, Operation
Trench, Lt Col 166
Tripp, Captain Charlie 185
tropical diseases 133, 144–6
Tucker, Ron 173
Tunisian Campaign 125

**US Forces**
*US Army* 15, 37, 57, 90, 99, 100, 159, 162, 170, 173, 177; Americal Division 54, 197
USAAF 73, 167
US Marine Corps 91, 98, 99, 116, 117, 163; 1st Marine Division 15, 45, 47, 54, 57, 176; 3rd Marine Division 95; 2nd USMC Parachute Battalion 179
*US Navy*
Naval Construction Battalions (Seabees) 76, 96–8, 104, 106, 122, 156, 163, 166, 171, 178; USS *Greenling* 96; USS *Missouri* 16, 193; USS *Philip* 99, 103; USS *Pringle* 99, 103
US Forces in South Pacific in 1943 68
US-NZ Mutual Aid Agreement ('Lend Lease') 128
US Troopships: USS *President Adams* 71; USS *President Coolidge* 42, 175; USS *President Monroe* 58; USS *West Point* 58

Vandegrift, General Archer A. 164
Vickers machine gun 89, 143

Wacquawai, Private 38
Wales, Brigadier J. G. 185
Walker, Private 143
Warambari Bay, Vella Lavella 80, 83, 85
War Memorandum Eastern 18
War Plan Orange 219
Washington Naval Conference 17
*Watchtower*, Operation 44, 158, 219
water 146–7; importance of clean drinking water 146; shortage on the Green Islands 146
Western Samoa 18, 24, 34, 37
Wickham, Frank 100, 101
Wilkinson, Vice Admiral Theodore S. 68, 95, 110, 112, 159–64, 167, 176, 186
Williams, David 144, 175, 180
Williams, Lt General Guy 31–2, 219

Yamamoto, Admiral Isoroku 14, 15
YMCA secretaries 154–5

Zivaneth, Lt 117
*Zero* fighter 39, 114